# WALLS

## Why Racism and Sexism
## don't matter...as much

I0413631

## Josh Nsangi

WALLS

Published by Royalty Bros Publishers

No. 207, 380 Murray Street,

Canada,

Ottawa,

ON, K1N 8W1

ISBN-13: 978-1546692447

To dad, mom, David and James: I love you so much.

**CONTENTS**

# Introduction

That institutions as Oxfam, today, frequently publish reports on the state of the world's inequality, is not unprecedented. Indeed, today we speak of the one percent wealthiest, and even of the crème de la crème class, of individuals in our highly globalized and intercommunicative world. However, the Gilded Age, as the "roaring 90s", bore fruit to similar predicaments, as regards both the distribution of wealth and the public's weary, if not envious protestations of such blatant abject inequalities. Much like the effects of acid, extreme ill-distributions of wealth serve as a corrosive agent, eroding the very fabric of the institutions of democracy that many have tirelessly toiled to instate, and, on several occasions, amend. In this book, one of the postulates I make is that one should conceive the state-apparatus as a buffer, an institution that keeps the masses at arm's length from the ruling classes. As Albert Einstein duly noted, insanity is "doing the same thing over and over again and expecting different results," it would thus be insane of us, to presume that the predominant elite circles during renaissance Europe were as insane as to continue their monarchical modes of rule, in the wake of several revolutions, as was notably seen in France, and much, much later on in Russia in the 20th century. Fears by the opulent minority, within various European societies, of the dispossession of capital wealth, incurred by the wrathful hands of the many poor peoples, begun to envelope most covert intimate discussions between and amongst elite individuals. Thus began the period of partly consensual forms of rule, within many an advanced society. This is mostly in reference to the state of world affairs in the wake of the (in)famous American declaration of independence, an era ushering in a means of rule mildly influenced by public sentiments, at least, more than in times prior (e.g. feudal system). However, as inequality within the society increases, through institutional means, this centralization of segmented accretions of wealth concurrently results in a corrosion of democratic institutions. The effect had by the accumulation of wealth by individuals, who upon grouping together, through institutions or other means, mostly hidden from prying eyes; is the accumulation of power, political as legal, and to some extent, even power of a militaristic nature. Hence, as mounted pressure descends from the top of the societal ladder, pursuant to interests of centralization, it is cordially met with resistance from the bottom rungs. The masses, the majority and poor people, if organized, pressure the state, and thus, make their voices heard on the political scene, and mobilize towards institutional gains in democracy. This antagonistic power struggle between the opulent minority and the poor majority is a recurring notion, evidenced in several societies, feudal, imperial, democratic, or otherwise. Thus, despite variations in forms of rule, that wealth is disproportionately accrued in progressively fewer segments within society, invariably entails the development of social antagonism, with institutions (established social constructions, e.g. patriarchal) being the means by which the ruling classes pressure society; a 'divide and rule' tactic, if you will.

Chapter one attempts to make use of historical and other scholastic accounts, approaching issues of race, racism and racial inequality from an angle that bespeaks socioeconomic disparities, and ill-distributions within a society. Furthermore, the discussion centered on a social fabrication/construction, race, as we have come to know it, according to the premise of my book, is a system of exploitation that ensures that some of the ruled (whites) feel superior to another segment of the likewise ruled (nonwhites), reducing the potential for mass organization (democratic rule). To the extent that a white person, from the 17th century to date, in communities within the US, in spite of the dire straits they may be facing, is able to console him/herself and the rumblings of an aching and foodless stomach, as being better off than most nonwhites; racism, or the use of race to keep the poor at odds with each other, has proven beneficial a tactic. In other words, "at least I ain't black" has always been comfort enough for those whites, found at the bottom of the socioeconomic food chain, to overlook their squalor, and in so doing, overlook the strength of their collective numbers.

Chapter two is a discussion, much in line with the 'divide and conquer' precepts attached to the evidenced racial antagonisms made mention of in chapter 1. The need for and origins of inequality, attached to gender roles, and even the antagonisms within a 'gender group' is alluded to, as a means of sketching a picture of the products of inequality. A good example of the troubling inconsistencies in all three waves of the Feminist movement can be seen, among other eventualities, by the preclusion or mis/non-representation of poor black women in a movement that, predominantly sees to the upholding of women rights for the educated middle-class woman. Traces of antagonisms between women of different classes is evident, with myths of the promiscuous black woman a longstanding tradition in the US, a principle which does not apply to the middle class woman (typically white), who, in choosing to be promiscuous is rather seen as 'modern' and independent.

Chapter three, in discussing the different cultures associated with the respective socioeconomic classes, in society, attempts to establish and bring together notions of racial, as gender antagonisms, in a bid to attribute the inherent exploitative methods of rule, by the political, power and socioeconomic elites, to a rule made possible by the initial disparities of wealth, which, in time, engender power. Chapter three, is where it all comes together, at least, on a local/national level.

WALLS

Chapter four and five are discussions, each in their own right, showing the power-struggles that take place on a more global level. Chapter four speaks of the need for actors, commercial, political or otherwise to maintain their system of rule, that is, to maintain the racial, ethnic, gender, class or any other form of societal conflict that ensures that the energies of the masses are lent to other preoccupations. It is in these last two chapters that the notion of soft-power is more expounded upon, as with other theories of power that have predominated the scholarly and political discursive realms. Together with the fourth estate, spoken of in chapter 5, the ideological battle for the hearts and minds of the many is being waged by several factions within varying elite circles, with each group or institution working towards the fulfillment of their respective interests.

That this book is not an in-depth analysis of the manifestations of inequality, both now as in times past, allows for a particularly interesting, and I believe, beneficial position from which to begin a global discussion on exploitation. Why have someone think for you, when you can be given information from diverse sources and times, and decide, for yourself, what and how to think, using the extensive research material to follow, as a guiding framework, of possible eventualities, rather than a set-in-stone prescription of a very dynamic and uncertain world.

# 1

# RACE

~*~

**B**oth, the rhetoric of fervent disgust and that of surreptitious lauding, in short, an emotionally charged atmosphere, were, to me, the prevalent moods, both during and after the OJ Simpson and George Zimmerman court proceedings. Francistown was as remote a city as it could get, yet, even in this quaint cadre of the globe, the evenings were imbued with the same charred notions of race or racism, of being black or white, with gray being an absolute no go area. For most, this betrayal was akin to the treacherous act levied on Jesus by one of his twelve brothers. Justice; at this point, was just another word relegated to the anthological realm of mythology. Not many people took an objective stance on the matter, that is, when finding themselves among friends, within the confines of their intimate circles, and where the politically correct garb could be rid of in preference of the speak your mind garb. The year was 1995 and it was October, the third day of what the Romans initially deemed to be the eighth month in the year. I at the time was enjoying some recluse time at the Thapama Hotel where I spent my last fortnight vacationing in Botswana. I woke up late that afternoon, and nonchalantly made my advance towards the assorted buffet of wild game meats and fresh produce, one of the ways I favored most for ridding myself of the nauseating hangover sentiments, which ensued from the care freeness with which I approached the night prior. Outdoors and protected from the vicious sun by a looming umbrella, the dry crisp air caressed my jubilant skin. I hadn't until then crossed paths with another black patron at the hotel, and it bothered me not one bit, but that afternoon, as I sat down eating, recuperating, the notion of being alone in a sea of non-blacks began to sink in as though hookworms overwhelmed my dermis. This must be how it feels like to be famous, like Mohammed Ali, or someone of the like grandeur, I thought to myself amidst the stares of repugnance that enveloped me. The patted down whispers that accompanied the glares were, of course, in stark contrast to the adulating, ear drum bursting screams of people chasing after their celebrity and idol of choice. "What did you do?!", asked my bemused younger brother James upon him hearing of my tales once I got back to Toronto at the end of that month. "Well MajeZ," I leaned over my beanbag, turning to look at him before carrying on to say, "I just smiled and waved". It's worth taking note of the type of place Botswana was during the early 1990s, sequestered in Southern Africa, and sharing a border with apartheid South Africa, this land locked country was at one point a protectorate of the British empire, before peacefully securing its right to sovereignty in the mid-1960s. Hence the notion of privilege and wealth was strongly attached to the whiteness in that region of the world, as is the case in most regions of the world, even in contemporary times. This was a place where the vestigial institutions of white supremacy still lingered, and lingered strong, as a pungent odor of a dead mouse hidden in some small crack in the floor boards in the attic lingers to the distaste of all those exposed to it. A young white couple sat across from me, no doubt, from the Afrikaans influence that troubled their English, that they were Boers. They, rather than settle for calumnious seeming whispers to one another, opted to engage me in conversation.

"Hi!" they both uttered, and to which greeting I smiled back in like salutation. "What brings you to these parts?" the man would go on to yell, despite my being merely four or so feet away. "I'm not deaf, you know!" Well, I wished that I had said that, seeing as I very much thought it, in my volatile and dazed state. However, beggars cannot afford to be choosers, as my good friend Samora always said. I, of course, in this analogy, am the beggar in question and needed all the allies I could muster, even the loud ones. "Food" I answered.

"You not from around here, ey?" this time he toned down on the volume

"So, what gave me away?"

"ah!" he exclaimed, finding some exuberance that I didn't know people upwards of twenty years old could get from rightly picking out foreigners, in this case a black one, against a white backdrop, most of them white South Africans. "I'm just good like that."

My dear boy, no human is purely good, the bad, often hidden to public eyes, tends to balance things out that way; I thought to myself. "It seems." I said, now tilting my head down as I presumed this was not an ally worth my troubles. The intended a priori need for silence, and mouth stuffing, took seizure of my mood once more.

"You American?" his partner interjected in the hope, maybe, of injecting some pace back into the attenuating flickering light of a conversation.

"Close enough, I'm actually Congolese." I replied.

"Oh." She said, as though she were a child at a candy store, forbidden from sampling the ample delicacies on display.

The man seemed now to have been pinched by a sudden bout of curiosity, as he proceeded to ask four questions in a long winded manner, which amounted to an inquiry on my background, perplexed at my being able to spend enough money to eat the heavy lunch I ate, at the pricy rate it was offered. I in turn felt obliged to reciprocate the air of openness that flowed from them to me, and went on to explain my background and how I, at that time, was living in Canada, and had been for over half of the preceding decade. My telling such said story seemed then to bring back the once had twinkle in his partner's right eye, either that, or I had mistaken the sun's reflection upon her eye for something much more than it was.

"Would you care if we joined you?" the man inquired, as he motioned his head, to his partner, in my direction.

"Free country! I hope," I said smiling youthfully. They both smiled back and took up no time hesitating, shifting both their persons and drinks alike in a swift swooping motion, settling down on my table, averse to any socially overtone queues I may have ambiguously been hinting towards through my feeble body language. "I'm Johan, and this is my wife Elize."

"Hi guys, I'm Yashuwa, but you can call me Josh."

"So Josh, what do you think about the O.J. Simpson case? Fair or unfair?" Elize wasted no time with further pleasantries. Well, there goes my appetite, I thought sardonically. Was this another trick question? For the sake of political correctness, I simply retorted to the fact that, "I don't know really, ey; thank God I'm not one of the jurors!" It seemed that I was not as funny as my mind purported me to be. No one laughed, but me, in my head, of course. This, though, was enough to provoke a response from Johan, as Elize shook her head in sheer disgusted disapproval, with the region about her mouth taking on a disfigured form, as though embittered by some vile thing she had just eaten. "Like, no man, the gun was still smoking! And that glove thing! Like, please man!" It was clear that I wasn't getting out of this anytime soon, and it seemed I was attracting the gaze of the public around me for longer spells of time than before.

"Indeed" I retorted, "but the justice system seems to have spoken, he was judged by his most capable peers, so then am I to do the judging? At least, that's partly my view."

"See!" interjected Elize, "it's this black and white race thing that has everyone lost for sense!"

"That's one way of looking at it," I replied to her comment. She was not too far from the truth, however, since, race has always been a highly charged topic in the world, let alone in America, and more so even in apartheid South Africa. It is hard for people; it seems, to be objective.

It is here that I wish to begin talking about race, firstly in the North American context, before moving on to the global implications of this social construction, which has grown into an animal in its own right. I wish, as much as possible, to tilt this book away from the annals of historical anthology, but a quick skimming over of conversations had by several historians would do some good in refreshing our memory a tad bit, just enough to allow for the contextualization of race in contemporary times as it relates to class antagonisms. To do this, I implore the reader's patience.

# What is- and is not- Race

To most, race is something real. Peter, a friend of mine, and I, got carried away in a deep-set discussion on race, with him appalled by the notion of me thinking of race as a fabricated phenomenon. He had not let me fully encapsulate the logic to my thinking that way. Indeed, I too thought of race along the same constructs, as did he and many others that both he and I had encountered, during the courses of our lives. Peter currently runs his own small private law firm, he and another friend I know not well enough about to speak. Peter is a middle-aged black man living in Toronto. In addition, his profession meant that Peter was well accustomed to wiggling his way out of any conversational tight spots in which he may have placed himself. Thing is, however, "race is not real in the way we think of it: as skin deep, primordial, and biological. Rather, race is a foundational idea with devastating consequences because we, through our history and culture, made it so."[1] Therefore, this accounts for the logic that; if two blonde haired, blue eyed white Norwegian persons were placed next to a dark skinned, dark brown eyed Sudanese individual; it could, in fact, turn out that one of the Norwegian persons shares more similar genetic material with the Sudanese than with his country folk. This is the essence of race being non-biological, as I shall later on expound upon. The reason for which Peter and many others like him around the world feel and experience race as a certitude, as something definite and real, partly has to do with paradigms, or otherwise said, one's world view. Race seems visually real. How so? On a daily basis, the outward difference in form, exhibited by people, as we cross paths in a grocery store, or brush shoulders on the street, escapes not a single person. This difference in color and morphological features is clear even to a seven year old. Funny enough-depending on your sense of humor,- rather than it having to deal with biology, race is real because of how we, on a daily aspect, interpret these outward differences in color and structural appearance, and, of course; the meanings that we invest into these 'biological' differences. It might seem counterintuitive- and counter-productive even,- but race is also biological to the extent that the idea of race, and more so how living in a racially stratified or varying society, with differential access to resources, has effects on the body. The afore-mentioned effects are manifest in infant and adult mortality. To give a pungent example of this, allow me to move away from the North Americano-centric or even Eurocentric view of the world, and take up a more global approach. The global South (Africa and South East-Asia), the breeding ground for the world's misfortunes and social ills, due to colonial and neo-colonial exploitation; on average, exhibits lower life expectancy and high child mortality rates. Thus, such social miscarriages have become synonymous with being black or being South-East Asian. The effects of unequal distribution of wealth (health and affluence), when presented statically, purports to show that whites and their infants, have a better chance of surviving past adulthood and to an older age than is commonly seen among non-whites. Another example of the implications of social marginality, can be seen in the proportion of crime related deaths and ills within 'Western' societies (black on black violence for example), lowering the life expectancy of non-whites in our more developed societies. Therefore, if race is an illusion, then it is an eccentrically powerful one (the product of centuries' long molding of societies). "There is human linguistic, cultural, biological, and genetic variation. [However] these variations are not racial in that they do not 'naturally' partition individuals into races. A key insight from anthropology is that what we see as real is often due to what our worldviews predispose our minds to see." [2] It is, thus, in much the same way that we used to think the sun revolved around the earth. Our conceited geo-centric notions of peculiarity were shattered, upon the discovery of the world being (at least somewhat) spherical, changing our worldview of what it meant to be human. Yet, the notions of our past worldview still effect our contemporary paradigms, since, we still make mention of the sun rising and setting, as though hinting to the fact the flaming fireball of gas in the sky is in motion, in the stead of the globe spinning. We, for example, do not say that the earth has spun towards light or to darkness, as a way of describing dawn and dusk periods of the day. It is much this lingering effect, despite our paradigm shift, that affects our view of race even today. As humans, we see variation as race, only because the idea is all around us and is unquestioned (or insufficiently questioned). In effect, race is not only a social construct, but rather, it is also a powerful social contract.

*"History is written by the victors"*- **Walter Benjamin**

Apart from the Quakers and a few marginal groups of the sort, it was commonplace, to most before the mid-17th century and Lincoln's proclamation of emancipation; that enslaved Africans were three-fifths of a person. The afore-mentioned logic was the rationale used as a means of justifying the inhumanity performed by the 'civilized' part of humanity. While the Thirteenth Amendment changed this formulation, the racial contract was, and still is, much deeper than laws and 'official' statements. Yet, despite that, the recognition of blacks as fellow humans pre-empted the erection of additional laws, against miscegenation (interracial marriage), guaranteeing, for one thing, the perpetuation of the inferiority complex amongst black communities in the US. This complex was particularly enduring because the idea of race, as a paradigm, had become, over time, deeply etched into our minds and institutions. Therefore, if we earnestly want to expose racial thinking today, then, just as weeds will return if not pulled out by the roots, we will not get beyond racism unless we pay attention to the roots; that is, to its foundational ideas. As fundamentally woven of an idea as race is into our minds and institutions, we still, I believe, can change the way that we understand race, and even, how race is to, from henceforth, embed itself in our institutions. Race and racism within our institutions, tend to be implemented into society three, and even four steps ahead of our collective understanding of race. The policies and laws which had been legislated from as far back as Abraham Lincoln's emancipation of black slaves, up until the civil rights revolution of the 1950s and 60s, and the subsequent forms of reform and 'reparations' offered to Blacks; are the instruments that spearheaded the march towards the renovating of society through institutional means. Still, resistance to such progress is but a given and the dropping of the guard by civil rights activists allows racism within our institutions to take up different, and never before seen variations and overtones. "It's always about race with you people," a term I hear all too often. However, before moving further with this section of the book, I wish to clarify that racial issues, in and of themselves, are not what I am here talking about. Instead, I wish to lay claim to the notion of *race, racism, sexism and all forms of marginalization, as being the product of class antagonisms*. Such occurrences, of inequality, are the manifest tools of the few to control the many. Hence with the above stated perspective of racism, as a strategic tool for control, it only thus makes sense that from the system of slavery, to the Jim Crow way of life and overt racism, up until our contemporary system of covert racism; the 'divide and conquer' strategy stays the same, despite the variant methods used to accomplish it. [3]

## Reflecting on the origins and development of the notion of race

One aspect that led to the emergence of the categorization of peoples in terms of race, had come about with the encounter of Native Americans ('Indians'), by the first Europeans to greet the shores of the 'new world'. The mere fact of unilaterally asserting that a diverse group of peoples, occupying vast stretches of land must necessarily come from one race, the Indian race; did not seem preposterous, is not short of perplexing to me. The likes of Christopher Columbus and Hernan Cortes, and the institutions that backed their ventures, men of sufficient mental capacity, ignored or refused to face the fact that humans, wherever in the world they may be, have complex relations with one another. The Natives of this 'new world', like any other 'world', had rivalries and differing customs/norms and mores, cultures, and heritages that were dissimilar to one another. Although, the cultures encountered in America by the European sojourners were in stark contrast to their own, and the Americans (and their differing cultures) were much closer to each other, when compared to the customs held by the men and women who came across the vast oceans. Still, equating every American person, at that time, to a monolithic people, was as outrageous as positing that the Chinese in the orient (who had been introduced to the West via the establishment of Marco Polo's Silk Road), were the same people as the Indians found on the sub-continent. Therefore, grouping the Aztecs, and Incas, and the high land dwelling Andeans (the subjects of the Inca minority, for the most part), as one block of peoples with unified aspirations and traditions and gods, allowed for the easy classification of them as the 'other'. This categorization, and mercantilist indifference towards the natives begun to churn the ideological machine that allowed for the subsequent labeling of 'us', meaning whites, versus 'them', meaning Indians or Blacks or Asiatic or anyone non-white. Through these texts, that is, in this book; I wish to discredit the type of thinking that is sometimes prevalent amongst peoples from minority communities. Often posited, by the aforementioned communities, is that the white man is the cause for all societal ills. The Nation of Islam even goes as far as demonizing the 'other', with the term "white devil" resting readily on the tip of their tongues for its next explosive use in times of argumentative confrontation. Instead, I wish to move away from the divisive rhetoric, which serves not the majority (the demos); I wish, rather, to instill a conversation starter that sees the acts done, at least initially, by a select group white people-backed institutions in our recent history (of the past 400 years) as typical of any hegemonic or ruling demographic.

Al Andalusia, or the Muslim ruled Iberian Peninsula (modern Spain and parts of Portugal), ruled their caliphate, and of coursed influenced most of Europe during the Middle Ages (circa 711-1490 AD) in quite similar manner. Indeed, the Berber (Black Muslim) and Moorish (Arab Muslim) elites, ruled by sectarian means. This province of the greater Umayyad Caliphate had splintered and ruled almost independently from its main polis and Caliph (Emperor/Religiously instilled leader) in Arabia. Reasons for this varies among historians, but what is plain is that great distances in those times amounted to less control, and often indirect ruling was preferred by most of the involved parties. Taxes and goods flowed easily, however, from the west via the Mediterranean Sea to the east. Just as is the case today, concerning white supremacy, religion, culture, and language were the main precepts by which the society in the peninsula was to be stratified. To avoid falling into the misfortunes of slavery, or worse, at the hands of the conquering 'barbarians', masses of merchants, elites, and scholars of the former Visigoth European civilization flocked to the tender embrace offered by Islam. The Islamization, primarily, and the Arabization, secondarily, precluded people from servitude by the invading force. Today, Black artisans (musical artists mostly) and business people, as well as scholars find that they have to adhere to the prevalent institutionalized norms of the ruling elite to see any moderate advancements in their endeavors. Such compromising maneuvering within an already established Western capitalist system has the effect of perpetuating white supremacy, and its changing forms across the changing seas of time. So today, despite any enacted policies and civil rights bespoken of by politically correct people and our leaders, the system is geared up to favor white Christian Anglophone males. Thus, the division within the greater populous continues unimpeded; to the detriment of the many and the opulent thrive of the few. Merit, only for the previously mentioned few, and but for a few exceptions, could carry the day and bestow great wealth upon the smart and hard worker in the New World, America. Yet, in this developing New World, the criteria for whiteness had been in constant flux.

White and whiteness, in the United States, according to linguistic anthropologists is what is termed as an 'unmarked' racial category/class or demographic. However, it is not often that one would explicitly come across such a classification, or an acknowledgement by the members of said scholarly community as the 'normal', a standard against which all 'others' are to be measured. Across the vicious seas of our individualistic capitalist society, this categorization serves as a north star, guiding us, and thus relegating other 'racial' groups to the realm of the exception, or the deviated ones, from said normal. As such, white racial identity is often equated, by some, with true or authentic 'American-ness'. It is tough to speak of the story of America and of race and of class antagonisms without making mention, even in the slightest, of the story of how whiteness came to be. The place is colonial Virginia, the year, 1691. This setting marks the first time that the term 'white' is legally used in a stature, the effect of which, among others, "expanded the range and severity of punishments for interracial marriage and sexual relations. This statute is an early example of how colonial leaders attempted to preserve the boundaries of whiteness *as they understood them.*"[4] As a consequence of such social manipulations by the higher ups of that colonial society, today, many individuals we see and treat as white would not have been so in 1691. What did it take to be white? Religious and national affiliations were in large part indicators of where one would lie on the racial spectrum. This white 'class' was reserved only for Protestant Anglo-Americans. At the time, German and Irish immigrants and their offspring were not yet quite white, and in addition, only the landowning class of the afore-defined white class enjoyed the full benefits of citizenship. "Like all racial formations however, the development of whiteness is an ongoing process or 'project.'"[5] As such, definitions and walled up boundaries of whiteness have changed throughout American history, with the expansion resulting from the strategic need, from place to place and time to time, for the balancing of nativist and anti-immigrant prejudices with the labor needs of a growing nation. The impetus that drove these changes, during the changing times and needs of the nation came from scientists, policymakers and other economically dominant actors.

For a better understanding of contemporary racial whiteness, we, like numerous other scholars and seekers of the truth, begin with W.E.B. Du Bois, the source of several critical expositions into what it is that makes or does not make for race or racism in America. In one of several masterpieces, *Black Reconstruction*, originally published in 1935, DuBois expounds on the notion of whiteness, and how being white was neither natural (based on phenotype) nor was it a foregone cultural conclusion in the US of A, and even in the context of racial slavery. Rather, he believed that whiteness, as is defined through European ancestry, was a well concerted and calculated racial solution developed by leaders of the colonies, for the eking out of economic and physical threats to the solidarity that begun to fester among the laboring or proletariat classes. Over the course of the 17th and 18th centuries, as the legal apparatus of racial slavery took root and hold, molded and intricately crafted by lawmakers on behest of the landowning/agrarian and political elites (who often times were the same folks in those days); revolts against exploitation from the elites was not uncommon. The coalitions that banded together in fervent protestation had as members individuals from all walks of the lower-rungs of life. Blacks both free and enslaved, together with the working classes of white farmers, and other disparaged white groups conspired and revolted in unison. As put by labor historian David Roediger, in his 1999 book *The Wages of Whiteness: Race in the Making of the American Working Class*, Bacon's Rebellion of 1676 in Virginia and the 1741 'conspiracy' to destroy New York, illustrate the seriousness of this threat to propertied class. To answer the 'lesser' folk, the white elites thus resolved to undermine interracial working-class solidarity. How so? They did so by granting virtually all European men full access to political or legal whiteness; the right to suffrage being not least poignant of these rights. In effect, during the first half of the 19th century, tax, property ownership, employment, and other requirements that had, before then, circumscribed suffrage to landowners, were now accessible to the masses, those of European descent. [6] The expansion of whiteness, in the wake of the 1741 'conspiracy', with Bacon's Rebellion also still in mind; was not a utopian-like banding of Europeans. Instead, this was but a successful attempt on the part of colonial elites to quash any forms of resistance to their reign, both present and future. [7] This newfound racial alliance with the elites, for DuBois, and on these terms, was insidious to society, since, working-class whiteness freshly baked in an elite oven, posited on the betrayal and suppression of shared class interests in favor of white supremacy and privilege. The acceptance of "personal whiteness" by European laborers as "something that could be owned as an asset and as an identity" (Roediger 2008) ensured continued political economic dominance by the landowning class. In exchange, they acquired the accrued material benefits typically associated with full citizenship, as well as the "public and psychological wage" (Du Bois 1935) of codified social distance and deference from their former allies. The political independence, with which the white workers were ostensibly blessed, was now an experience that their former black allies found non-relatable. Thus, a powerful and enduring economic incentive for systematic working-class racism established itself, because of the lowest social stratum consisting exclusively of nonwhites (and primarily of blacks). The Du Bois-style assessment of political, personal whiteness as the stark contrasted opposite of racial blackness, till this day informs critical analyses of the legal and economic consequences of white racial formations on their nonwhite counterparts (scholarship such as: Cheryl I. Harris; "Whiteness as Property"; Harvard Law Review 106: 1707-1791; 1993. George Lipsitz; "The Possessive Investment in Whiteness: How White People Profit from Identity Politics"; Rev. and expanded edition, Philadelphia: Temple University Press; 2006).

During the late 19<sup>th</sup> and early 20<sup>th</sup> centuries, in response to demographic shifts and cultural pressures, once more, the enlargement of the prerequisite criteria took hold. This time, to be included in the prestigious league of the 'normal' and ostensibly monolithic race were the Italians, Germans, and other 'Nordics', who gained greater acceptance as 'true' Americans (although, of course, still decidedly less true than Anglo-Americans). The newly enfranchised group already possessed the legal and political privileges afforded white males, and so, as a means of reaffirming and reinforcing the boundaries of whiteness, their enhanced racial standing (and psychological wage), this time, was meant to offset the fast growing numbers of southern and eastern European immigrants. More white bodies of a more agreeable 'stock' were thus needed to offset the 'lesser' whites. These 'new immigrants', for example, Jews, Poles, Russians, and Italians, brought differing customs and traditions from those of the 'old immigrants' of northwestern Europe. The newcomers were often looked upon as being little better than barbarians, or having an antiquated and bizarre culture to that of the older immigrants. They were, to other whites in Europe of inferior quality. William Z. Ripely, in *The Races of Europe: A Sociological Study*, alluded to the victimization of these older migrants, through discriminatory restrictive immigration policies designed to limit their numbers via quotas. Therefore, once in the US, they resumed the taking up of the inferior mantle, relegated to walk through life alongside indigenous peoples, Hispanics, Asians, and African Americans. [8] However, despite such hurdles and underarm treatment, new immigrant groups soon found their way to whiteness, although relegated to an ethnic variety of this whiteness. Even so, their almost immediate acceptance -due to their skin- as white, although legally, politically and economically enfranchised within the society, did not translate to social or cultural acceptance. In effect, as in the past, when acceptance finally came, it did so unevenly, creeping at a snail like pace for some groups than for others. At the turn of the century, for instance, most Anglo-Americans had found it easier, I am even tempted to say, more convenient to receive Germans, Scandinavians, and other old immigrants into the white racial fold than they did the Irish. Such prejudices are a reflection of the historical relationship between the British and the Irish, and the political subjugation of the latter by the former in Europe. To add gasoline to the smoldering heat, inflaming matters, tied to the bad blood was Catholism among the Irish, and the disparaging of said doctrine of papal supremacy by the English. [9] On the other hand, Jewish and Italian Americans seemed to remain in somewhat of an in between state, in constant flux between nonwhite and white racial identities. World War II; may be considered as a marking or reference point. Until then, these groups, the primary targets of the 1924 immigration quotas, were, in fact, deemed somewhat less white than those of European descended factions. By the middle of the 20th century, however, all European émigrés and their offspring saw themselves, and were in large part recognized politically and culturally as white people. This, then, was the third widening of the whiteness bin. The 1940s and 50s saw these groups of the 'third phase' benefit from the discriminatory federal housing policies that helped create and nurture suburban middle-class whiteness in contrast to increasingly 'colored' inner cities. Increasingly so, also, they enjoyed favorable popular portrayals as 'normal' whites, despite the harsh realities of popular culture serving to remind them that they in fact did not match up to the idealized aesthetics of Anglo-Americans.[10] "This was a crucial period in U.S. history, when white and new immigrants became "ethnics". From this point, only Hispanics, Asians, African Americans, and Native peoples had been marked and measured as racially different."[11]

*"...[There's] a vast and growing literature that documents race as a social/historical/cultural construct: a system of ideas identities, and material relations that emerged slowly in the context of Western European imperialism and colonial expansion beginning in the 15th century. In contrast to popular belief in race as an empirically validated, innate, and defining human quality, they point out that the first laws designed to establish and patrol racial boundaries and hierarchy did not appear until the middle of the 17th century, when the 'racial worldview' was a new thing under the sun..."* [12]

Having this paradigm as a reference point, human races are no longer, or at least should no longer, be perceived as biological units. Despite the global contemporary scholarship and mainstream affinity for referencing through presumably shared physical (and, increasingly, cultural) attributes, races are in fact political entities resulting from our social actions. As such human races exist solely because we created them and only in the forms that we perpetuate them.[13]

~*\*~

Ten years on from my tanning spree in Botswana (is it still tanning if you are 'black'?) and the incendiary O.J. Simpson race-coated trial of the century; not much on global racial relations had changed. The remnants of an amazing fun-filled, and at times flabbergasting touring of Brazil, was, for me, coming to a close; as the intonations of the Fall season, and the busy schedule that went with it reared its visage discretely. I always loved Toronto in September, but was not yet sure of my want to rid myself of August 2005. Those easy breezy sentiments of mine would not last long enough. Calamity and sheer humanitarian disaster (both natural and human-made) shook the foundations of interplay between rhetoric and practice. Hurricane Katrina happened. Before peering through, on even the most superficial of levels, at the manner in which a disaster, rather than bringing a nation together, wrought it with tension and division; I wish to take you a fortnight aback and unfold a story of a more personal, and somewhat, maybe, trivial manner. On this, the above-mentioned summer trip of mine, I decided to leave the hustle and bustle of the concrete jungle of Toronto, for a more lush, herbal and serene Amazonian milieu. I was to leave my busy life and fly to Rio de Janeiro, where my younger brother David had already opted for a head start on all activities fun and dire. He had no patience for spending a single summer day in Toronto when he could be "enjoying it somewhere cheap and spicy". When asked if he was confusing Brazil with India, he retorted on how the women and men were of a spicy nature there. I nodded, pretending to know of what he spoke. Having once been kidnapped (a story I will elaborate on later), I got into a rent-a-cop habit. I hired an armed bodyguard to accompany me throughout my shenanigan-filled escapades in Brazil. Was I taking the scare a bit overboard? Maybe. However, since I get no satisfaction visiting a place without footing around the shantytowns and ghettos at night, I figured, 'what the heck', it would not hurt hiring one, no matter how "corny" I looked. David on the other hand, had no such impulsions, to live as the poor or even the lower-middle classed people did, in contrast to my belief that one has not partied until he or she has done so in a shantytown, spurred on by a local 'guide'. In Rio, that summer, as amazing as it was to let loose of several of my normatively held inhibitions, partying, like anywhere in the world, is a dime a dozen. It is the people and interpersonal relationships that I tend to remember, and dare I admit, even pride myself on doing. Two things were the 'sore thumbs that stuck out', to reference the clichéd metaphor that needs no further hinting from me.

### The First Sore Thumb:

Danny, my suited muscle for hire, was Brazilian born and was already at high altitude levels before we had even boarded the plane, having not stepped foot on home soil for just over four years. We warmed to each other rather quickly and thus I had no qualms about asking of his recent history. I was curious as to what drew him to Toronto, and more so how he found himself doing what he did best, for people like me. Did he always want to guard another body with his body? Of course, I had no impressions of him taking a bullet for me. My thought was, and still is, that no one would be willing to take a bullet for another person, unless on ideologically spurred notions. However, a man licensed to use a firearm for the purposes of self-defense in Brazil, was, by no small measure, a welcomed edition nonetheless. In tandem with the conversation, flowed some beers and too the fluid appreciation for any type of Dutch beer, but the pre-vacation libation was put on halt before it even took off. A middle-aged man found his seat adjacent to ours. Still waiting for the rest of the passengers to board the flight, and overhearing how excitedly we spoke to one another of what to expect in Brazil, he decided to engage us in conversation. We, indeed, obliged his engagement. He had these bright green eyes that peered at us in sheer curiosity, sizing us from head to toe, not so briskly that we would make note of him then, but subtly enough so as to have picked up on it later, upon further reflection, and once that a bit more of his personality become apparent to us. He seemed genuinely interested in what we had to say, since we spoke of the crime rate in Brazil, and him dubious about his second trial venture at fun, since, it seemed, the year before had ended in malevolence. He was one of the many guests whom each year have their luggage ruffled through and ransacked. In addition, the crème de la crème moment came when robbed of his great-grandfather's pocket watch, an heirloom that he was on his way to give to his son living in Rio; he wound up in hospital for a few days, healing from a knife wound/slashed flesh. He spoke with a thick British accent. I crossed out the possibility of him being from Liverpool, I was confident of it, since, that was the only accent I knew. A pale man he was, so much so that I began to worry over his vitamin D intake, in mind only. After much talk on the economy and the social life in Brazil, and now pulling away from the tarmac to take to the air, he blurted out a question much laced in suppositions and fiction. The question itself seemed to be veering off the avenue that led to the realm of inquisition and steered more to the principality of assertion.

"So what kind of professional sport's player are you?" the man seemed to have lashed out without warning. He shook his hands almost theatrically as he asked that, a gesturing that he had not once done prior to this inquisitive aberration.

"w-who...? Me?" stammered Danny, taken aback by the random introduction of the tangential question, having just laughed at a political joke not more than a couple of seconds prior.

"Oh sorry- I- I just...what do you do?"

Danny and I were both young black men, and both our phenotypes are non-expressive of any racial mixing having taken place in the past two generations of our families' trees. I am somewhat athletically built (am I exaggerating a bit? Who cares?), despite the five-feet-ten inches of vertical height that I take up in a room. Danny on the other hand was six-feet-eight and made my 'athletic' morphological features seem quaintly 'cute,' a term unwelcomed, as pertaining to one's appearance, by one incapable of being emasculated, the product of a young man raised in rural Africa. Still, if you were to assume of someone, as your typical black sports professional sitting in first class, I would not have faulted you for having bet your buck on Danny boy. The fault would of course lie in that you had indulged in a harmful assumption of social life in the twenty-first century. Harmful for both parties involved, but not surprising only to the recipient of the manifestations of said types of assumptions.

"If I told you, I would have to kill you," Danny retorted. His face showed no creases, which would have hinted to the rendition of an awful and outdated joke. Of course now, the man would never know if we actually were part of an illegal or dangerous organization, like the mafia or something, I thought. I suppose that it is fair to confess that I too may be guilty of pre-supposing his paradigm, in view of his question. Therefore, I chuckled, and opted to fess up to what we were to another and the broader picture of all things vacation. He was an investor and managed all types of funds throughout his portfolio-expansion driven career. Once we were safely in the air and cruising at a constant altitude, we turned our conversation inwards and only turned back to wave goodbye upon arrival in Rio.

### Second Sore Thumb:

I am all in favor for the unhindered flow of culture, *cultural traffic,* between and amongst different communities, both on a national and global scale. However, how proud can one be when the representation of an 'ethnic group's' culture is biased to the depictions that caused the same ethnic group, or at least a segment of it, to imitate 'artistic' depictions, rather than the art being founded in the factual representation of said group's culture? Should I be okay with the term nigger? How about: pronounced by blacks to blacks and spelled, as 'nigga', under the guise of 'endearment'? Would it be ok for a white person, with close 'ties' to the 'black culture' to say it to a black person (I am going along with the misguided view of black people belonging to a monolithic ethnic group, for now)? In addition: would it be right for the person to utter the word, in reference to a nonblack person? I could go on…

It was my second week in Rio, and the last day before heading to Sao Paolo. David, Danny and I opted for a relaxing day at the beach, with plans of exerting the least amount of energy throughout. Once at the beach and having established a semi-reclusive spot that was a stone's throw away from a shack, with an impressive resume of liquors; we entrenched ourselves, the sand covering half my lower body, as we gazed at the shimmering clear wavy giant body of water that stretched on, touching the bright silhouette line of a horizon. A man and two women, all ostensibly in their 20s approached our imagined sand-fortress of solitude. They looked hip (is it hip to say hip?), with dreadlocks that sprouted from all three heads, belonging to the respective waving arms of greeting. I would make for the worst possum, and so never bothered to play one. With that being said, I must go on to admit that it was the chiming blended melodies of Miles Davis, echoing out to the world through our portable speakers that called them into our universe of tranquility. Accompanying them, however, was the pungent alluring odor of something both David and I had not smelt since our days as undergraduate scholars.

"You guys smoke weed?" The shorter of the two girls called out in her stride. "Of course they smoke!" Retorted the man, now standing above us, before he went on to asset that, "all black tourists smoke! Especially on vacation! Wassup ma niggas?"

"No thanks!" I signaled my hand refusal to both the offer and state that he treated as a truism.

"I'm down!" rang out David, with Danny smiling in egregious anticipation. They sat down, only standing up an hour later. Growing up as a black person in North America, in general, and in Toronto, in particular, I long ago found that many of the overt forms of ignorance, as it relates to race could no longer invoke sentiments of surprise in me. Being black, to most people, meant that one had lived in a harsh manner, somehow, someway and at some point in their dark lives. Therefore, the probability of them being comfortable with the consumption of drugs was that much more elevated in comparison to whites, and a few other stereotyped nonwhites, or so went the tale from the taller of the two women, Brandy was the name. Justin and Christina were ethnically white Brazilian-born Americans, showing their good friend the "temptations and vices worth indulging in." They figured to have known a thing or two about what to do and where to do it whilst in Rio, the young Rastafarian couple, for the past decade, never missed a year without embarking upon this vice-full pilgrimage to their homeland.

"How rampant is the blight of racism in Brazil?" I sat upright, lifted my optical UV-blockers and showed off my dark brown eyes, looking to Justin for an answer.

"Man, it's pretty mellow out here," he said, paused, and then carried on to emphasize that, "Brasil is a rainbow nation." This was all too reminiscent of South Africa's new motto, moving away from their days of white supremacist rule. I have always considered racism as a mental/cognitive blight, which affects all societies on earth. This was a human-made blight, initiated by the ruling class and passed on from mind to mind, throughout the days of our lives, in differing dosses, as it interacts with our own predispositions of the social and 'concrete' worlds around us.

"You must really proud to be Brazilian then?" David inquired, knowing that it would spark several avenues of inquiry from me.

"Yea, yea, of course! We will even host the FIFA world cup here!" yelled out Christina.

"Hey, don't jinx it guys! I hope it is in Rio though, it would be amazing!.. Give me an excuse to come back here again!" retorted Brandy

"How many people live in the favelas?" I put the question out for testing.

"In Rio or the whole of Brazil" retorted Brandy

"Good question," was the reply from my younger brother, now facing me at a non-hygienically close distance.

"Indeed," I replied, "which ever one you thing you're competent enough to speak of."

"Man, I don't know anything about my competence on the matter, but I took a few courses on Brazil while at NYU. What I can say is that there is more than there needs to be. The world's getting greedier, man."

"I love how you knit pick my words, which makes this conversation that much more swell," I conceded, "competence is a lot to ask of anyone these days, I doubtless think that I am hugely incompetent, but I do know that over one million people live in such shanty-town-like conditions....most of them are black."

"That's so true..." Justin whispered, he now had his neck curbing at the weight of his troubled head. "In my opinion, there is something very wrong with the system, I mean, black people are the poorest of peoples, on average, compared to other ethnic groups globally."

"South-East Asians too... they've suffered through their fair share of poverty," retorted Vade, my little brother, in dire approval of Justin's assertion.

"Plausibly so..." I answered whilst leaning back and closeting myself in a world of thoughts on the matter.

"I guess it's not as rainbow and colorful as I would like to think," postulated Christina. "I think that the real world troubles shame even the most vehement human rights activists, not too many people would wish such a lifestyle upon themselves, let alone attempt to live in such a way, placing all their privileges and luxuries aside for even a couple of months."

We all agreed, nodding away in lulled comfort, with the bar being a 'tough' long walk for us at this point. The irony was not lost on us.

When the three smoking travelers initially made their way towards us, and with their pronouncing of the first few exchanges, I had the impression that I was dealing with some airheads who were quite ignorant on matters concerning race. The impression that stayed with me was still not too far off that mark, but then again, I think of myself in like regard. Thing is, I was initially very hesitant to 'chill' with them, and converse, only because of the manner in which he came to conclusion about my character and personality by merely looking at my skin. In leaving, I reminded him of it, and proceeded to pointing out why his approach, and him speaking that way was offensive to not only me, but also all forms of struggle for political (and hence social and economic) parity. The last fifteen minutes that we spent together went into talking about the use of the "N" word, and asking how it made him feel to use it, as well as how it made Brandy, a biracial woman, feel about her friend being so friendly with such a historically unfriendly term. Political correctness in the public arena, in my humble view, is as the act of sprinkling perfume on a piece of bull turd. The masking of our words, by filtering out our thoughts, the very thinking generated by our predisposed respective minds; leads us nowhere nearer to pointing out the faults that we would inevitably find to lay in each one of us. Tolerance, although an unstable concept, is easy to enact, by this I mean, easier than what's required of us for the continuous renovating of society; understanding human beings as complex systems, and more so, understanding the different influences of ethnicity in the different people. Why bother renovating of society? I believe it to be necessary, to keep up with the changing elitist strategies of conquering through division.

New Orleans at the end of August 2005 was the epitome of 'us', the collective Western society, saying one thing only to act in a contrasted manner. The majority of the desperate "refugees," fleeing from the wreckage wrought by the hurricane were black. Yet as citizens, as I will further show in the proceeding section, these scattered individuals from several communities ostensibly had to prove their citizenry. The notion of a unified and tolerant nation crumbled in the face of the stratified reality, made bare by nature's havoc wreaking. It was visible to the whole country, and embarrassingly for said country, the whole world, that there were different classes of Americans, even among the poorest classes of Americans. Once more, it was a white and black issue, for some, and for few more, it was an issue of power relations and a vivid depiction of exclusivity.

## What is- and is not- Racism?

Racism is *"a form of knowledge"*- Thomas Cleveland Holt

66
*In every human order there are always going to be some groups for whom knowledge of the totality is necessary, seeing that it is only with knowledge of*

*the totality that their dispossession can be brought to an end.* 99 - Sylvia
Wynter

Calling someone a racist, as I have found along the course of my error ridden life, is to the effect of single handedly bestowing on them the title of lord governor over all the slave holding masters of the eighteenth and nineteenth centuries, as well as being one of Hitler's most esteemed right hand men. Thus, I rarely lash out at someone that way anymore, as it does more harm than good in the long term, with the long hoped for resolution to injustice in the world ushered in by goodwill. The interplay between the different cultures and races, globally, made bare by the conditions and the actions we see, and not by the flamboyant, and maybe even well intentioned rhetoric we hear from our peers and leaders alike. Rather than continually embalming the world with ill borne words and sentiments, having no afterthought for the aftermath, since, knowledge giving (of what you deem to be a taboo) inefficiently translated to the person under reproach, will next time, maybe, not be given a sympathetic ear and thus maybe result in a "it's always about race with you people" situation. No one likes an "it's always about race with you people" moment, neither the embarrassed pronouncer, upon realizing "you people" is just as inflammatory as the N word, nor the recipient who becomes ever the more convinced of his 'agitator' as a racist. Well founded in the science of knowledge translation, the issues of racism and that of pedagogy have strongly bonded strands of mutual tethering. This is where counts the adage: it is not what you say but how you say it. The misunderstandings brought about by the avalanche of misinformation assimilated by us all, presented to us on most media platforms, screens and flashy lights, and systematically sustained by the pillars of our civilization, our institutions, be they academic, political or economic in nature. In essence, our progression to enlightenment as a global village depends on how best we can put our conceptions across, of what our grievances are as they regard our actions to one another, as between races, so it is between varying cultures within those same racial categories even. As the only black child in an otherwise exclusively white school in the suburbs of Oakville, Ontario, in Canada, relatively earlier on, my need to adjust and be flexible socially became apparent. As an African immigrant, the culture into which I was raised, that is to say, the mentoring style adopted by my parents to teach and guide me through life's early and crucial challenges, was markedly different to the tone and approach my school teachers had. My teachers' expectations of me, although not explicit, were regardless clear for all to read. Our social interactions, both between that of me and my peers, as well as of that of me in relation to my academic molders, were ostensibly as immiscible as vodka and a bowl of cornflakes. On the surface of it all, the vodka would no longer be distinguished from the milk, but if unaddressed, and with time, the vodka could be a seen as a blight on either or both aspects of your social life or/and your health. Hence, bothering to understand how I saw things or the reasons for my seeing them the way I did, eluded most of my peers and teachers alike. The underachieving bar set by most my instructors, for a time, had now become the glass ceiling that not only halted my progress but also worked to reaffirm its validity. Such self-fulfilling prophecies are not unheard of. In a post-slavery and post-Jim Crow society, where the wealth that encompasses you screams of the exploitation of the marginalized, both at home and abroad, racism is the tool used by those who have monopolized power and wish for a perpetuating of the like conditions that were favorable to their ascent. It is the overlords' coup de grace. It is racism, I postulate, that accords for the inferiority complexes, among other conditions, that acts as the ball-and-chain and whip, bearing high over the psyche of nonwhites.

What never escape my wonderment is the hypothetical scenario, of the possible life prospects, how would look the sphere of opportunity for hundreds of millions of people had civil rights activists not been vociferous about the injustices that enveloped them? Every day, apart from my family and the state of my health, I am thankful for the tribulations that such activists overcame. What I am also conscious of, however, is the need to refuse to settle for 'better than,' as concessions by the elite and ruling classes only occur by truckloads of resistance. Therefore, one cannot be content with the present norms and rigid guidelines of our working system of a society. After all our civilizations are still progressing, and we humans are the agents applying the adequate selection pressures which drive this progression. Hence, thinking that racism is finished in the year 2017 is no different from thinking that all of the evils of racism, indeed, were wiped out with the stroke of honest Abe's pen. Later in the book, we will see how capitalism as an ideology and economic system, intrinsically premised on the exploitation of some for the advancement and wellbeing of others, is a driver for the ongoing global inequality. My point being that, no matter the number of policies erected to level off the playing field of opportunity, there will always be an even number of other, often not well-known policies, which counter the effects of progress. What we are then left with upon this push back against actual progress is the semblance of moving forward in moral terms, as a collective human society. As stated in the preceding sections of this book, the concessions made by the elites through policies and the renovating of institutions are very much real. Rosa Parks and the reverend Martin Luther King Jr. and sundry activists achieved true mile stones in the fight against human injustice; the fight for human dignity. However, the strategies once used to keep the masses at each other's throats become obsolete upon said concessions. Also worth noting is the likelihood of enlarging the basket of undesirables or 'exploitables'. As was the enlargement case previously discussed, in relation to who could become white, so too could the notion of enlarging the bin of the poor be possible. As my good friend Adam once pointed out to me; we are all economic niggers and slaves in view of the exploitative system that liberal democracy has championed. Adam is white, needless to say that I am severely paraphrasing him as it regards the 'N' word. Racism, however, remains a favored tool of control and of dividing the masses of people. The rule via racism happens to remain the case for several reasons, of which one of said reasons has to do with the organic growth with which social constructs tend to exhibit. The seeds of socially built paradigms/realities once sowed, blossom into a network of complex interactions. This in turn means that despite the seemingly level footing of poor blacks in comparison to poor whites, their respective accessibility to resources differ, regardless of their parallel class statuses. It is this residual truncated benefit system in favor of some groups of people over others that is the newly taken up form of racism. The disparaging of a little-known scholar merely based on his or her name not sounding European enough, for example, that translates to racism and inequality in contemporary times.

I have read countless articles and blogs, and listened to many a person talk to me about how, in North America, the act of racism is something that can only be levied against a nonwhite person by a white person. How, the persons benefiting from this unequal system are uniquely in the position of ignoring the rewards this system grants to them. That said; they, then, are the only parties eligible for blame if racially motivated or biased actions are undertaken towards people of color. As well thought out as these hypotheses are, I would like to be the emboldened bearer of constructive skepticism. In tandem with the central premise of this book, I believe that (since this all chalks up to opinions); the need to empower one group of people using the same means as that which was used to subjugate them in the first place, is akin to us sinking to the level of a self-tail chasing mammal. All forms of bias and hate perpetrated against someone on the basis of their skin color is racism, regardless of which person is doing the attacking. I am an advocate of color-blindness, but not in the traditional sense, as one who ignores the variety inherent in the different races. These differences are not because of genetics, of course, but rather due to the ethnic and cultural backgrounds strongly linked to 'race'. Hence, any policy enacted must necessarily take into account the historical and social contexts of the demographics it influences, directly or indirectly. Throughout time and circumstance, a pyramid like hierarchy has always been present in delineating the beginnings and ends of different classes. Our civilizations happen to be well founded in discrimination, not only by culture as was often the case in times prior, but in race as well. The Greeks are often looked to as the torch bearers of enlightenment, a pillar of democracy (that is rule by the many). Yet, even in such a highly lauded society, although race did not translate to one's social and political standing, culture was very much the indicator of one's civility or brutishness. Fast-forward a few millennia, nothing much has changed in that regard. The notion of race is so deeply rooted in our societies that it is often an indicator of one's cultural upbringing, although not an accurate one. "In fact, it is sometimes difficult to distinguish between ethnocentrism and racism because of the increasing conflation of culture and race (Harrison)."[14] It takes a substantial amount of schooling in the values brought about by other cultures to, for example, look at a black person, as a nonblack person, and not see fried chicken, even though the nonblack individual is accustomed to more buckets of fried chicken than the person he or she is predisposed to have such judgments about. Even though black people hale from different cultures and ethnicities, we nonetheless simplify matters, as is a practice evident in all humans, and group all black people under a single umbrella. Stereotypes, as is often said, are the gateways to an entrenched form of racism. The point here is to elucidate the paradigm shift in human relations. The shift I speak of is from primarily focusing on learned practices and traditions to fixed notions of physical and essential characteristics. By and large, pre-racial conceptions of diversity did not halt or inhibit one from recognizing and/or acknowledging the shared capacity for human learning and the capability for all humans to be able to participate fully in any society (irrespective of phenotypic characteristics later used to distinguish races. This shift, therefore, is from slightly harmful cultural hegemonic practices to the severely pernicious racial-cultural hegemonic form.

## I Don't See Color

In the wake of war, all victories are of the pyrrhic type, at least, so I opine. The American civil war was no different, and I perceive there to have been two losers upon the proclamation of the war's end. Still more, the South continually sought for ways to propagate the a priori culture and economic system predicated on the exploitation of African Americans. In turn, the nation amended the constitution for the fourteenth time, mandating the "equal protection of the laws." From then up until now, waged from the east to the west coast is the debate over what these amorphous terms mean. However, today the prevalent interpretation of this is that the equal protection clause strongly disfavors any governmental use of race. In shorthand, this stance is what is often referred to as colorblindness. How we, therefore, interpret the policies and laws that we erect in one epoch subsequent epochs later, depends on our worldview (paradigm) of human relations. Such talk deems that Justice John Marshall Harlan's dissent in *Plessy v. Ferguson* be not amiss. In Plessy, an 1896 decision, the majority announced the "separate but equal" standard that eased on decades of Jim Crow racial oppression. [15] In an emphatic idealistic roar, Harlan declared that, "our constitution is colorblind, and neither knows nor tolerates classes among citizens." [16] At the time, one could imagine, given the dragged out, sorry history of racial subordination in the US, there was immense rhetorical appeal to this utopian vision of a future society in which race no longer correlate with privilege or disadvantage. Yet there is a difference between colorblindness as an ideal and as a current practice. As current practice not 'seeing color' would be detrimental the already marginalized segments of the population, of which segments need the judicial system to guard them from the oppression of the many. In other words, we have not yet, as a society, reached the level of equality and parity among races and sexes to be able to apply the law indiscriminately. We have not yet earned the right to be idealistic and uniform about how we deal with the descendants of slaves and those of former colonies.

Throughout the twentieth-century colorblindness is a story that has shifted from a progressive demand to a reactionary one. In the late 1940s and early 1950s, Thurgood Marshall, as counsel for the National Association for the Advancement of Colored People (NAACP), repeatedly encouraged his colleagues to uphold Harlan's famous injunction and to argue that, "classifications and distinctions based on race or color have no moral or legal validity in our society. They are contrary to our constitutions and laws." [17] In this instance, colorblindness was invoked upon in an attempt to attack the racial degradation given constitutional sanction by *Plessy.* Marshall's argument was premised on the notion that the use of race lacked moral and legal validity precisely when deployed to oppress. The dominos fell with such constant selection pressures from men and women of the likes of Marshall, coopting the Supreme Court to dismantle Jim Crow "with all deliberate speed."[18] However, as mentioned above, influence-bearing forces within the nation swiftly maneuvered their way around the system and work, to good effect, to counteract said policies. This made the Court fearful of having taken on more than it could chew. They particularly sought to avoid abruptly declaring unconstitutional –and by extension, immoral- the emotional core of white supremacy, that is; the ban on interracial marriage. With time, scholars and policy makers alike attested to the wisdom inherent in the act, that of not flatly prohibiting governmental distinctions based on race. Once more, it would be facile for us to imagine that the stroke of a pen could erase all forms or targeted forms of well-entrenched social ills. By the mid-1960s, leading up to the famed civil rights movements, it became evermore apparent, to both advocates and foes of racial emancipation, that segregation readily and gladly continued even in the presence of formal racial neutrality.

*"As late as 1965, less than one in one hundred black children in the South attended schools with whites, and the number of whites in predominantly black schools was infinitesimal. Civil rights lawyers dropped their demands for colorblindness and began to stress the necessity of race-conscious remedies to achieve integration and substantive equality, winning support from the Court in a series of decisions spanning the late 1960s and early 1970s."*[19]

Then the shift came, as the opponents of integration became the new patrons of colorblindness. Thurgood Marshall himself had acknowledged that colorblindness as a remedy promised tepid change, despite posing a radical demand for immediate freedom from all Jim Crow oppressions. Colorblindness, as presented and interpreted, required only an end to explicitly segregationist laws, not actual remediation of the harms wrought by racial oppression.[20] To the opponents of integration, which meant opposing colorblindness, this indeed was not lost on them. As was so abrasively yet still concisely well-articulated by a South Carolina district court in 1955, as a counterargument to integration: "The Constitution does not require integration. It merely forbids discrimination. It does not forbid such segregation as occurs as the result of voluntary action. It merely forbids the use of governmental power to enforce segregation."[21] Again, despite the policy having been erected, the manner in which said policy was interpreted in the different regions of the republic, according the predispositions and prejudices harbored, was what ruled instead. Hence, from such a starting point, it is but a short escapade to the contention that colorblindness affirmatively prohibited race-conscious integration measures. Such race-conscious integration measures in schools and neighborhoods was deemed unconstitutional/immoral, the housing discrimination and inherent socio-economic biases within the system, which restricted most colored people to urban cites notwithstanding. This movement, made manifest in several locales within the state, of which one said locale was North Carolina, which in 1969 would then go on to pass the law that, "no student shall be assigned or compelled to attend any school on account of race, creed, color or national origin."[22] In 1971, however, the Supreme Court intervened and unanimously struck down this law, declaring that the rigid limitations on government efforts to use race in a remedial manner had no place under the Fourteenth Amendment. North Carolina's strategy was relatively transparent in view of the Court, which recognized that "the statute exploits an apparently neutral form to control school assignment plans by directing that they be 'color blind'.; that requirement, against background of segregation, would render illusory the promise of *Brown v. Board of Education. "* The Court would then go on to explain that: *"just as the race of students must be considered in determining whether a constitutional violation has occurred, so also must race be considered in formulating a remedy. To forbid, at this stage, all assignments made on the basis of race would deprive school authorities of the one tool absolutely essential to fulfillment of their constitutional obligation to eliminate existing dual school systems.*[23]

By the end of the 1970s, the shift for colorblindness had completed its transition of camps, from a progressive emancipating standard to a more conservative (reactionary) stance. In essence, the rhetoric of colorblindness had been repurposed to suit the glove that laid attack on affirmative action. Justice Marshall Thurgood, the former counsellor, found himself urging the Court in its first full affirmative action case to reject colorblindness. "It is because of a legacy of unequal treatment that we now must permit the institutions of this society to give consideration to race in making decisions about who will hold the positions of influence, affluence, and prestige in America."[24] Marshall, unfortunately was once more faced with defeat, having faced it as a proponent of colorblindness whilst a lawyer, and then later against it as a justice. There is of course another side to colorblindness, other than its unyielding opposition to affirmative action. A side that has done more harm and limited racial progress than is often noted. In defining "racism as any use of race, colorblindness simultaneously defines what counts as "not-racism", that is: all government action not expressly predicated on race, no matter how closely correlated with racial hierarchy or how disproportionate the harm to nonwhites. This aspect of is best epitomized by a 1987 Supreme Court decision, *McCleskey v. Kemp.* The court turned its sights, disregarding what was at the time the most sophisticated and exhaustive survey of capital sentencing, rejecting the claim that racism tainted Georgia's death penalty machinery. Despite the Court's acknowledgement of the fact that the state of Georgia sentenced to die blacks who murdered whites at twenty-two times the rate for blacks who killed blacks, it opined that these statistics proved, "at most…a discrepancy that appears to correlate with race."[25] Taking cover behind colorblindness (now the reactionary form of it, of course), the Court reasoned as if racial discrimination was not an issue at play for their contemporary times. For racism to have been deemed to have played a part, the record had to maybe include a racial epithet or a confession of evil intent. Most critiques of colorblindness pay much more attention to its role as ammunition against affirmative action. However, regarding government practices that discriminate against nonwhites, colorblindness also serves as a shield. Affirmative action, it is argued, should be forbidden, say the proponents of colorblindness, on the premise that it encourages racial factions, invites reliance on stereotypes, and stigmatizes its supposed beneficiaries. Opponents, on the other hand say that the real source of factions, stereotypes, and stigma in society is continues and even resurgent segregation, after which they go on to claim that race-targeted approaches offer the only feasible solution. With time though, government officials, as is often mentioned by critics, have learned not to announce their discriminatory motives, this in turn means that protection for the 'little guy' from discrimination requires looking beyond the words of state actors to the impact of their actions, also, to historical patterns and the larger context (the larger worldview). For critics of the new wave of colorblindness, they in addition often point out that today much harm done to nonwhites occurs though embedded disadvantage, through the inertia of past injuries, and that government then has an obligation to at least not exacerbate the in-pitfall situation. What often escapes the American imagination is the aspect that;

> *"Courts have the power to overturn the will of the electorate. When the Court does declare an act unconstitutional, it asserts that the basic law of the country forbids what the majority seeks. On one cut, this is anti-democratic, for it involves a small-unelected body overturning the will of the voters. On the other, it is de4mocracy-perfecting: it gives expression to the nation's deepest democratic values in moments when voters seek to use the power of numbers against vulnerable groups or disfavored ideas.*

Put in epigrammatic form, courts protect democracy by guarding against the tyranny of the majority. Colorblindness as an interpretation of the Constitution must be evaluated in this light, not simply as a policy argument against the use of race. How does colorblindness fare when evaluated as an interpretation of the Constitution?"[26]

Colorblindness is perverse in striking down affirmative action while doing nothing about continued mistreatment. Colorblindness, coming from as humble an opinion as mine, is the politically correct garb that prevents an efficient 'grassroots' exchange of opinions, negating some of the potentiality required for the best possible bettering of our understanding of race, and race relations, in North America. It exemplifies the adage, "everyone is the same under the skin," This injunction was the 'grandmaster flash' of all clichés during the civil rights era, and was not a sociological claim but rather a moral demand. This clichéd catch phrase, aired out in most places, was an attempt to counter some of the biases people have towards others based on skin color or complexion. Today, however, the notion of race as skin deep serves as an ostensible description of social dynamics. Under said vision, racial groups serve the purpose of lumping individuals, and thus free moral agents, into irrationally constructed groups, with only arbitrary differences in physical appearance. Not constructed by the plunging into the furnace of history, that is, a history of subordination and exploitation, the aforementioned groups, as such, find themselves differentially situated even today. Seeing as, then, race is only a color; race says nothing about individual or group position in society. When made bare of any historical context, this superficial definition of race in turn undergirds the colorblind understanding of racism as every single advertence to race. Therefore, in this light, to take cognizance of race, whether to segregate or integrate, is to, according to colorblind activists, ostensibly treat people differently based on an arbitrary characteristic that is devoid of any social significance, a phenomenon found beyond the confines of control for the individuals concerned. What is worth noting about this vision is the manner in which it comprehends and encompasses racism in individual and symmetrical terms. Individual, in that racism is pernicious to the person classified by race (the 'other'), and symmetrical in that there is nothing that distinguishes the group positions of whites and nonwhites. This turns affirmative action into group discrimination. The exclusion of nonwhites under the overt system of white supremacy is no different from the preference given these disparaged individuals, in furtherance of social repair. In the words of conservative Justice Clarence Thomas, "government-sponsored racial discrimination based on benign prejudice is just as noxious as discrimination inspired by malicious prejudice. In each instance, it is racial discrimination pure and simple."[27] In light of this understanding of colorblind practices of race, the racist appears to be the first person in the room to use the word 'race'. This, more often than not, happens to be the person vociferous about the persistence of discrimination or advocating for racial, and as such, social repair. An accurate elucidation of this reactionary practice is the atmospheric change of racial relations and rhetoric levied against former President Obama whenever he referred, however obliquely, to the continued presence of astringent racial relations. Cries and proclamations of him to not choose sides, as he's the president of a whole nation and not just blacks is emblematic of this reactionary backlash. The next section of this very chapter will have us taking a closer look at the relationship between race, racism and inequality. However, having stripped race and racism of almost any significant content, colorblindness finds itself incapable of explaining the continued correlation between race and inequality in the United States. The correlation between race and inequality, even globally speaking, escapes not even the least perceptive and astute of us. Just to pick out a needle in a haystack of other needles, black median wealth, being said needle, lags far behind that of whites, even as African Americans have suffered disproportionately in the past recession of 2008/2009. The New York Times reported that, "as of December 2009, median white wealth dipped 34 percent, to $94, 600;" while the comparative demographic of black people saw theirs drop by "77 percent, to $2,100."[28]

What's worth noting, however, is the manner in which any reference to group culture is treated as not being racist. Eduardo Bonilla-Silva (2003: 28) speaks of cultural racism, a phenomenon that has greatly contributed, in his view, to the paradigm of colorblind racism. Cultural racism is the frame the accounts for stereotyped arguments such as, "Mexicans place little emphasis on the need for education" or even how "blacks have too many children" or "all black people love chicken." Such generalizations, in part, are an attempt to explain the standing of minorities in society. Under these rules established by the different advocates of colorblindness, only open references to skin color or the use of explicitly derogatory racial slurs and epithets end up counting as racism. In addition, the mention of 'cultural or behavioral deficiencies' often attributed to nonwhites, seems to bear no relation to racism and xenophobia. The type of rhetoric and the vocabulary used during the 1980s and 1980s of; 'super-predators', 'gang bangers', and 'welfare queens,' typifies this cultural racism often not thought of, especially at the time, as being racist. In contemporary times, we have to contend with having to listen to the type of rhetoric that paints Mexicans as mostly illegal immigrants, the newest edition to the boogy-man (next to black men), as well as the mention of Muslims as terrorists. Of course, only the bigoted among us actually voice such sentiments, but my point here being that, being inundated with such negative depictions of nonwhites on a constant basis, has an effect on our perceptions. Our perceptions of the non-relatable, of what we are not exposed to often, is greatly affected. Let us say that the total knowledge held in your mind is given the value of 100 percent, of which one percent of what is known to you is of matters concerning Mexicans and African Americans. Yet, only a tenth of said one percent of knowledge (so 0.1% of your entire knowledge) is borne from genuine experience and exchange of ideas with people from those demographics, while the remaining nine tenths are acquired by media consumption and peer-peer talks. In light of this, despite our best wishes to be politically correct, our conditioning, which strongly correlates with our accumulated knowledge, factors in the biases we then embody. Even I, as a black man, am not immune to this conditioning. When I, for example, working on my pc at a public library, have the need to take a break or pick up my phone away from the quite floor, I more often than not ask my white neighbor to my left rather than my black one to my right, to keep an eye on my belongings. Education on matters of race and race relations help to counterbalance the predispositions with which I was raised, but only to an extent. How are such biases eliminated in a society striving for and preaching about racial parity? For starters, genuine exchange of knowledge needs to take place between the races and classes within and without these different races. Secondly, the rhetoric spewed by our leaders and peers need to not stop only at 'better than yesteryear' policies, but such practices must be institutionalized with a more progressive understanding of colorblindness than the current reactionary one. No matter the hysterical commentary or punitive governmental actions may be, colorblindness, or the advocates of, insist that race is not involved so long as the focus is on failed cultures or bad behavior, even when such characteristics are attributed to whole groups in a manner that bears uncanny resemblances to the racial stereotypes of yesteryear. Thus, for advocates of colorblindness, and a large and growing part of US population contend that: groups have, largely, earned their relative accent, or deserved their relative disadvantage because of their made choices, values, and the abilities inherent in the groups themselves. Illegitimate social engineering is often the term of recourse when one seeks to alter the ill-mannered distribution of privilege and hardship. This ubiquitous societal inequality is, by the framework of colorblindness, rationalized as legitimate, warranted and earned, as such, society is morally forbidden to do anything.

*"Quite frankly, the present incarnation of colorblindness seems geared to preserving the racial status quo. The great triumph of the civil rights era lies in the defeat of white supremacy, not only as a set of ideas but in its most egregious practices. This tradition of struggle against racial injustice continues, even as discrimination has evolved and remains stubbornly entrenched and even sometimes actively pursued. Colorblindness originally boldly demanded that Jim Crow be dismantled. Contemporary colorblind partisans wrap themselves in the moral legitimacy of this history, loudly trumpeting their opposition to already defeated practices and seeking to arrogate to their use the heroes and slogans of the civil rights era. But in practice they defend continued inequality. Using the rhetoric of colorblindness, they oppose affirmative action, refuse to look critically at discriminatory practices, attack as racists all those who speak forthrightly about continuing racial problems, and tolerate and even promote rank stereotypes so long as masked in cultural and behavioral terms."*[29]

## Hi Katrina

Hurricane Katrina made landfall, devastating the land and sentient beings with her saying of hello. Yet, it is the our reaction as a nation, proud enough to the point of rejecting any aid from other nations and allies alike, but also lacking in pride in its barbarous treatment of her own citizens. The aftermath ceased the world's attention far more than did the actual catastrophe, however short-lived this attention may have been. The pillars of societal information sharing and awareness promotion, our media platforms, played a pivotal role in dampening said global and even local attention of the catastrophe's aftermath. For this reason, I have devoted an entire chapter on the media and the public relational endeavors undertaken by the federal government. For now, however, I wish for us to peer into the veneer that is racism and race relations as it regards the elephant in the room. By elephant, I am referring to the massive chasm present between our rhetoric, as a nation and a western-style civilization, and the practices we undergo daily and yearly. If you wish to know more of a person's character, the saying goes, one ought not to analyze an individual during lush and comfortable times, but rather, better judgement of the person takes place in the wake of discomfort, malaise and unexpected disaster having befallen said person. Therefore, I don't think of myself, and others making similar claims of the nation's abandonment of its citizens, as being nit-picky when analyzing US practices during its hours of moaning and teeth-gnashing, rather than doing so only during times of solace. I do not intend for us to spend too much time on what is already becoming an expansive literature, but a quick peering through of this façade of equality and colorblindness will do us some good and add some form of continuity to our ongoing discussions.

Sequestered at home, entertaining some guests that had flown in particularly to see me, old friends from Liverpool, with whom most of what came to mind I could say without the unease of feeling judged. We sat down around the television for hours, as most people did, and after a while went ahead and muted the reporters' voices, believing that images have a way of speaking out to us more. It is a habit that I later adopted when watching the news, upon, of course, having gotten a healthy dosage of rhetoric and having listened to the most eloquent wordsmiths of our time, I then revert to soundless footage in an attempt to (re)interpret what I saw. A number of things stuck out to us visually, one of which was the need for residents of New Orleans to wave the American flag and show off some of their patriotic spirit. It became very clear to us, and even clearer, I am sure, to the marooned thousands upon thousands of people, that they were not as American as upper-middle classed and mostly white suburban citizens were. The notion of second-tier citizenry was at play and ostensibly unambiguous in appearance, seen by an entire world with aspirations of themselves being a 'land of the free.' Some of the typical rhetoric on civil rights and human rights underwent rapture from the realm of practice. While some of the rhetoric on black stereotypes and crime as it relates to black-majority-communities were intact, concurrently at pace with the practices now under observation. Our paradigm or otherwise said, the proverbial glasses through which we see the world, both the physical and socially constructed world, made it easy for a significant number of people to go along with the ramblings of the mainstream media platforms. As is oft the case with racism, such prejudice and discrimination is best received and used, when the 'attacker' is under the impression that the 'other' is not all too human in the first place. This dehumanization does not require one party to physically strip bare the other, nor does it entail the whipping and stripping of the name of the person under attack. That strategy, unfortunately (for some), has run its course. While on the matter, I will go ahead and share with you one form, or strategy, I believe, of dehumanizing individuals. When and if a terrorist organization lays siege on a city with the typically ill minded placing of a bomb, what images are shown of the survivors and unfortunate fatalities? Well, it depends on where the attack happened. If this sad display of power by this terrorist group takes place on European or North American soil, we see Facebook and family-provided pictures of the person while they were alive. These images have a powerful ring, almost as if to say, "this could be you or me next time…this loss of life is an attack on everything you (we) believe in. However, the flip side is that if such an attack were to happen somewhere in the Global South, in a 'third-world' country, then the images are to be vastly contrasted to what would be shown to us of our 'western-society.' On several occasions, I found myself pointing this out to some of my colleagues and friends, how pictures of the survivors or the fallen would be of them after the fact. The bloodied bodies laid out and scattered all over the place, the surreal disarray of first responders and bystanders is thrashed onto your faces. Made to feel less sympathetic for the victims the more that these images are shown to us and soon forgetting what is supposed to be a horrific display. This unsympathetic approach to reporting the news has in great part added to the dehumanizing process and inherent system of exploitation greatly favored by hidden capitalist elites. Also, it takes the killing of great masses of people and the bloodiest displays for people to speak out in protestation and even go as far as changing their profile pictures on social media sights as a show of solidarity. While, in Paris for example, world leaders and peoples from all over showed their strength with the 'Je suis Charlie' phrase, for that to happen, it took the taking away of a dozen lives (all lives are precious, and human lives are even that much more valuable…or so we say). Now back to the story at hand, and how the systemically dehumanized people of color, left to fend for themselves, feeling betrayed, rejected and once more, as devalued and demoralized as ever, acted humanly in kind to one another.

    I once stood on my balcony, gazing out at the world that went on thirty stories below me. I was with my younger brother James, who was in the mood for playing read-the-motions. This game is not unlike what we do when watching the news, in that we attempt to guess what activities are taking place with as little sensory information as possible. We watched a procession of people in black clothes walking by and tried to guess what the event meant. There were shouts of "it's a funeral man! Obviously! ...I win!" and I was more content in thinking of it as a Black-Panther movement, the first that I had seen in Toronto. It could have easily been some other organization, one that favored black as a shade, to be worn on all their outings. My point being that, without proper reporting and narration, it is hard to judge the occurrences taking place. On the other hand, what happens when the reporting suits the agenda of the media-owning bosses and their counterparts rather than strive for truth seeking? Therefore, not buying too much into the rhetoric used to describe the events taking place in the wake of Katrina, while also paying attention to visual detail, could go a long way in analyzing the scenario. This method allows for an open mind, knowing that all-knowingness is a grand task on its own, in this age of disinformation and mass information. The coupling of reading-in-between the lines and visual footage analysis allows me to fall on grounds I find more comforting than those laid out for me for simple tilling. Black residents accused of looting, drug abuse, homicide, and rape during the disaster-evoked chaos, was the typical go-to response for people predisposed to envisioning the black man as the boogieman. Stereotypes of what 'black' behavior ought to be, added gasoline to the flames of a dilapidating social structure, a structure now exposed to the wiles of a natural disaster. Most of these media-reported crimes, as has become common practice and as is to be discussed later, were never substantiated and later research showed that extensive pro-social behavior, and not crime, was the primary response of survivors in the days following Katrina.[30] The Katrina disaster, as mentioned much earlier, is both natural and human-made. Those desperate survivors were depicted as a bunch of dangerous criminals and good-for-nothings was, in large part, due to the racialized nature of the Katrina disaster. June 1971 marks the modern day commencement of the 'war on drugs,' with former President Nixon spearheading the charge. Since then, for most Americans, more especially the wealthier segments of the population, enveloped in their bubble and away from the day-to-day harsh realities of their exploitative prone society; crime has been linked with urban African American and Latino/Latina communities. Despite decades of research in sociology, political science, and psychology, in an effort to demonstrate the facile link between race and crime, the (mis)conceptions of nonwhites, as easily prone to crime and drug abuse is still as prevalent as ever.[31] The early reporting that took place as a consequence of the nature-induced Katrina disaster focused on, and followed through with a long old traditional formula of representing black people as dangerous criminals. In their article, "Metaphors Matter: Disaster Myths, Media Frames, and Their Consequences in Hurricane Katrina," sociologists Kathleen Tierney, Christine Bevc, and Erica Kuligowski argue that this framework of crime is not only racial, it also has roots in "disaster myths." They go on to show that there are multiple prominent disaster myths that affect their framing by the media. "Following Hurricane Katrina, the response of disaster victims was framed by the media in ways that greatly exaggerated the incidence and severity of looting and lawlessness."[32] Government officials in-turn voiced their denials of any such laissez faire attitudes having possessed them. Black Americans, however, grew increasingly convinced that their government had abandoned them. Ray Nagin, the Mayor of New Orleans at the time, voiced his frustration with an angry but yet anguished plea for federal assistance during an interview with WWL-AM, a local radio station on September 2nd. This defining moment for the disaster and the mayor's political career alike could, of course, not be ignored for too long, for reasons of public relations both at home and the world abroad. The mayor's implications were clear; he felt that the unfair abandonment by the government of victims affected by the hurricane was "breaking [his] heart". "We're getting reports and calls that [are] breaking my heart from people saying, 'I've been in my attic. I can't take it anymore. The water is up to my neck. I don't think I can hold out.' And that's happening as we speak…" the mayor would then go on to add that, "you mean to tell me that a place where you probably have thousands of people that have died and thousands more that are dying every day, that we can't figure out a way to authorize the resources that we need? Come on man… I need reinforcement. I need troops, man. I need 500 buses, man. This is a national disaster." This reaction by the government and the nation it has custodianship over, or rather lack of reaction, is eerily emblematic of the lackluster mobilization of aid that is commonly seen in 'third-world' nations. The uproar one would expect of the greatest advocate of aid and civility, as it relates to human rights, was nonexistent in said advocate's own playground. It was not only black people who were affected by this disaster, but it was black people who were disproportionately in the cross-hairs of the incident, and who bore the grunt of media depictions of them as savages, thugs and not quite as American. That is racist.

~****~

My social death by a thousand cuts came in the form of a thousand glares and stares during the summer of 1995. Still, I have always loved and will always love my trips to Botswana, a land of pride, partly due to the graceful humility shown by its inhabitants, who let the atmospherics and optics of the place speak of and for their own. That, however, was not my first ever experience with the place, as I had lived there for a couple of years before my parents decided to emigrate to Toronto. I was seven years old the first that I waved the place and the continent goodbye. Seeing as I had left that part of the world at such an early age, their very few memories still available to me. It sometimes saddens me when I think about how little I remember of my continent of birth, much less my country of birth, the Congo. Such sentiments do not linger for too long though, since, it once dawned on me that the little I did remember was seared and hard-pressed onto my mind, never to escape the grasp of my conceptualization. I was content to have had vivid but few memories (quality) rather than to have had been cursed with a stampede of thoughts, from memories that were not all too clear (quantity). One such memory involved my dad picking me up from school. Despite me having the option to take the school bus back home, seeing as the yearly subscription for said bus company's services had been taken care of for a consecutive year; my dad still wanted all the time he could spend with his children and so I seldom took the bus. As medical doctors, working for the government of Botswana, my folks understood the value of time, and the need to spend as much of it as possible with those you love, for they all too well also understood death. On our way back home, David, the youngest of his three sons asked a question that we all were thinking.

"Dad?" (This is the question yet).

"Yup?" replied my dad, he gave a quick glance at Dave (aka Vade) through the rear view mirror before looking right and then turning left (they drive on the left side there). Such multi-tasking always kept me in awe, I, a seven year old child whose dad could do no wrong or harm, or be defeated in a hand-to-hand combat, even against six bulldogs.

"How come white homeless people never exist?" David carried on in all perplexed and candid curiosity. My father laughed, a lot.

"Well David," he said upon having had regained his composure, "let's see…" he pondered on how best to address the matter. My father always believed that there was beauty in simplicity. "Yesterday, before going to bed, what were you watching so attentively that mommy had to drag you to bed?"

"oh, uhm, the frosty the snow man marathon!" David replied jovially, having by now forgotten about the sadness he felt of not being able to watch a couple more hours of Frosty on a school night.

"okay, so before seeing snow on tv, or having heard about it from mom and me, when we read to you about Frosty, did you know what a snowman was?"

"No…I'm not born knowing everything dad!" he trumpeted.

"good answer, except: you're born knowing very little in fact," my dad said pleasantly, with that patient gentle smile that was a trademark, "just because you don't know about or haven't seen something before, doesn't mean it doesn't exist…that was a great question though, want to know how I would have phrased it if I were to ask about white homeless people?

"yes!" we all cried out in unison, harmoniously nodding our heads to the rhythmic-like tutelage on display.

"I would have said something like: hey dad, are there any white homeless people?" he then paused for a bit of a while, we paused too, trying to figure out why didn't give us a one sentence answer which explained the inexistence of white homeless people. But we had over twenty minutes to go before catching view of the black and red gate that was the portal to our home, and that was enough time for things to sink in and be otherwise explained to three year-old, kindergarten attendee of a little brother.

A couple of months later, we travelled to Pretoria, South Africa, a bigger city and country than the less than one million people that populated Botswana. It was there that we saw, as is the title of a book I enjoy, our first "black swan". In his book, black swan, Nassim Taleb makes mention of the occurrence of the unexpected, the black swan, which for a long time was thought to have had not existed, since for thousands of years all swans seen were white. We saw our first homeless white man, asking for money from us home-filled black people. It blew our minds.

"….simply focusing on diversity and acceptance, as is common today, misses the deeper roots of race, racial thinking, and overt racism. On the other hand, a purely scientific and objective approach fails to tell the full story of how race has shaped historical events and continues to be a powerful influence on individual lives. It certainly does not tell all about the variation in how race is experienced among individuals and over time and place." [33]

# Race, Racism, and Inequality

South Africa, Brazil and Haiti, among many things, what these three countries have in common is the disproportionate number of people of color, and black people in particular, who find themselves entangled in and entrapped by an exploitative social matrix, with their presence hidden away from and on the outskirts of the formal economy, in their shanty-towns and ghettos. That society acknowledges racial mixture does not translate to racial parity and the absence of racism, as is evident in the aforementioned countries. The history of America too, wrought with such prejudicial preferences and outlooks, -the blue vein societies, brown paper bag tests, and light-skinned privilege- attest to the happy relationship between multiracial identity and racism as it regards white supremacy. [34]

*"More often racial legacies persist in classrooms, workplaces, banks, courtrooms, and a host of other institutional spaces where life chances and material realities are significantly enhanced or diminished. In such settings, the seemingly impersonal nature of procedures and interactions may easily conceal underlying race-infused assumptions, biases, and power relations. Especially through the enactment of "race neutral" and "colorblind" policies, these routine interactions can invoke and reinforce racial stereotypes and power relations in subtle and but potent ways (Haney Lopez)."* [35]

The early colonies, in the US, are distinctive medleys of 'Old' and 'New' World ethnicities. As was aforementioned regarding the evolution of whiteness with time, one notices that these Old and New World ethnicities lived and loved together without recourse to race or racism. Instead, dissimilarities in religion, Christians versus heathens or Catholics versus Protestants, and also the difference in nationality initially weighed more heavily on the pioneering minds of the first colonists than did skin color. Audrey Smedley, the renowned anthropologist, describes the change in societal mood and mores when the wealthy land owning elites created race for the purposes of justifying chattel slavery, claiming the land on which indigenous peoples lived in for thousands of years, and so as to promote division among an increasingly dissent-ridden class of Native American, European, and African laborers. "The development of a heritable and permanent slave status for blacks contrasted starkly with slavery as a practice in other societies and the nation's founding principles, including the burgeoning notion of freedom and liberty as inalienable human rights." [36]

People often have the (mis)conception of slavery in the Americas as the continuation of ancient practices and traditions, something that at even at the pinnacle of the Atlantic slave trade was a commonly held practice the world around. I mean, ancient Rome, so gloriously touted, did it, so too was the case of the Gold Coast (Ghana) in the 17th century, or 19th century Virginia. However, owing to the nature of race-based slavery in the Americas, this happens to be a misconception, as this was without historical precedent. An economy unlike any other had burgeoned, the 'Atlantic World' economy. Mercantilist Capitalism was the prevailing economic system of the 17th century, a century that produced defiantly dissatisfied thinkers of the likes of Karl Marx and Fredrick Angles among others. Any contrary economic systems offered up by the intellectual and scholarly class, as suggestive of changing the global order, always had been met with swift opposition. As is the case in our contemporary times, so persistent, and filled with defamation, the damaging to one's reputation, comes the backlash from institutions that set worldly trends, with full backing from the very elite under criticism often the case. However, as we will later make mention of in this book, dynamics of power relations are not so clear cut, with feuds and conspiracies against one another constantly taking place among the elite circles. Apart from the highly lucrative nature of the slave trade, another thing worth noting about what distinguishes North American based slavery from other forms of slavery having had taken place prior to then, was the extent of the social alienation between the slaves and those who 'owned' them.[37] Taking advantage of the ancient old tradition of tribal conflict, deeply entrenched in West-Africa's daily political, social and economic life, took place at an organically gradual pace. The taking advantage aforementioned, done at the behest of mercantilist capitalist profiteers, seeking to establish new wealth while further enriching their aristocratic backers, was often ruthless and unabated. Unchartered land yielded the promised potential of retiring back home for these profiteers, in Spain, Portugal, Holland, England and the New World, among other densely populated colonist elite regions, which hold significant sway over global activities and social constructs/contracts. This global economic system (Atlantic Slave Trade), naturally, created a widening unhealthy rift in economic inequality, with the slimming out of the middle class and the creation of centralized accumulated extreme wealth for a few at the expense of a marginalized majority. While in other slave owing societies, in most of Africa and the Middle-East, enslaved individuals mostly found themselves integrated into the social fabric, the bottom rung, and bottom-feeders, if you will, owing to a biological and fictive kinship ladder. In said societies, however, as farfetched as the notion of human equality may have seemed to the elites, they usually deemed it not necessary to call into question the fundamental humanity of those they enslaved, whether through conquest, debt or other means. In addition, slave status did not directly translate to an intergenerational curse designed to ensure an enslaved labor force, as was eventually the case in the colonial Americas. Thus, the former type of slavery could be thought of as, 'societies with slaves', and the latter, sprouting from the colonial Americas, as 'slave societies'. "Classicist Frank Snowden (1983) clearly illustrates this fact in *Before Color Prejudice,* his seminal study of 'the black image' in Egyptian, Greek, Roman, and early Christian art and literature. [He warned] against the temptation to read contemporary social issues into the historical record." There is a self-feeding and reinforcing agent at play between history and culture. Contemporary culture greatly influences a nation's, a society's, or a community's history, the very history that in turn subjected to contemporary cultural perspectives, sees each proceeding generation within the same culture interpret their history in a slightly different way, sometimes much contrasted, in some aspects, from past generational beliefs and notions. "Snowden observes that interactions in the ancient Mediterranean between peoples today classified as black or white- even among political and military rivals- were devoid of 'acute' color consciousness and any type of racial discrimination. He points out that these societies never observed blackness as the basis of slave status."[38] In societies with slaves, unlike slave societies, the prospect of freedom was more likely, if not for the slave then for their children. The refusal to perceive slaves as humans, and grant to them the decency that came with such an acknowledgement, posited on race, as a justification of this new form of dehumanizing slavery. Following this trend, Native Americans at the height of this large-scale 'importing' of people, and after having been safely relegated to the margins of society and into Federal Reservations, were often depicted as (sometimes 'noble') savages undeserving of their lands. By 'noble', I wish to infer my disapproval for the attachment of values of nobility according to perceived notions of this term in a Euro-centrically cultural aspect. In my opinion, apart from the differing colonial experiences endured between blacks and Native Americans, the fact that the latter could 'sometimes be noble', unlike the former, was justification enough to posit the superiority of Native Americans over Black people, thus maintaining the much desired social ladder based on pigmentation. The darker the skin, the lower ranked the racial group. What such an ideology further did was to justify -making easy the mental (empathetic) burden- the notion of slavery and why black people were genetically adapted or constructed (maybe divinely) to be slaves, unable to even 'sometimes be noble', since such 'cultured' values and norms could not be, by definitional fiat, nurtured in them. The reverting to old feudal European systems now taking place in the New World invoked only a few batted eyelashes from the wielders of influence and power, who ironically knew the burdens of taxation and imposition of unwanted policies that benefitted an overlord. Policies, such as the abolition of slavery, continued transfer of financial capital in the form of taxes, to a king on another continent, made the American elite class dreary about and weary of the status-quo. The top-down revolt against the British crown successfully took hold, a tale so bespoken that it needs no retelling. However, the aristocratic English colonists in the United States were acutely aware of the moral contradictions, indeed, as time passed; they evermore tussled with the fear that enslaved communities might draw inspiration for large-scale rebellion, especially in the wake of the Haitian Revolution. Hence, the subsequent tactical inducement of division and infighting amongst the lower laboring class by the elite, through the means of race, a prejudicial ideology taken root, upon having had grown over the centuries of ever-growing reliance on the exploitation of Africans.

## Mr. and Mrs. 'Savage'

The human animal is more fragile, and vulnerable to the groaning pangs of life's uncertainties, both the unknown and the unknowable, create the need for constant facile mental conceptualizations, contraptions and constructs. We tell ourselves the appropriate narrative at the appropriate time, in conjunction with the accumulatively altering and evolving ideology of who we tell ourselves we are. One's identity, in itself, is a fluid and unstable construct, rigged with uncertainties. One tragic car accident, a single event involving the loss of a loved one, for some, and to some degree, can alter the persons' views on life, and greatly alter and affect the principle probabilities surrounding their life-trajectory. These stories we tell ourselves to keep relevant, productive, motivated, secure and focused, among other virtues and needs, limit not themselves to the case of an individual, but stem and branch out to the societal network of many individuals, across a region. Therefore, culture is what dictates to a society, as was a priori said of the individual, the accumulatively altering and evolving ideology of who we tell ourselves we are. It follows then that culture forms the matrix on which the fragile human animal is in constant contact with, drawing from its essence and remaining socially healthy.

"As fish need the sea, culture with its timeless reassurance and its seeming immortality, offsets for the frail human spirit the brevity, the careless accidentalness of life. An individual human life is easy to extinguish. Culture is leaned upon as eternal. It flows large and old around its children. And it is very hard to kill. Its murder must be undertaken over hundreds of years and countless generations. Pains must be taken to snuff out every traditional practice, every alien world, every heaven-sent ritual, every pride, every connection of the soul, gone behind and reaching ahead.."[39]

As such, it is this common rhetoric, manifested in a way of life within a society, which is always the subject of imposition on the marginalized segments of the very society. The demographics within a society with the least influence, politically and economically, endure grave psychological harm. The remnants of their collective identities disintegrate with creeping ease, its ashes blown aside by the winds of disparagement and the dehumanization of their very souls. Since time immemorial, whether between distinct societies or within a society, the wealthiest of the parties involved, and the power wielders and influence bearers, tend to look down repugnantly at the 'other' culture. The other is referred to as a clan of savages, or an uncivilized amalgamation of individuals, often considered as not meriting the privilege or right to think for themselves, let alone hold some of the levers to power. These 'brutes' have their cultures ridiculed and equally have their achievements downcast, downtrodden and down-right discredited. It is this preference singularly for an exclusive number of cultures globally, in general, and in particular, in the US, which fuels the inter- and intra-class related tensions and divisions within the multitudinous communities. Race, as a social construction, was deployed as a tactical maneuver, against the conspiring and concerted efforts of the labored class, from varying races and differing life-experiences, as well as ethnic backgrounds. Having divided the laboring class, and over time, the new face of the lower classes was often nonwhites, and more especially African Americans. History shows us that with the parallel between poverty and blackness readily made, reactions within the collective of the 'black race', the black elites, the middle and lower classes, sowed further divisions and reclassifications. The brown paper bag test or the blue vein society, are but a few of the many manifestations of self-hate observed among African Americans, the exploited class, on whose backs, minds and souls, the established global imperialist/capitalist system thrives on. The brown paper bag test was a perverse embracing of blackness only as far as their pride of 'white' ancestry allows them to appreciate. Fraternities and the like social clubs established policies that dictated that members should have a complexion at least as light as a brown paper bag. Apologists of the brown paper bag society sometimes claimed that their experiences, as African Americans were different to their darker skinned 'race-mate' citizens. Indeed, at some point during the first half of the 20th century, the treatment of African Americans with a white father was relatively better than the attitudes endured by black people who had not a white parent. The manner in which the social system rewarded racially mixed offspring, favoring them over pure black individuals, is among the main causes that begot this prejudice, and resulted in weakening the resolve of black solidarity within the American society. In short, colorism, this prejudice based on skin tone, rather than race, hinted at the power-struggle between two dangerous, bigoted and exploitative ideologies. Racism as an ideology had to contend with the rise of colorism, a thought-construct largely an offshoot of North-American racist ideology, and to some extent, a compliment to the system of white supremacy. Privilege has long been linked to skin tone in US society, in general, and in particular, in the African-American community. The relationship between US history and colorism stems back to the days of slave-based racism, with mixed-race individuals of white fathers often given preferential treatment, ranging from more desirable work, the right to acquire a formal education, the freedom to purchase property, which in turn translates to the seldom grant of freedom. The contrasted social and economic selection pressures between mixed-black and black individuals, has had a significant effect on the development of a culture based on colorism. This contrast also accounts for the divergence in dogmas and mores and traditions practiced by black and mixed-black people. The development of a rift within society, based on skin tone was, in hindsight, unavoidable. It is after all natural, for the purposes of maintaining relevance and a healthy livelihood, for people to work within the system and according to its dictates, thereby readily receiving recompense, than seeking to overthrow a centuries-old established system.

African Americans more than contributed to colorism, one could even say that they championed the perverse ideology. Mixed-blacks jumped at the opportunity to climb a step up the social ladder. As was the case with working class white American citizens, upon the widening of the 'white bin', the segment of the laboring class, whites, given more rope on their leash settled for something than nothing, despite the meagerness of said something. The adage that speaks of being grateful in the face of affliction since someone, somewhere is experiencing greater odds and challenges, well exemplifies the logic of settling. For an individual, upon the solemn realization of how much better life would be with a pair of shoes to warm and caress his feet, slight gratification is induced when the person realizes that they are in a better off position when compared to the persons without feet. It follows, then, that blacks competed amongst each other and even amongst other marginal groups within society, in an attempt to gain relevance in view of their peers, and the in peering 'white world'. Most, of course not all, mixed-black people who benefitted from colorism under the overt-racial order, seldom were not in a hurry to distort the status-quo. As with most people immersed in this radicalized (dis)order, the reluctance to fight against a system of oppression, among other things, came down to the fear of the uncertainty, of not knowing whether one system would be substituted for a worse establishment of norms. As such, the contention that being second last was better than the unknown was, one can imagine, a key proponent in the propagation of such prejudicial social and economic relations. The "Blue Vein Societies", as is suggestive within the name, adhered to the precepts that a glass ceiling largely reliant on the notions of skin tone, should bar people too dark-skinned, and whose blue linings from their veins had readily failed to be seen. The 'Blue Vein' Society thought of itself as sharing more European ancestry than most African Americans, the brown paper bag also being among the downcast lot. There was a pride in being linked to European ancestry. The origins of the brown paper bag test, for example, was found to have had its origins in the French colonial era of Louisiana, New Orleans.[40] New Orleans had a tradition of segregating the classes of free people into three categories.[41] The test was a manifestation of perceptions of beauty at that time. The idea that lighter skin and more European features were more attractive still haunts the global collective of views on beauty today. During the first half of the twentieth century, paper bag parties/societies mostly took place in the major American cities with a high concentration of African American population. During the height of such folly, many churches, as with fraternities and nightclubs, used the brown paper bag test for admission into their establishments.[42] Starting in New Orleans, the denied entrance into the social club, is the commencement of an established rift, alienating the black aristocracy from the rest of the masses of black people, caste lines were drawn along color lines within 'black life'. Howard University, a historically black institution, endorsed the practices of colorism among the black community. This, of course, comes as no surprise, since the private academic institution happens to be one among several jewels possessed or influenced by the black aristocracy. Howard University's interests necessarily coincided with that of the black nobility, as it needed all the funding it could muster. Thus the use of brown paper bags to test a person's eligibility for admission, distorted the natural 'free-market' social and economic mobility of darker-skinned blacks. A Jim-Crow system rested on ideologies of colorism, applied to the white supremacy mode of Jim Crow, already ubiquitous within the nation, propagating the caste social and economic models of the time. Academic institutions evolved a practice of requiring a photograph along with the prospective student's application; Howard University was thus by far not alone in this regard.[43] There was a clash of cultures, even within what white Americans considered to be a monolithic culture, 'black culture'. Multi-racial persons, freed before the American Civil War, tried to distinguish themselves from the many newly freedmen who filled the metropolises after the war. These newly freedmen appeared to be, mostly, of African descent, with the confined system of slavery the only thing known to them. The distribution of the number of mixed-blacks among blacks owed much to a law, established in Virginia and other colonies in the 17th century. Indeed, some mixed-blacks were born free. It is worth noting that during the early colonial era, working class people, regardless of race, worked closely together, and slavery was not as much of a racial caste. Slave law dictated that the legal status of mixed children was to be determined by that of their mothers, in opposition to the patriarchal traditions of English common law.[44] As early as the 18th century, there were tales, by travelers, of the variety of color and features available to slaves in Virginia, as European ancestry was obvious. Some of these mixed-blacks were educated, or at least allowed to undergo enlightenment. At times, cases whereby a white father arranges, say a two-year stint of apprenticeship for his mulatto son, only to see to the child's freedom upon completion of his learning. This 'liberation fever' was more prominent in the first two decades after the American Revolution, when numerous slaves were freed in the northern-segment of the South. It is in this region that we find an increase in freed people of color, from one to more than ten percent, between the end of the Revolution and the year 1810. By 1810, however, 75 percent of black people in the state of Delaware were free.[45] In reference to the three-tier class caste system inherent in New Orleans' everyday life, Creoles of color constituted this third class during the years of slavery. These Creole persons and communities achieved a high level of literacy and sophistication under French and Spanish rule. Many became artisans, property owners, and sometimes slaveholders themselves. However, after the United States negotiated the Louisiana Purchase, more and more Americans opted to settle in the colorfully, artistic, musical and lively New Orleans. These immigrants from other colonies within the US brought with them their binary approach to society, whereby persons were classified as either white or black. The privileges initially owed the Creoles of color were gradually curtailed.[46] Still, the sense of entitlement and level of education attained by these mixed-blacks translated them to a different cultural plane than both whites and blacks. They wished to be of a racial category of their own. Such divide and conquer tactics are not necessarily planned from beginning to completion by the ruling class. Rather, upon the establishment of a system of exploitation, confusion and division, the machine of a social construct exhibits a nature of its own. Great attachment to one form of vice, for an individual, often leads to the partaking of other vices, a slippery slope. In like manner, one system of inequality and exploitation, gives rise to several dysfunctional systems and power dynamics of social and economic life. Still, injustice, no matter what shape, color, or form it is presents itself in, is still just that; unfair, and discontent has a tendency of fermenting until explosive release. Ask the French King about it. Oh, yes, that is right; we are deprived of that possibility.

Cultures within a society are in constant contact due to human interaction and integration, of a network of several individuals available to a community or society, with each person enveloped by their respective cultures (norms, self-serving stories, and values). Society is segregated along racial lines, it also is, as was afore-hinted to, divided according to notions of colorism and so too cultural antagonisms. Cultural antagonism is as archaic a concept as rivalries centered on class, predating the racial prejudices later seen within human society. The American Civil war is a good example of a struggle induced by inter-cultural conflicts, race-relations, elite economic practices and interests at clash. As just mentioned, culture-clash is among the several interplays of conflicts that led to the war between the Industrialist, new moneyed elite from the north and the old-fashioned agrarian ruling class of the south, the south's culture claimed that their system was fairer than that of the North. A clash of cultures, and the social constructions of the reward and economic systems that came with it, inflamed a nation in civil war. In the end, for me, it boils down to the north unable to stand high and blameless when accusing the south of committing great travesties and abominable injustices through their system of slavery. As to why the north could not get away with proclaiming this as a legitimate grievance, alongside the other many interests at economic odds, is because of the actual nature surrounding the industrial revolution of the nineteenth century. The industrialist north worked its laborers, mostly not unionized, and as such, prone to the hazardous terrain that came with limited rights. The economic machinery of the north was set up unlike that of the south in that, the former favored a mode of wage slavery over the system of outright chattel slavery. Some might petty proclaim that wage labor is nonetheless a step forward, I will hand it to them. Unfortunately, it is not a step high enough to claim moral, hence, cultural superiority over the other. While the south outright 'owned' their fellow human beings, the north settled for the more efficient mode of 'renting' out human beings. The lack of rights among workers, and the larger the available labor force within a community, then the easier it becomes for the ruling classes to exploit the little guy. Well known are these principles within contemporary literature. Known to us is that, for example, sweatshops and massive assembly plants are the favored system of profiteering in the 'free-market' global economy. Located in poor developing countries, these organizations, contracted by a major corporation based in the US, are not accountable to any governing body. The low levels of living standards in places like Bangladesh, China, Taiwan and Indonesia; just to name a few, allow such human rights abuses to go on unabated. This need to maximize profits is very much inherent in the system of capitalism. In his 1974 book, "Obedience to Authority, an Experimental View," Stanley Milgram, while at the University of Yale, sparked intrigue for, and uproar against psychological experiments on humans. The Milgram experiment and his in depth book on the human pathology as it regards obedience to authority, showed the lengths to which humans will go in the name of duty. Ostensibly controlling the inducement of increasingly higher voltages shocking a participant person in the next room, the test participants in the experiment, mostly, went on shocking their ostensible victims for the sake of the experiment. I apologize for the offshoot, or digression the conversation has taken. However, I wish to emphasize and shine light on the capabilities humans have for detachment, depending on the rhetoric or story that they without cease tell themselves. The elite classes of the different races, through the systemic dehumanization of the exploitable classes, unable or unwilling to empathize anymore with such masses of people, have formed a detached mindset. Therefore, submerged in their respective cultures, absorbing desirable traits within other cultures in society, while still maintaining exclusion, exclusivity and superiority; these elites feel unconnected to the vast world. In some way, it becomes akin to the pushing of the button, for the sake of 'racial' preservation, systemic maintenance of the economic system, without care for the consequences had on masses of people, resulting from their policies and interest pursuits.

If culture is the collective story pertaining to a peculiar group of individuals, then the rhetoric told about whites and nonwhites in the intellectual and moral space, add to the perceptions attached to a 'singular culture', which in turn affects how this perceived culture views itself. Although black people in America, let alone globally, do not share a monolithic culture unique to them, the linking of race to poverty and then in turn placing a parallel between race and culture, paves the illusion that all black people share a single culture. The effect that this generalization of several ethnicities based on a simplistic notion of skin-deep politics has on the several varying cultures, of black people in the US and the world beyond, is that it paints social and race relations with a single simple brush. It thus simplifies the problems inherent within the society, and in so doing, simplifies the solutions or the means of going about such a possible resolution. Linking race to culture, not only as it regards black people, among other things, also has the effect of propagating stereotypes of race and of culture being non-adoptive to a significant number of black persons. Black people in the US and the greater African Diaspora at large have had to face conflicted ideologies of their identity, their culture. Racially painted notions of culture has contributed to the idea of global black solidarity, but since culture is only affected by outside influences and perception of it, and not subservient to it, the reality of confusing rhetoric and harsh social and economic afflictions, has the effect of ultimately dividing the several people under the racial banner of blackness. Together with a long history of black people betraying their kind to have a foot in the door, so to speak, there's an affinity within black communities in the US to denounce a person, as not pertaining, in their eyes, to the racial category the white world view them in. The notion of blackness, acting or not acting black enough, of real or true 'niggas', has dominated the airwaves. Once established, social constructions such as the linking of race to culture, grow into their own 'man,' so to speak. The people depicted in this cultural light, are a people rigged with the curse of self-fulfilling prophecies. They advocate for and champion this system of how one ought to comport and carry him/herself, as a black individual. Inequality is thus maintained and money is made, from this 'cultural-urbanization' of blacks. Black culture and anything to do with black people is, surprise, surprise; belittled and ostensibly a poor culture and a culture of the poor. In this matrix, in which the human animal draws on to remain socially health and relevant, culture, can and often is the source of a great deal of debasement, ridicule and humiliation, to the carriers of a culture that happens to be deemed as doomed. Such debasement and inhumane perceptions of blacks, especially poor blacks, is something done to their mothers and their fathers, children, and their children's children and their children after them. "And there will come a time of mortal injury to all their souls, and their culture will breathe no more. But they will not mourn its passing, for they will by then have forgotten that which they might have mourned."[47]

Leading up to the proclamation of emancipation by the Grand Old Party (Republican), and perpetuated past then and into our modern epoch, the perception of black people as endowed with a culture of dependence, long-suffering, and in need of paternalism, took centre stage in 'white' discourse. In 1852, for example, "Uncle Tom's Cabin," was a theatrical production that is indicative of part of this dialogue/discourse.[48] Indeed, whites were so fascinated by black cultural production, as they perceived it, that replication of it was done on a mass scale, with little attention paid to accuracy. In addition, there was a lack for the need to understand a culture deemed as lesser, which in effect portrayed all 'black culture' as entertainment of the highest value, with no to little intellectual and artistic foundations. All art and culture that ran parallel to the depictions of blacks, had by whites, significantly swayed the development of inter-personal relations within black communities, and also between black and white people in the society. The eighteenth century "Negro jigs" and other similar dances, exemplify the absorption of cultural products by whites on plantations in the US.[49] Still sticking to the trend of global trends in racial relations as it regards to culture, the 1870s birthed, in

England, Ireland, Wales and Scotland, the likes of the Fisk Jubilee Singers. Their initial singing tour of England resulted in dissatisfactory reception. Fifty years of blackface performance in England had nearly undermined their appeal. People were often bewildered at the offer by blacks to perform, since; the prevalent ideology brought about the inquiry of what real blacks had to offer as songsters that was different from the singing of minstrels. That indeed, was the raging question. English blacks, in turn, in an economic and social system that had few occupations open to them, worried about the singers' presentation of serious, morally upright spirituals before white audiences who had grown used to the gimmicks of minstrelsy. However, as is known to us, the singers indeed succeeded on new stages, creating new constituencies for black music among both working and elite peoples.[50] The fascination with intermingling of differing cultures, reshaping and reconstituting the characteristics of the entangled cultures, is of growing steadiness among the contemporary intelligentsia, and literature on culture. Relations and inter-relations within a society have, for decades been in the spotlight among scholars incline to such intellectual persuasions. The transfer of cultural material, referred to as cultural trafficking, happens from both the top-down and from the bottom-up. The elite classes of all races, whether to show off their extensive knowledge of the downtrodden, with the sort of pride and fascination only a tourist spectator at a zoo could have, or to simply feel 'in' with the latest but most admiral trends of all cultural kinds, 'borrow' cultural materials from the middle classes. I, of course, have nothing against spectators at a zoo, or their pride and fascination over the unconfident and battered beats they have played a part in creating. This flow of cultural material, that is, tastes in food and music, for example, are often in flux within a society, as each class segment peers into the superficial social construction of a veneer that delineates it from the other two main class groups. Unknown to many a social and anthropological scholar are all the steps that lead up to the phenomena of other cultural practices or material, taken into the fold of a foreign particular class. The aforementioned is an exchange that catches fire in the imagination of a segment of a class group, through contact with another class' cultural production. However, the exchange of cultural material, although can be considered as an encouraging and even a progressive occurrence, could, nonetheless, lead to disastrous and unintended consequences to, more often than not, the more depraved of the two classes in question. Consider the prominence of minstrelsy in the US and around the globe, what in millennial years would seem as having had happened not too long ago. There was no genuine exchange of cultural material between races and the cultures accompanying those races, of all classes. By this, I mean that the power struggle (e.g. for access to resources) was not one between equals.

The cultural traffic that takes place, then, as is the connoted view on 'traffic', becomes something akin to a crime, something stolen and used, never in a good way. As such, I used the term 'borrow' when describing rather than 'acquire' or 'learned,' when describing the adoption of cultural material by a (if you will) foreign class or race. Since true assimilation and genuine cultural exchange between factions can only take place with the genuine exchange of knowledge, then the burrowed culture does more harm in reconciling old rivalries, and injustices, than good. A breeding ground for stereotypes burgeons under such luck luster and ignorance driven motives of exchange. In the ideal notion of cultural exchange, it is encouraged to mix up a blend of cultural margaritas. When gospel, jazz, the boogie woogie, rhythm and blues (R 'n' B), and country music are mashed up, we get Chuck Berry, Joe turner and Elvis Presley, what we get, is some good old fashioned rock n roll. However, when cultural practice, unlike curious musical intrigue from one musician to one else he or she considers a peer, borrowing without genuine knowledge exchange is a perversion. It is indicative of one class' paradigm, unaltered and yet, still, imposed upon the cultural product, with said class' prejudices fueling and influencing the growth of the newly integrated cultural material into consolidated norms and practices.

The anecdote-rich and eye-opening, "100 years of Negro in Show Business," was, in 1954, the first look at a history of black entertainers from the 1840s forward, told from an insider's perspective. The subtext to this account, however, is the struggle by blacks to gain legitimacy and primacy in the performances where black culture was in representation. They sought for monetary recompense from the (mis)representation of black material. The economic infrastructure that benefitted from white, and as such, wealthy persons' longstanding captivated imaginations of Africans, was not lost on the exploited communities. In the case of the Fisk Jubilee Singers' tour, for example, they needed to take part in the profits made around black misery, in part, as an attempt at collecting funds for Fisk University. Even as estranged a place (for most Americans) as South Africa, the cultural transfer of jazz there, created a system of sustaining both the music bands and the vibrant marketing of illicit liquor in the 'shebeens' where the bands performed.[51]

Still, it stands to reason that with a segregated sense of culture among the collective black community, drawn up by class distinctions, and with the 'sell-out' of some blacks to the successful economy of black misery; certain black cultural performances have not been embraced by black communities. Jazz and its prominent rise, for example, in hindsight, and with the application of revisionist history, is often perceived as an assured ascendancy. However, the early years of this unprecedented musical genre was quiet wrought with opposition, mainly coming from voices within the black middle-classes.[52] In the early 1920s, jazz had not yet won broad support from the black intelligentsia and respected opinion shapers of many types, who would later cluster around it, endorsing and explaining jazz's performance values. With all black people globally being lumped into a single culture, despite the potent ethnic and cultural diversity within this racial group, the notion of black solidarity against global injustices was unable of taking flight. Black people everywhere sought to distinguish their community, ethnicity and culture from the rest of the heterogeneous 'black-race' group that they been joined to. Hence, another example of black communities' resistance to importing black cultural material came in the form of the post-independence intelligentsia of the 1960s and 1970s. They were often a crucial opposing force to the adoption of African American cultural exports within their communities. The much-touted Afro hairstyle of the 1960s met unrelenting resistance in West Africa by local writers. These writers saw the hairstyle, among other modes of Afro-American fashions, as inconsistent with traditional African body presentation, a truth often left out in today's histories of the Afro.[53] In 1970s East Africa, the late writer Okot p'Bitek, a critical and creative thinking powerhouse, dissented from what he called, the youth's cultural "apemanship," relating to their absorption of black cultural material from the West. He wanted a reversal of cultural traffic, asking, "when will the youths of Africa influence the youths of the world?" That black cultural material was contested within the global multi-ethnic black community, is of no surprise. However, why was there a need for the Africans to dissociate themselves from Black American culture? Was the 'respectable image' a conception imposed on Africans by their former colonial turned (economic) imperialist masters? After all, Africans were the latest to be overt captives of or slaves to Eurocentric hegemony. Could it still be that African people still limited themselves to these norms and values, that is, to a foreigner culture? Or could the new 'true' African culture be a mélange of European and past African ethics? Could, in turn, the different outlook had by African youths in Bamako (Mali) and Accra (Ghana) be the ascent of a new global culture of acceptance of one another, of liberal thinking and rebellion against past structures of local and international hegemony? Indeed, these questions have no simple answers, especially not from a simple man as me, or any one scholar for that matter still. Post-colonial nationalism brewed fervently during the 1960s and 70s in throughout the African continent. For the older generations, the more educated, independent and influential segment of the populations, a deviation from conservative traditions of morality, both in the Eurocentric manner as in the African conception of morality, was to be the plight of a nation barely taken flight. Academic and political institutions molded and wielded the reins of power handed down to them by former European colonialist rulers, during this period of neo-colonialism or free trade imperialism. As such, some of the youths in the relatively large metropolises of Bamako and Accra, rightly felt duped by both their former fair-skinned authoritarian authorities and their elders and community leaders alike. The counter-revolution against war and discrimination that dominated the radio waves, not only in the US, but the world around, was had taken a liking to the youths in these ostensibly post-colonial regions and they it. Therefore, while hairstyles like the Afro, or dress styles like the mini-skirt, were frowned upon by the African ruling elites, as well as the middle classes, the youths from all classes within the society thought of them as elements or symbols of rebellion and liberating-anarchy. Indeed the mid-70s produced a band of youngsters who refused to take on a pan-African approach to liberation, let alone a nationalist one. They tried to repair the injustices of the past by moving forward into the future, with little mental recourse to the heartaches gone by. Globalization was on the tip of the tongues and minds of the new generation. This 'respectable presentation' was thought of as a recourse back to the need to adhere to the beauty standards of the European past, and away from the rebellious expression of pride in global blackness; as well as global unity, regardless of class or race. The youth of Bamako and Accra were well aware of racism, that's why they took up the mantle of anarchism, but they also were all too aware of the need to built themselves up to achieve perceived parity with the Euro-centrists. They indeed saw Euro-centrists as fellow humans, and knew of the pangs that needed to be undergone for said humans to view them on par, as fellow inherently capable humans. They saw themselves as citizens of mother earth, no matter how cold she had been made to be. Unlike in today's Ghanaian and Malian societies, the understanding of class antagonisms was in the forefront, with the cold war deeply etched into world affairs. A global anarchism based on individual racial pride but collective global class culture was what they strove for. The idea was that youths' black solidarity movements would grown into a youth solidarity movement, which in turn will consolidate class distinctions altogether. Naïve? Maybe. Maybe idealistic.

---

# Notes

[1] "Race: Are we So different?"; Alan H. Goodman, et al; 2012; pg 2.

[2] Ibid.

[3] It is important to note that even within the same racial strata one finds a hierarchy and division of said group by classes (that is: black elites and middle classes, as well as white lower classes ['white trash'] and upper classes). Similarly in terms of gender, one may find that lower classed black women and white women find it hard to relate to the, often university educated middle class black and white women, who are often the promoters of feminism. These upper classes, both in terms of race (within the races) and in terms of gender (within the 'gender group'), tend to disparage the lower classes, showing solidarity only amongst their own classes.

[4] Winant, Howard; 2001; White Racial Projects. *In* The Making and Unmaking of Whiteness. Brigit Rasmussen, Eric Klineberg, Irene Nexica, and Matt Wray, eds. Pp. 97-112. Durham, NC: Duke University Press.

[5] Ibid.

[6] David Roediger; 1999: "The Wages of Whiteness: Race in the Making of the American Working Class". Rev. Edition. London and New York: Verso.

[7] David Roediger; 2008: "How Race Survived U.S. History: From Settlement and Slavery to the Obama Phenomenon". London: Verso.

[8] William Z. Ripely; "The Races of Europe: A Sociological Study"; 1899, New York: D. Appleton and Company.

[9] John Hope Franklin, "Ethnicity in American Life: The Historical Perspective", in *Race and History: Selected Essays, 1938-1988, pp. 321-331.* 1988; Baton Rouge: Louisiana State University Press.

[10] Karen Brodkin; "How Jews Became White Folks and What that Says about Race in America"; 1998; New Brunswick: Rutgers University Press.

[11] Melissa V. Harris-Perry; "Sister Citizen: Shame, Stereotypes, and Black Women in America"; pp. 46; 2011; Sheridan Books.

[12] Cited in: Alan H. Goodman, et al; "Race: are we really so different?"; 2012; pg 10, 2013.

[13] Blakey 1999; Mukhopadhyay et al. 2007; Harrison 1995

[14] Cited in: Alan H. Goodman, et al; "Race: are we really so different?"; 2012; pg 11, 2013.

[15] Haney Lopez, 1996; "White by Law: The Legal Construction of Race"; New York: New York University Press.

[16] *Plessy v. Ferguson,* 163 U.S. 537, 559 [1896] (Harlan, J., dissenting)

[17] Brief for Petitioner, *Sipuel v. Bd. Of Regents of the Univ. of Oklahoma,* 332 U.S. 631 [1948] (No. 369), at 27.

[18] *Brown v. Bd. of Educ. (Brown II),* 349 U.S. 294, 301 [1955]

[19] "Sister Citizen", Melissa V. Harris-Perry, 2011, pg 82-83.

[20] Christopher W. Schmidt; 2008, "Brown and the Colorblind Constitution", Cornell Law Review 94:203, 234.

[21] *Briggs v. Elliott,* 132 F. Supp. 776, 777 [E.D.S.C. 1955.

[22] N.C. Gen.Stat. 115-176.1 (Supp. 1969), quoted in N.C. *State Bd. of Educ. v. Swann,* 402 U.S. 43, 44 n.1 [1971].

[23] Swann Report, pp. 45-46.

[24] *Regents of the Univ. of Cal. v. Bakke,* 438 U.S. 265, 402 (Marshall, J., concurring in part, dissenting in part).

[25] *McCleskey v. Kemp,* 481 U.S. 279 [1987].

[26] "Race: Are we So different?"; Alan H. Goodman, et al; 2012; pp. 84-85.

[27] *Adarand v. Pena,* 515 U.S. 200, 240-41 n.1 [1995].

[28] Michael Powell, 2010, Blacks in Memphis Lose Decades of Economic Gains. New York Times, May 30.

[29] "Race: are we so different?"; Alan H. Goodman et. Al; 2012; pg 85-86.

[30] "Rising to the Challenges of a Catastrophe"; Rodriguez, Trainor, and Quarantelli; *The Annals of the American Academy of Political and Social Science;* Shelter from the Storm: Repairing the National Emergency Management System after Hurricane Katrina (Mar., 2006). Vol. 604.

[31] Some of this research include: Jeanette Covington, "Racial Classification in Criminology: The Reproduction of Racialized Crime," *Sociological Forum 10 (*1995): 547-568; Mark Peffley and Jon Hurwitz, "The Racial Components of 'Race-Neutral' Crime Policy Attitudes," *Political Psychology* 23, no.1 (2002): 59-75; Vincent Sacco, "Media Constructions of Crime," *Annals of the American Academy of Political and Social Science* 539 (1995): 141-154; and Lincoln Quillian and Devah Pager, "Black Neighbors, Higher Crime? The Role of Racial Stereotypes in Evaluations of Neighborhood Crime," *American Journal of Sociology* 107 (2001): 717-767.

[32] "Metaphors Matter: Disaster Myths, Media Frames, and Their Consequences in Hurricane Katrina," *Annals of the American Academy of Political and Social Science* 604 (2006): 57-81.

[33] "Race: Are we So different?"; Alan H. Goodman; et al; 2012; pg 2.

[34] "Passing and the Problematic of Multiracial Pride: *or, Why One Mixed Girl Still Answers to Black*", *by* Danzy Senna in: "Black Cultural Traffic: Crossroads in Global Performance and Popular Culture"; 2005; University of Michigan Press.

[35] "Race: are we so different?"; Alan H. Goodman, et al; 2012; pg 10.

[36] "Race: are we really so different?"; Alan H. Goodman, et al; 2012; pg 12.

[37] "Generations of Captivity: A History of African American Slaves"; Ira Berlin; 2003; Harvard University Press. & "Anthropologie de l'esclavage: le ventre de fer et d'argent"; 1986; transl. 1991 as "The Anthropology of Slavery: The Womb of Iron and Gold".

[38] "Race: are we really so different?"; Alan H. Goodman, et al; pg 11; 2012.

[39] Carol D. Lee; 2005; "Black Education: A Transformative Research and Action Agenda for the New Century"; pg 45.

[40] "The Future of the Race"; Henry Louis Gate Jr.; 1996.

[41] Maxwell, Bill; *"The paper bag test"*. St. Petersburg Times. Tampa Bay Times. *Retrieved 23 October 2015.*

[42] "Did Hurricane Katrina reveal a historic reality?" Excerpt from Michael Eric Dyson's "Come Hell or High Water"; 2006.

[43] Kerri, Audrey Elisa; "The Paper Bag Principle: Class, Colorism, and Rumor and the Case of Black Washington"; p. 93; University of Tennessee Press; 2006.

[44] "Paper Bag Test: Letter From 1928 Addresses Black Fraternity And Sorority Colorism At Howard University"; *WatchTheYard*; Retrieved on 31 October 2015. & *Williams, Heather*; "How Slavery Affected African American Families"*; National Humanities Center. National Humanities Center.* Retrieved 21 November2015.

[45] Peter Kolchin; "American Slavery"; *1619-1877*; New York: Hill and Wang; 1994; Pbk; pp. 78 and 81.

[46] Ibid. pp. 83.

[47] R. Robinson (2000); pg 217-218; "The debt: What America owes to Blacks"; New York: Dutton; cited in: Carol D. Lee, 2005, "Black Education: A Transformative Research and Action Agenda for the New Century".

[48] Clare Midgley; "Women against Slavery: The British Campaigns, 1780-1870"; London: Routledge, 1992); pp. 145-46; "The influence of uncle Tom's Cabin".

[49] Katrina Hazzard-Gordon, Jookin': The rise of Social dance formations in African American culture (Philadelphia: Temple University Press, 1990), 51, has collected reports of several eighteenth century plantation dance episodes and of whites in attendance. Cf. also Albert Murray, stomping the Blues (New York: Vintage, 1976), 62-66; and Josephine Wright, "Early African Musicians in Britain," in Under the Imperial Carpet: Essays in Black History, 1780-1950, ed. Rainer Lotz and Ian Pegg (Crawley, Eng: Rabbit Press, 1986) 14-24.

[50] Doug Seroff, "The Fisk Jubilee Singers in England," in Wright, *Under the Imperial Carpet*; *pp.* 42-54.

[51] "Traveling While Black"; Kennell Jackson, in "Black Cultural Traffic: Crossroads in Global Performance and Popular Culture"; 2005; University of Michigan Press.

[52] Pianist and bandleader Dave Peyton's "The Musical Bunch" from the *Chicago Defender*, 1928, is presented as "A Black Journalist Criticizes Jazz", in *Keeping Time: Readings in Jazz History,* ed. Robert Walser (New York: Oxford University Press, 1999), 57-59.

[53] Nina Darnton; "Lagos Hairstyles Reflect African History (and the Afro is a Put-on Wig)"; New York Times; January 6, 1977; 1-3.

[54] Okot p'Bitek; "Pop Music, Bishops, and Judges"; in *Africa's Cultural Revolution*; Nairobi: Macmillan Books for Africa; 1973; 5.

# 2

# Gender Relations

## and the

# Feminist Struggle

## (or: "You Throw like a Girl!")

**

---

*"The more famous and powerful I get the more power have to hurt men."* – Sharon Stone

*"So de white man throw down the load and tell de nigger man tuh pick it up. He pick it up because he have to, but he don't tote it. He hand it to his womenfolks. De nigger woman is de mule uh de world so fur as Ah can see."* [1]

Are the biological differences inherent between women and men a sure fire sign of their places within society, boiling down to 'us' versus them', or that divine statutes have ordained the subjugation of one sex in view of the other? Does the right to vote make obsolete the need to struggle against any purported injustices? Are women who choose to not have children traitors to the human race, or in turn, should women who decide to have children but not rear them be considered just as traitorous, or a little less so? How about if a woman decides to both have children and dedicate the best part of her life to raising her offspring, is she a traitor to fighting women, is she part of the problem, another person with ideologies that feminists must denigrate?

The general consensus among scholars of the social sciences, using the postmodernist approach, is to differentiate between something made real and something that is real. By this I mean that human conceptions (social constructs) or the framework to ideologies are to be regarded as something made real over time. While some truths about the world, for example, that it is not flat; remain just that, truths, and are not anything but in spite of our assumptions. The world will not cease to be almost spherical in shape because we prefer to think of it as flat once more. As such, moving forward, it is important that we attribute our conception of women in society to millennia old human practices. Women have contributed to human history to a far greater extent than they are given credit for, due to our interpretation of history through contemporary cultural lenses, we read less into their roles of excellence. Also, because of a long history of misogyny and unforgivable subjugation, women have often contributed to the intellectual, political, social and economic spheres, among others, only to do so in secret, for fear of reprisal. These truths are well known to a significant segment of the population in developed nations. In this section of the book, I wish to bring to the forefront a discussion on the evolution and current affairs of gender relations and also the struggle for equality, of which may or may not be the same as feminism. It is easy to brush off an opinion, which at the end of the day this book is, when said opinion goes counter to one's core beliefs; it is, however, harder and more noble to hear out a thinker's opinions and agree or disagree through discourse rather than approbations. As was said regarding to race, there needs to be an *exchange* of knowledge between the parties for true progress to move along its gradual course with better efficacy. This means all parties involved need to be thought of and treated as equals, this means respecting (not agreeing with) their convictions, as much as you respect your right to have one. Moving away from a rotten paradigm that we inherited from our forbearers and into a new and more progressive, more tolerant of diversity, and more inclusive epoch, is a collective thing and not up to one segment of the population to dictate, unless the main goal is to obliterate all males, then I have no counter-argument, and no time for such a radical and intolerant approach.

# No Right to Speak for Me!

The need to speak for others remains relatively unquestioned in the citadels of colonial administration, among activists and even still within the academic domain. It elicits a growing unease and in some schools of discourse, it is being rejected. Within feminism, there is a strong, albeit contested, ideological construct which holds that speaking for others is arrogant, vain, unethical and politically illegitimate. The libertarian scholarship, as an agenda, almost exclusively requires that female scholars speak on behalf of other women. However, the problems and intricacies of speaking across racial, class, sexuality, cultural and power lines are becoming ever more apparent. Such notions within the world of feminism abound, as Joyce Trebilcot, in her paper, "Dyke Methods", offers a philosophical account of such a view. She abdicates the practice of speaking for others within a lesbian feminist community, arguing that she "will not try to get other women to accept [her] beliefs in place of their own", on the grounds that to do so would be to practice a kind of discursive coercion and even a violence.[2] The problem of speaking for others, and how this is to be addressed and maybe mitigated, is not a notion exclusive to feminist discourse. Is it justifiable to speak for others, and furthermore, would such representations even be adequate? Trinh T. Minh-ha explains her grounds for being skeptical of the need to speak for others, when she points out that anthropology is "mainly a conversation of 'us' with 'us' about 'them', of white man with the white man about the primitive-nature man…in which 'them' is silenced. 'Them' always stands on the other side of the hill, naked and speechless… 'them' is only admitted among 'us', the discussing subjects, when accompanied or introduced by an 'us'…"[3] Given this analysis in our post-modernist, post-structural era, even ethnographies written by progressive anthropologists are to now be seen as regressive due to the structural features of anthropological discursive practice.

The supposition that speaking for others is to be looked down upon is posited on two principle claims. The first principle has to do with the growing awareness that one cannot rise above the environment that nurtured their nature. The position that one finds him or herself within the hierarchical/caste systems in a society is greatly tied to a person's knowledge, with said knowledge confined, owing to the limitations of approaching matters through a single lens, that is; a single perspective. In other words, both the meaning and truth of what one says are affected by the collective experiences of the author, or the position from which one speaks from. As such, the author's social location or social identity has an epistemologically significant impact on the author'/speaker's claims. Following this logic, most scholars within studies of African American and Feminist discourses and schools of thought, among many, are keen to ride this train, thus serving as the prominent voices that (dis)authorize one's speech. One can even go as far as to posit that the creation of Women's Studies and African American Studies departments were founded on this notion. That the study and advocacy for the marginalized must be endeavored by the oppressed themselves, is largely a post-structural philosophical approach, well received by many a significant scholar. Indeed, this much is clear, that acknowledgement must occur as it regards the systemic deviations inherent in social location between speakers and those spoken for, as this has a significant effect on the content of what is said. The second principle is posited on the claim that not only is one's social identity/location epistemologically salient, but goes further in declaring that certain privileged identities are discursively dangerous. Allow me a brief moment to place the term privilege within the proper contexts. In reference to the power and knowledge structures in a society, privilege here points to the more favorable, mobile, and dominant position that persons may occupy within our exploitative post-modern societies. As such, privilege often substitutes for the need for rigorous critiquing and limits the discursive checks and balances needed in a healthy scholarly community. Privilege, for example, and among a plethora of such, carries with it the presumption in one's favor when said individual speaks. "Certain races, nationalities, genders, sexualities, and classes confer privilege, but a single individual (perhaps most individuals) may enjoy privilege in respect to some parts of their identity and a lack of privilege in respect to other parts. Therefore, privilege must always be indexed to specific relationships as well as to specific locations."[4] I mean not to exclude those attaining discursive power through proper merit, they are, however, rarely pure. To zoom in closer to the mark of what I mean by privilege, I'll continue to use Linda Alcoff's view, that is:

"...some persons are accorded discursive authority because they are respected leaders or because they are teachers in a classroom and know more about the material at hand. So often, of course, the authority of such persons based on their merit combines with the authority they may enjoy by virtue of their having the dominant gender, race, class, or sexuality. It is the latter sources of authority that I am referring to by the term "privilege."

Back to the second claim of the two aforementioned presupposed principles needed to run the 'do not speak for others' machine. The general consensus among the academic literature, in favor of not speaking for others, is driven by the underlying notion that; not only is location epistemologically salient, but that a certain of the aforementioned privileged identities/locations are, in and of themselves, "discursively dangerous." This principle was made poignant in the arguments levied against Anne Cameron, despite her track record of going on the record to emphasize dialogue between the privileged and the disenfranchised, claiming to speak with the marginalized and not for them. Anne Cameron is a white Canadian author who has written several first person accounts on Native Canadian women. She faced an unpleasant backlash while at the 1988 International feminist book fair in Montreal, an event to which she was invited to speak, on matters 'well-known' to her, dealing with the social conditions of Native women, or at least, some of them. Native Canadian writers suggested that she "move over", on the grounds that her writings are disempowering to Native authors. It is worth noting that Cameron's intentions were never in doubt, it was, rather, that the effects of her writings were argued to be harmful to the needs of disparaged authors. After all, it would be Cameron and not the 'other' who will be listened to, and owing to this receptive ear, as such, Cameron, or other much needed contributors from a similar social location, will have their books read by persons interested in the social dynamics surrounding Native women. For people belonging to a dominant group, speaking for others comes with the perks of being perceived as "authenticating presences that confer legitimacy and credibility on the demands of subjugated speakers," thus perpetuating the hegemony on knowledge and its transfer.[5] For this reason, a great number of scholars and authors have come under criticism by members of the very disparaged groups spoken for. Within feminist schools of thought, certain groups dispute the legitimacy of being spoken for by such speakers, who are seen as having little resemblance to them, in terms of social identity. An example of this within the feminist struggle is evident among African American and other black women. As I will try to elucidate in later sections of this chapter, these women are estranged from not only partaking in the conversation, but likewise asked to espouse an ideology that isolates them from their communities.

In the wake of the 1989 elections in Panama were overturned by Manuel Noriega, for U.S. President George Bush made a public denouncement of a man that the U.S. government once backed, that his actions were an "outrageous fraud" and that "the voice of the Panamanian people have spoken." Before going on to plan the invasion of Panama, the former president would go on to add that, "the Panamanian people want democracy and not tyranny, and want Noriega out." Should the voices of the people continue to be ignored, despite that being the case for several years prior, when the toppling of said tyrant was inimical to US interests? Should speaking for others be done a selective basis? And who would be doing the selecting needed to legitimate an author or a speaker? A good place to start is by asking ourselves whether this is ever a legitimate authority, if so, what are the criteria for legitimacy? Once more it begs the question; is it ever valid to speak for others who are unlike me or less privileged than me (in terms of social location, or identity)?

*"...we might try to delimit this problem as only arising when a more privileged person speaks for a less privileged one. In this case, we might say that I should only speak for groups of which I am a member. But this does not tell us how groups themselves should be delimited. For example, can a white woman speak for all women simply by virtue of being a woman? If not, how narrowly should we draw the categories? The complexity and multiplicity of group identifications could result in "communities" composed of single individuals. Moreover, the concept of groups assumes specious notions about clear-cut boundaries and "pure" identities."*[6]

That a part of the demographic in the developed nations, that is; human beings born with penises, are often berated and rebuked whenever they wish to engage in civil interaction and collective discourse, on topics revolving around feminism, means that exchange of knowledge is inefficient. Liberal capitalism, with its emphasis on free-trade and globalization, has always advocated for, or better said, has used democratization and global democracy promotion as a scapegoat, with a 'stable world' the supposed intended outcome. To springboard off of this, I need little in the way of proof as to the prevalence of democracy promotion in the political rhetoric, profusely diffused in media platforms for more than the past four decades. Democracy as an ideal, calls for an engaging and heated arena of societal knowledge exchange, among humans, as equals. To be sure, I do not condone or justify the patriarchal binary system of 'us' versus 'them', not unlike the process used to define black people, when aspiring to fashion the ideal of 'the white *man*'. This need to describe or characterize what man was, upon which doing, place all negative and unwanted values onto the other, in our case, onto women, can be attributed to the mental modes of construction begotten by modernist structuralism. As it regards democracy promotion, then, the US' hypocritical approach to global geo-political relations, has surely not escaped the vast number of astute observers the world around. Needless to say, the shady dealings at times perpetrated by the pentagon or the CIA, or the existence of a 'detention' facility, funded by taxpayer dollars, outside mainland USA; has over the past several decades weakened American credibility in view of the values they claim to espouse. Most would agree with the logic that saying one thing yet manifesting acts to the contrary, is ill-advised and harmful in the long run. It is hypocritical. Imagine now, what would happen to the mood in global relations vis-à-vis the US, when you denounce the act, say, of terrorism, and yet yourself resort to infiltration of such deeds, as is the view of the US by a growing number of people in several nations, particularly in the Middle-East and Latin America? Allow me to carry the analogy on to the topic at hand, feminism and the fight towards equality, a given human right. Wouldn't it be somewhat hypocritical if women were to fight for freedom and actual democracy between peoples, regardless of sex, gender, race, creed, or any such socially constructed notion, and yet deny the right of a significant part of the population, to participate in an aspect of democratic practice? Indeed, once more, as it regards patriarchal norms and practices that still linger profusely in the atmosphere, some women rightly point to the fact that male authors and contributors to the discourse on feminism, would continue to benefit from the old patriarchal reward system economically or otherwise. However, one cannot deny the dangers inherent in not maximizing exposure to criticism, and the richness that comes with multiple perspectives and unique individual contributions to any scholarly, political, economic and social endeavor. As a lover of knowledge and libertarianism, as well as many ideological notions of progressive post-structural visions of the world, I find myself saddened and disgruntled at the quashing of human potential. For democracy or even for the global free market economy (which isn't what we have currently) to function as intended, the masses of people must be well informed in many a field of knowledge. This informed public can thus better understand what they're signing up for in their elected officials, or better yet be readily cognizant of matters gone awry in the public space, and thus move to counter circumstances unfavorable to them. Of course every author should be aware of their contribution to the status quo of global inequalities, whether man or woman. As will be further elaborated upon, no one woman, as is the case for a man, can claim to speak on behalf of all women. No one person universally shares a cultural identity with any and every oppressed group. As such one has to be aware of his or her view as limited and only suggestive in nature, a piece of a much larger conversational pie. One needs to know from whence they socially stand and shun any reverting to former norms, taking into account the multi differing relations, not just between men and women from a broadly varying spectrum of life experiences, but between the differing socially situated women themselves. In historical terms, the constriction of women from intellectual participation is only a blink of eye's time ago.

Resting on the position that one should only speak for 'oneself' raises a few questions. Namely, if I do not speak for the less privileged, in view of the current system, who then will take up the mantle? Or in the words of Linda Martín Alcoff, one of the greatest thinkers of our age:

> *"Am I abandoning my political responsibility to speak out against oppression, a responsibility incurred by the very fact of my privilege? If I should not speak for others, should I restrict myself to following their lead uncritically? Is my greatest contribution to move over and get out of the way? And if so, what is the best way to do this---to keep silent or to deconstruct my own discourse? The answers to these questions will certainly depend on who is asking them...some of us may want to undermine, for example, the U.S. government's practice of speaking for Guatemalan Indians. [7] So the question arises about whether all instances of speaking for should be condemned and, if not, how we can justify a position which would repudiate some speakers while accepting others."*[8]

In the creation of a personal identity, as is the case for cultural identities, and in speaking for myself, I paint myself in a certain light, occupying a certain social position, and have some characteristics and not others. In so speaking for myself, I temporarily create my 'self', in like sense, when I speak for others I create them as a public, a discursive self, a mental fabrication that is more coherently constructed than any subjective experience can support. Indeed, the publicized personal identity will in most cases affect the self that one experiences inwardly. What I am trying to show in a roundabout way is the inherent dilemma of representation that underlies all cases of speaking for, whether one does it for him/herself or for others. However, as was discussed in the chapter prior to this one; mental representations are not circumscribed to the realm of fiction. These narratives that we tell ourselves aid in forming our individual mental paradigms and too our collective cultural mind frames. As is the case with racism, in spite of its origins as a mental construction for justification purposes, its material effects, and the material origins which led to the need for said constructions, are too real to be read into by society as one would a fairytale. These representations, however, are always mediated by discourse, power, and location, in complex ways. Of course the complexities in human social relations when speaking for others are generally more intricate than the simplified aforementioned analogy of representations. The problem of speaking for others is a social one, and it should not be assumed that individual act free and autonomous in their choice making but that the options available to us are socially constructed. However, to remove all human agency and as such, human accountability from the equation is something I would also argue strongly against. We are responsible for the words we say even if it was our intention to perpetuate a patriarchal tradition of subjugation.

It is worth noting that group identities and demarcations are both permeable and ambiguous with the delineation of identities always partly arbitrary. How specific does an identity need to be to confer epistemic legitimacy? As regards this legitimacy, and for advocates of *groups speaking for themselves*, can a white woman speak for all women, even women of color? Can a woman of color speak for all women, including women of color and also homosexual women? And so on…

One of the few things that critical theory, discourses of empowerment, psychoanalytic theory, post-structuralism, feminist and anti-colonial theories have agreed on this century, is that the neutrality of the speaker or author (the theorizer) can no longer be upheld. After all, "[w]ho is speaking for [who] turns out to be as important for meaning and truth as what is said; in fact what is said turns out to change according to who is speaking and who is listening."[9] The current social infrastructure helps to account for the presumption against a woman when she speaks, while equally in favor of a speaking man's ideas, usually taken seriously.

*"When writers from oppressed races and nationalities have insisted that all writing is political the claim has been dismissed as foolish or grounded in resentment or it is simply ignored; when prestigious European philosophers say that all writing is political it is taken up as a new and original "truth" (Judith Wilson calls this "the intellectual equivalent of the 'cover record'.")…The rituals of speaking which involve the location of the speaker and listeners affect whether a claim is taken as true, well-reasoned, a compelling argument, or a significant idea. Thus, how what is said gets heard depends on who says it, and who says it will affect the style and language in which it is stated. The discursive style in which some European post-structuralists have made the claim that all writing is political marks it as important and likely to be true for a certain (powerful) milieu; whereas the style in which Africa-American writers made the same claim marked their speech as dismissible in the eyes of the same milieu."[10]*

# 'De Mule uh de World'

When the Equality Rights Amendment (ERA) was initially written out and sent to Congress in the early 1920s, it was done within the confines of a male-generated elitist paradigm. Not unlike the framework of attributing to one segment of humanity three-fifths of their value, during our 'slave society' epoch, proponents of equal rights in the 1920s saw some portions of the population in a much less favorable light than they did others, still in tune with the discriminatory practices of society at the time. At that time, Americans were behooved by their fears of the other, suspicious towards people of Japanese descent, melancholic towards black people, and nothing short of patronizing towards nonwhites and women. The (mis)conception that the fight for equality by women and for women, then as now, was done with all women in mind is readily apparent in the extensive, idealized literature of the 20th century. The truth, however, shows us the extent to which class distinctions, more so than racial dissimilarities, have affected and even guided the trajectory of progress, as it regards equality between the two sexes. To the extent that class is influenced by racial elements, race distinction becomes one morsel, among many others, within the various organizations that have been set up for the benefit and uplift of women in our society. Before we venture on to discuss the role of race within the feminist struggle, it behooves me to firstly contextualize feminism in contemporary times, by the somewhat superficial telling of parts of its history.

The backlash to the perceived threat of the consequences to accrue from the enactment of the ERA bill came in the guise of outcry from several prominent civil rights groups, the National Consumers League, the League of Women Voters, and the Women's Trade Union League, who among others went on record "opposing 'blanket' equal rights bills, as the NWP formulations at both the state and federal levels were called."[11]. Their refutation of the bill, as is the case with color blindness, poses several questions, some such as; how best do we understand the implications to the policies we pass, and what world will result from said policies, furthermore; are we all in agreement with that picture of our world? Not unlike colorblindness, passing policies in a nondiscriminatory manner, has little benefit for the bulk of the population these statutes aim to empower. The root problems within society are yet to properly be addressed. There is little authentic knowledge exchange taking place. Knowledge, like power, its kindred entity, always seems to accrue and centralize beyond the access of the ordinary woman and man. Opposition to the ERA bill pointed out that this broad brushing was "too undiscriminating an instrument," further adding that, "objectionable sex discriminations such as those concerning jury duty, inheritance rights, nationality, or child custody would be more efficiently and accurately eliminated by specific bills for specific instances".[12] The opposition to the Equal Rights Amendment bill was revived when the second wave feminists attempted to reintroduce the ERA. As with the first wave of feminism in the 1920s, prominent critics arose in the early 1970s to counter the ERA, one of whom is Phyllis Schlafly. Schlafly, a conservative Catholic mother, wife, and lawyer, led the charge against the underlying notions of shifting society towards the devaluation of the role that women within our societies play. She was not advocating for the continuation of the status quo patriarchal subjugation of women, despite her opposition to the promotion of values and policies that threatened to change some of these norms and values. One reason among many which translated to Schlafly leading one of the most notorious and almost triumphant campaigns against the pro-ERA movements of the 1960s and 70s, as with the case during the 1920s; was the focus on women as a singular group, who would have their interests solely tied to their gender.[13]

*"The NWP posited that women could and would perceive self-interest in 'purely' gender terms. Faced by female opponents, its leaders imagined a fictive or abstract unity among women rather than attempt to encompass women's real diversity."*[14]

Phyllis Schlafly saw in the ERA revival, forces not dissimilar to the previous wave of feminist pro-ERA factions within a broad and diverse feminist struggle. She was able to mimic the anti-ERA efforts of the 1920s, and much unlike her opposition, she portrayed women under the light of family, as "daughters, wives, mothers, and widows with family responsibilities". She made public her acknowledgement that the "promise of 'mere equality' did not sufficiently take those relationships into account."[15] Unlike the fight brought to the forefront of the public's attention by opponents of the ERA bill in the 1920s, Schlafly's concerns were not limited to women's equality, racial, or labor issues. She, instead, noted the many accomplishments that had so far been achieved to promote equality, including the Equal Pay Act, Title VII, and countless court battles audaciously fought and won.[16] Schlafly had noticed the inherent potential consequences of ERA, to actually cause harm to women, radically altering social and cultural mores. For her, and in the words of Christina Hoff Sommers, this was "a blueprint for a radically new society".[17] Schlafly's peers, the likes of Betty Friedan, were highly critical of women in the domestic sphere, they went as far as to "attack a postwar culture that consigned women to the domestic sphere," and even warring against "the domestic sphere itself and the women who choose to live in such a world.[18] The ERA effort, according to many women, was looked upon as something different, as something much more radical, yet, overlooked by the major part of politicians, who felt encouraged to follow along uncritically in a bid to win over a key constituency.

As cited by Hoff Sommers, in tandem with historian Jane Mansbridge's view, "by the mid-seventies most feminist leaders held that 'the ERA would require the military to send women draftees into combat on the same basis as men.' They did so, she says, 'because their ideology called for full equality with men, not for equality with exceptions'."[19] There's a constant need to prove that women can do any and all things that a man can. This, in my view, is still within the confines set up by our traditional patriarchy, a paradigm where manly or man-like values, as they were once envisioned, are favored, lauded and rewarded. Men can't birth, but they can child rear. We value the ability of child-birth, as it is not given to all women, but we value such said biological manifestations through the lenses of masculine dominated norms and perceptions, defining womanhood in terms of their fertility. I believe in the need for attributing child-birth to womanhood, but not that such a primitive activity be the sole criteria for defining what or who a woman is. Child birth and rearing, and the confinement to a domestic milieu should not necessarily mean backwardness and subjugation, not if that mode of living is the woman's choice. It is in understanding that some women take pride in having such a life, that solutions can best be drafted up for a society that seeks to be all-inclusive and somewhat harmonious. It goes without saying that members of pro-ERA groups were not pleased to have as effective an opponent as Schlafly working against their cause. In the view of several pro-ERA individuals, Schlafly was essentially a sellout, and attained success reaching "out to vulnerable women and [playing] brilliantly on cultural anxieties."[20] Schlafly to this day, remains vilified by feminists for her right-wing views, and who is apparently "Still a Cranky Asshole Who Doesn't Get It," according to a Jezebel article that, at the time, undertook a crusade against one of her most recent books. This antagonistic response, beginning with second wave feminism in the 1960s and transcending to third wave feminism throughout the late 1980s to the present, attempts to portray freedom for women as the liberation from biological essence, in a uniquely postmodern way. The idea was that, if women do not seek for radical egalitarianism and legislation much like the ERA, then this meant that a deeper and larger social force was at play, something that served as an obstruction to the perceptions of the masses; obstructed from seeing the light. As was noted by Sara Evans, "Many New Left activists came to believe that the American society was not salvageable and required a total transformation."[21] In the eye of such a storm, the feminist climate became increasingly and readily intolerant to any dissent. Evans, in her book on the history of modern feminism, depicts the shift as a "search for purity" and for a "'true' feminism in the realm of ideas and the formula for a perfectly realized feminist life. The pursuit of perfection made it difficult to entertain complexity, sliding easily into dogmatism. Differences in opinion and lifestyle betrayed the "true faith" and could not be tolerated."[22] Shlafly and Evans were part of a faction that betrayed the values of another feminist faction, the latter of which Anna Snitow was a proponent. Snitow, in a personal diary excerpt, published in "Conflicts in Feminism," expresses her desire for the feminist movement to allow her to escape from womanhood.

She, in one instance, had the recollection of a conversation she had with one of her friends.

"How can someone who doesn't like being a woman be a feminist?" to which Snitow replied, "Why would anyone who like being a woman be a feminist?"[23] She goes on to express her joy in the realization that "now I don't have to be a woman anymore. I need never become a mother. Being a woman has always been humiliating, but I used to assume there was no exit. Now the very idea of 'woman' is up for grabs. 'Woman' is my slave name; feminism will give me freedom to seek some other identity altogether."[24] Snitow's views, like many of her peers, present the most extreme versions of feminism, which goes beyond the desire for equal-pay or the right to vote. Snitow and others equate their freedom with liberation not only from passive and active discrimination, but also from biological or cultural expectations or restrictions. Such a view has enable some to argue that it is not only possible but that it would be necessary "for the biological difference to wither away as a basis for social organization, either by moving men and women toward some shared center (androgyny) or toward some experience of human variety in which biology is but one small variable."[25] What's worth noting, is that, inherent to the liberation from biological essence mindset, is the commonly held belief in the social scientific view that many behaviors and institutions are a social construction. Marry Wollstonecraft, is perhaps from whom such a belief was initially derived. Among the first prominent feminist thinkers, Wollstonecraft, in 1792, in "A Vindication of the Rights of Women," she mentions how "what was new then and remains fresh, shocking, and doubtful to many now: that sex hierarchy- like ranks in the church and the army or like the then newly contested ascendancy of kings- was social, not natural."[26] However, upon rightly positing that gender roles and even gender are socially constructed, feminists like Snitow can easily follow these ideas to their extremes, making the case for liberation from biological and cultural essence. If gender is not a real and absolute category (which it is not)- "then there is no way to defend it, let alone impose specific gender rules and expectations on all human beings."

Simone de Beauvoir entertained such notions, immensely influencing feminist and postmodern frames of thought, and largely known for works like her publication "The Second Sex," released in 1948 France and translated into English for American readers in 1952. One of her many publications, in 700 pages, "The Second Sex" is one of countless examples of the reflection of liberation from essence paradigm in her work and within feminist thought. In her words, "one is not born, but rather becomes, a woman". Ultimately, it seems, woman can but escape the strenuous hold place on her by society at menopause, the inverse of puberty. This line of thought allows us to further strip womanhood of her biological and cultural attributes. Changing our collective identity at a speedy rate, what can that do? Are we ready to experiment upon the collective human psyche, without a full understanding of the implications hidden behind the veil of progress? Simone de Beauvoir, Snitow, and others would take the notion of transcending biological essence to further pinnacles of thought. The notion that woman is no longer the prey of external forces of imposition, upon attain the stage of menopause, she is herself, she is one with her body. I've often heard that at a certain age, women constitute a 'third sex'. Aforementioned notion has some ostensible truth attached to it, since according to de Beauvoir and others, while such women are not males, they likewise are no longer females. Following this train of logic, cultural expectations of this 'third sex' are altered. Of course to me, such line of thought is to presuppose that child birth and rearing are the obstacles to the empowerment of women worldwide, and not that such dogmatic ways of living are in and of themselves indicative of deeper underlying notions of patriarchal power pulls and tugs. Why not aim at having a society where women who choose the domestic lifestyle, as a means of ensuring a certain upbringing for their offspring are not vilified? Why not aim at a society that in equal measure respects the choice of women to abstain from either child birth or child rearing, or both? I somewhat naively believe that, although there may be different ways of achieving an inclusive society, in tandem with the high moral ideals of universalism that we hold, the desired result should be a civilization that offers people, regardless of sex, the option to map out their life's trajectory, without fear of losing a solid footing within economic, political and social discourses.

Still, the question remains, how fast do we wish to change our culture, and what impact will that have on society as a whole, furthermore, who is to benefit from such New Left feminist radical policy changes, since, as we saw, not all women feel represented within many a feminist organization. In Zerubavel's terms, the ideology pivoted about the liberation from essence feminism, are a thought community convinced that their perspectives and ideals are "social facts." The prevalence of such lines of thought, and their ascendant influence in the public and academic spheres, is cause for some concern.

## Bye Katrina

The still and motion pictures depicting, for the most part, black mothers carrying their post-Katrina and post-traumatically stressed infants, maneuvering their way through filthy, chest-high waters, was an enduring image of desperation and fear. It was through the suffering and resilience of black women in the wake of Hurricane Katrina, that the media told the story. As aforementioned, a few sections prior; the dehumanization of the poor by bourgeois and elite circles, in all predominant media platforms, is in part the reason for the need portray black people as having within their ranks, mothers and children. Through a patriarchal commonality held by most race categories, we expect society to be protective of its women and children. However, having dehumanized poor people, of which group black women are disproportionately representative, there seemed to be a need to show raw, painful human emotions expressed by women and children, so as to overlook the "thugs," "rapists," and "criminals" among their ranks. Such adjectives are typical of white America's view of black men. It took such depictions of suffering to spur on new conversations on race, class, and vulnerability. It is on the bodies, minds, and lives of black women that the story of Katrina drew inspiration from. The agonizing realization, for some, of inequality in this country of theirs was, at the dawn of the twenty-first century, made bare for a global audience. America, it seemed, was cementing its reputation for talking big and failing to back up such grandiose moral claims. Within five days of the storm, media reports nationwide shifted away from the representations of black men as looters, rapists, and snipers, and instead focused on black women and children trapped in the city's evacuation centers. This target segment within the abandoned black community of New Orleans became the sympathetic victims of the storm. New Orleans, in the wake of the deleterious storm, is a good enough place to begin taking seriously the idea of black women's experiences acting as a democratic litmus test for the republic. Lani Guinier and Gerald Torres, both legal scholars, offered the useful metaphor of the miner's canary as a means of understanding how the political and economic realities of marginalized segments of the population, indicate the democratic and economic health of the nation. Canaries are known for their sensitive respiratory systems, as such, miners used these birds as alert systems to indicate the presence of poisonous gasses in the mine's atmosphere. Not unlike this alert system, vulnerable communities of black and brown Americans foreshadow the inherent problems likely to poison the nation's system. Thus, August 2005, marked a point when the black women of New Orleans became the nation's canary in a mine one may refer to as the US of A.

The warning signs of a cringing and teeth gnashing society are visible to us, and matters concerning race, gender and class inequality affecting black women's lives in America, is the canary that points to problems enmeshed in the national fabric. Katrina was thus the chemical reagent that exposed these inequalities, rendering more visible the hidden heterogeneous elements within an ostensibly homogenous society. For one thing, the inadequate evacuation capacity illuminated America's failure to invest in its public, the neglect of maintenance and improvements to the country's modern public transportation systems. The levee failure that left communities vulnerable to the storm's destructive prowess, for example, was indicative of America's dilapidating infrastructure. While, on the other hand, the delayed government response pointed to "the limitations of federalism and a harbinger of compromised homeland security".[27] The urban poverty made bare by the storm was the foreshadowing of an impending economic crisis, of course, it is much easier to see this in retrospect. The disproportionate burden of the disaster needed to be shouldered by black women, was but a symbolic portrayal of the morbid intersections of race, class and gender. Such an intersection describes a typical day in the life of a black woman, more especially black women in the lower cadres of the socio-economic ladder. How best to evaluate the level of attained civilization in our 'western' societies in general, and particularly in the United States, is to analyze the manner in which the poorest elements of society are treated by their own. There is a certain prestige in being a member of a wealthy and powerful society, for example, the pinnacle of Roman civilization entailed free grain to all within its city limits. In like sense, relative to other societies the world around, Norway and other Scandinavian nations can boast about, their treatment of the most disadvantaged amongst them, their social security net. I would be remiss if I do not make mention of nineteenth- and twentieth-century educator Anna Julia Cooper, who so eloquently pointed out the hidden in plain sight reality that, "only the black woman can say 'when and where I enter, in quiet, undisputed dignity of my womanhood, without violence and without suing or special patronage, then and there the whole…race enters with me."[28] As such, it is colored women, in general, but particularly so, it is black women in the American society, surviving at the nexus of racial, gender, and classed dis-privilege, who mark the level of civilized progress attained.

*"If black women were free, [that] would mean that everyone else would have to be free since our freedom would necessitate the destruction of all systems of oppression."*[29]

In advocating for gender equality within a patriarchal society, it is necessary when critiquing the ill elements of that society, not to throw the baby out with the bath water. Not everything about our traditions and dogmas should be downtrodden, as there, sometimes, abounds some benevolent survival logic behind it all. Take for example the notion of saving women and children first in the aftermath of an unforeseen catastrophe. In a country that where tradition and dogma demand that women and children be paid particular attention to when evaluating pragmatic survival solutions, "the abandonment of poor black mothers and their children argue that these chivalrous impulses rarely extend to African American women. They shamed the nation because the narrative is triumphant and collective. Americans take great pride in understanding themselves as an uncompromised liberty."[30]

## Mammy and her Jezebel of a Daughter

Charting the experiences of black women during slavery, Jim Crow, and up to the present era, the myths and narratives told about them, in the newspapers, on the radio and television, and even in the stories we read to our children before they go to sleep, formulated narratives of who the black woman is are not amiss. Throughout the twentieth century, upon realizing the significant role played by stories about ourselves, in relation to the other, scholars of black women's experience, among other anthropological and social scholars, began to highlight the role played by projected images and myths. Such said narratives and societal myths aid in the creation of powerful ideologies that once blatantly supported economic and social structures as Jim Crow. The constant renewal of consequences, materialized when some power wielders, policy makers, act on presupposed information about a particular demography. Guided by the myths handed down to us, the result, more often than not, calls for choices that disproportionately affect the lives of black women. As alluded to in the first chapter of the book, many a myth was told about black people in general, to justify white America's treatment of them. Under such light of reasoning, black people had to be stripped of their humanity, while in the spirit of self-proclamations, white people half-way deified themselves, needing to carry a cross, that is; the 'white man's burden'. The dual notion of describing oneself, along with their community by renouncing what they are not, while at the same time placing these unwanted qualities onto the 'other', has been the cause for many a problem dealing with cultural and racial disparagement. In societies filled with male hegemony, in order to describe and define man and what constitutes manliness, through several influential esoteric institutions, white men firstly defined who they do not see themselves as, placing the remaining unwanted qualities onto women. Women, in line with the expected notions of chastity and humility of the Victorian era, were placed on a certain moral pedestal. Being a slave society, America had to come up with justifications for the normalizing of oppressions directed at black women. Using the power of myths to achieve dehumanization and produce repugnance towards black women and men, can be noted throughout American history. Historian Deborah Gray White, for instance, points out one of the many myths attributed to black women, that of a lusty and promiscuous Jezebel. This parallel of representing black women as the embodiment of libidinous evil, worked towards the capitalist paradigm of exploitation; in the self-denial of white men, for the sake of appearing to uphold moral standards within a rotten society, justified the sexual abuse of enslaved women.[31] Such reasoning is not unlike that used by medical practitioners when, as pointed out by legal scholar Dorothy Roberts, black women's assumed sexuality was used as the justification for involuntary sterilization en mass.[32]

Well entrenched in American life are the different myths that have been put in place to better describe the different social locations or identities. According to contemporary civil discourse, it is easy to forget the extent to which these self-reinforcing mythologies were normalized. In Thomas Jefferson's 1785 publication, "Notes on the State of Virginia," he concluded that white women were superior to black women. Following the precepts of his argument, black men, across the board, preferred white women to black ones, in a manner akin to "the preference of the Orangutan for the black women over those of his own species."[33] Since that epoch, rampant is the retelling of slightly different versions of the same myth, bespoken of which is the potentially dangerous desire of black men for white women. It became a truism that black women, and their urges, were somewhat animalistic, going so far as to suggest their willingness to have sexual intercourse with apes. Boundless in their blame of the black woman, white America vilified black sisters, mothers and daughters, as the incarnation of Medusa, this time luring white men away from their more cultured and more chase female counterparts. African American women were the most favored scapegoats for the easing of the white male conscience. Emblematic of this derogatory shadow cast on black women were public proclamations of influential persons, famous biologist Louis Agassiz's 1843 publication being one such example, who according to him, "as soon as the sexual desires are awakening in the young men of the South, they find it easy to gratify themselves by the readiness with which they are met by colored house servants."[34] The like proclamations prompted, and continue to invoke indignation within circles of the African American intelligentsia; one such backlash came in the form of "black women of the early twentieth century club movement [who] resisted the lie of black promiscuity by leading a movement of temperance, modesty, and respectability".[35] Indicative of the ranging spectrum of resistance by black women, from black intellectuals to domestic workers, the latter of which resisted the ideology entailing mammy-like devotion to whites, by living outside their employers' homes, in addition to protest of unfair and exploitative labor conditions.[36] It is worth noting that under the banner of female unity and solidarity, little to nothing about the racial overtones of society's narrative of black women was vocalized by clout-bearing upper and middle class women. During the telling and re-telling of the nature of African American women, it is all too natural for the disparaged to seek to counter such inaccurate projections about their supposed identities. In light of this backlash-phenomenon, some questions come to the fore, notably, as pointed out by Melissa V. Harris-Perry: "is it possible that black women's organizing efforts and public reactions to issues of sexual assault are linked to their beliefs about the stereotype of black women's promiscuity? Does the pervasive notion of Mammy help explain why black women are suspicious of coalitions with white women? Do black women often defer to black men's religious, familial, and political leadership because they reject the idea that they are angry and domineering?"[37]

Melissa V. Harris-Perry, considered among the leading experts of our times, authoring several books regarding contemporary black life in the US. In tandem with her book publications, she organized and conducted focus groups in Chicago, New York, and Oakland. This focus group made use of a relatively small sample size of forty-three African American women across communities in all three cities. In August of 2003, the Center for the Study of Race, Politics, and Culture at the University of Chicago hosted three focus groups. Lasting approximately two hours and amounting to eight or in some cases nine participants. For their participation, the involved persons received fifty dollars compared to the seventy dollar incentive awarded to participants to the two focus groups at the Focus Suites in New York. The participants of Harris-Perry's focus groups came from a variety of households, each beholden to a wide range of socioeconomic conditions and statuses. All participants had a GED or higher level of intelligence, lived in their respective urban areas, and excluded persons in the fields of marketing, advertising, market research, health care, counseling, or higher education. To supplement the research with geographical variety, two additional focus groups were conducted in Oakland, California at Laney Community College. During a warm-up exercise, participants came up with a coherent picture of black women, as they saw them. Working in groups, the discussion turned into a lively session of knowledge exchange about both the facts and myths attributed towards black women. A consistent portrait was painted, in spite of the fact that these women lived in three different cities, spanned several generations, and haled from different socioeconomic and familial circumstances. In line with the three main stereotypes pointed out by many researchers of African American women's experiences, the participating women, through personal experience, independently arrived at the same conclusions. They identified versions to which black women were said by society to adhere, namely; Mammy, Jezebel and Sapphire. It was concluded during this preliminary warm up stage of the focus group that black women were seen and constantly depicted as "oversexed" or as "fat mammies who aren't thinking about sex at all". The black woman, history tells us, is either promiscuous or asexual; it was as simple as that. Words like "Jezebel," "maid," and "Mammy" were all too redundant in the vernacular blurted out during these initial discussions. In the words of Margaret, a fifty-two-year old woman from the West Beverly neighborhood of Chicago, "just because we are African we're supposed to be wild and all this. We are supposed to be from the jungle and like to have wild sex. Like that is all we think about. Folks think we're hot or trot. Or they think we're Aunt Jemima. It's never in between." In addition, it seemed that the women would be remiss in not making mention of the "welfare queen," alive and well in the American psyche. During the preliminary discussions, which were as much an eye-opener as the core inquiry presented by the focus group, nearly all the women rejected the hypersexual and Mammy stereotypes. However, several participants concurred with the welfare queen myth, with one woman voicing her belief in it as "…not a myth," claiming that "[it] belongs on the 'fact' side of the page. [since to her] there are a lot of black women out here living on the system." Still more, everyone was in agreement that not all black women related to the welfare cheat of an image, with most participating women arguing that the stereotype was detrimental, despite the appearance of some truths. The group rightly noted that black men and women also perpetuated deleterious narratives and myths about black women. Other intra-racial depictions of African American women were accompanied by words like, "haters," "gold diggers," "overly demanding," and "argumentative. As exemplified by the proclamations of one professional in her fifties, "black men always try to say that we are manipulative and too bossy and too demanding. They act like they don't know that black women are the backbone of the family. We keep things together. The man may be the head of the household, but we are the backbone and the backbone has got to be strong."[38]


## Racial, Class or Gender Solidarity, or High Water


For African American women, the euphoria had from belonging to a community or group -the primitive concept of strength numbers very much at play- is not a feeling that lingers with them as they face the harsh marginalizing forces of real life America. Whether involved and encouraged by racial solidarity, they still found themselves unable to relate to the general experiences undergone by black men in general, and African American men, in particular, in spite of overwhelming similarities. What's more, the realization that a conglomeration of memberships in the different solidarity groups, racial, gender, or otherwise, for black women, did not amount to any comfort, came to them as a woeful chagrin. Their experiences, as at the time, women, black persons, and disproportionately a part of the lower socioeconomic classes within society; was akin to no other. Within academia and civil movements, persons had come to the realization that, neither racial, gender, nor class exploitation, could be overcome without sincere opposition to society's treatment of African American women. Black women, it seemed were destined for disparagement, even within the confines of their racial communities. A good place to begin our exploration into the fray, that is, the 'collective' experience of black and African American women, is by lending attention to the actions set into motion by the legal system. In 1991, accused of sexual harassment by Anita Hill was Supreme Court nominee Clarence Thomas. Anita Hill happened to be a woman, a black one, and in addition, she also was a former co-worker of his. The survivor of rape soon turned into the topic of much blame from within her own racial community. For three days, Hill underwent gruesome, and I'm sure traumatizing questioning by a Supreme Court justice. Thomas, on the other hand, infuriatingly referred to the questions launched at him as a "high-tech lynching." The use of ideology to unite people in the African American community, preying on the subconscious fears of a people, was masterfully wielded by Thomas. Accompanying the invocations of notions of lynching was Thomas' approval ratings, which sky-rocketed to nearly 50 percent. It is worth noting that for a conservative justice, whose decisions ran counter to the prevalent norms and advocacies of civil rights organizations, his approval ratings would never again know such heights amongst black Americans.[39] However, garnished with the garb 'blackness', and how that translated to America's history of racial violence directed at black men, Thomas received significant support from the black community.[40] Thus following centuries old traditions of depicting the black woman as the personification of Medusa the seductress, it was Hill and not Thomas under the line of fire, the former, it seemed, warranted questions of her behavior, in particular; what she had done to provoke or encourage the harassment. Hill was relegated to 'race-traitor' status, since according to a significant number of black persons; she had allowed her story to be used by powerful white opponents to harm the reputation and credibility of a black man.[41]

The year was 1992 and former heavyweight boxing champion Mike Tyson was charged and found guilty of raping Desiree Washington, an African American woman. Serving half of his six-year sentence, Tyson returned home to jubilant praise, hailed as black America's returning messiah. Who, you ask, was part of the welcome parade? Apart from a large segment of African Americans, and a great number of boxing fans the world around, including several prominent African American political and social leaders, the Nation of Islam and even the Reverend Al Sharpton voiced their welcomes.[42]

It seemed that having willingly met Tyson at the hotel, Washington's actions suggested to the world that she had invited sexual contact, and as such put Tyson's guilt into question in the minds of many an American. One would expect an equally significant number of black persons to be outraged by these developments, or even large groups of women, in a show of feminine solidarity. That, however, is a reality befitting a fictive Disney animated production. Let for one moment, then, entertain a short thought experiment, one in which Desiree Washington was a blonde haired, blue eyed American woman. I believe, since I can't prove a hypothetical, that regardless of whether Tyson was a black or white man, the outrage not only within society, but also within the legal system, would be more severe and punitive. My point here being that, such a plethora of moments in America's history hint at the continued power of stereotypes in shaping paradigms, of which mental constructs in turn fashion individual daily lives. Although black women in the US are assigned every shape and texture of qualities, and of characteristics, unwanted by almost every demographic in society, the most predominating stereotype, might just be that of her seductiveness and tendencies towards promiscuous, sexually immoral activities. As a teenager, I always found it ironic that white women, and more especially persons within feminine movements of empowerment, were encouraged to express their sexual needs and desires as do men. The reality, however, painted a different picture, while for a white woman, promiscuity spelled out independence and a libertarian lifestyle, the same could not be said of black women in general. Such moments in history also reveal the extent to which black women within the African American community are misrecognized, and the complicated responses that come with said misrecognition. In both the Thomas and Tyson cases, in spite of the perpetrators' punitive recompense, the women were bequeathed a legacy of shame in their communities, denounced as "fast", with the community rallying behind the enforcers of wickedness. As such, it is worth mentioning that although "black women's hyper-sexuality may have been historically created and perpetuated by white social, political, and economic institutions, its contemporary manifestations are often seen just as clearly in the internal politics of African American communities."[43]

# Inter-Cultural Knowledge Exchange

I continue to advocate for the genuine exchange of knowledge between different parties in society, noting that even a group ostensibly as monolithic as black women in the US, even accounting for similar socioeconomic, political, and familial situations, there are great variations between the women. It is genuine knowledge exchange, I believe, that will work towards eradicating gender discrimination and stereotypes, and understanding our history and its subjective nature is as a good place as any to start. As mentioned in the prior sections, culture is grossly linked to a person's social location/identity. It thus needs no mentioning that, in line with this wellspring of reasoning, black women in the US occupy their own collective, yet heterogeneous, social locale or identity. Knowledge transfer is indifferent to whether the information passed from one party to another is grounded in truth or is predominantly mythical. By stating the aforementioned, I wish to allude to the fact that it is the knowledge held by ruling white men in the world's history that amounted to constraints placed on all women. Misogyny, I opine, is the result of bigoted conceptions of the world, another useful elite tool devised to further divide an already fragmented society. One can trace the roots of the promiscuity myth that has contributed to the denigration of black women in the former slave society of America, to the trickled down values of the Victorian-era. The Southern slaveholding society was a machine that churned by incorporating elements of a gendered social and moral code. True womanhood was an ideal that followed the precepts of strict codes of piety, purity, submissiveness, and domestic-virtues, values believed to be inherent in feminine nature.[44] Aiding the elites to clearly divide the public and private realms, was the adherence to Victorian social codes. White men were the sole authorities within their households, while such the evidence of power was 'given' to white men, their female counterpart fared miserably. Married white women were dispossessed of their property and legal personhood, helping to cement the beliefs of women as essentially chase, innocent, and weak. The lives of African American women sharply contrasted with that iconic perception afforded to other women. For instance, during slave auctions, black women were subjected to forced nakedness, and were later in life seen to labor under harsh conditions, needing to have their skirts hiked up. As punishment on plantations, they often were either partially or fully stripped. Also, they were, of course, legally forbidden from marriage.[45] "The myth of black women as lascivious, seductive, and insatiable was a way of reconciling the forced public exposure and commoditization of black women's bodies with the Victorian ideals of women's modesty and fragility. The idea that black women were hypersexual beings created space for white moral superiority…justifying the brutality of Southern white men."[46]

Within middle class feminist bourgeois culture, one finds a huge chasm, a divide that alienates them from the lower and quasi-proletariat segments of the society. Given that black women in general find themselves disproportionately represented among the lowest classes, but more so in reference to African American women; feminist culture is a world away, and out of touch with the experiences of most these women. As discussed in the chapter prior to this, even within such a variegated racial category, say for African Americans, there are fragmentations; cultural clashing and meshing among black Americans. It would be patronizingly presumptive to think that differences don't exist, even within marginalized racial communities in a society, let alone across class and racial lines in the case of feminist organization. To group the voiceless within society along with the more 'educated,' middle class women, across multiple racial lines, often results in the interests of the more powerful and influential groups favored over the marginalized others. Often left out of the conversation, the lower classes of women, both white and nonwhite, have little to no say in the policies that shape the lives of their lives and that of their families. Having lower literacy standards compared to other socioeconomic classes in the US, their word amounts to little sway within policy shaping discourses. Furthermore, the organizations that these women erect fail to garner the support needed to successfully lobby their proposals and interests in Washington (D.C.). Dehumanized persons in the lower classes, in general, often find their pleas fall on very few borrowed ears. These ears, so to speak, are governed by the cultural hegemonic standards which aid in fueling the repeated feed-back loop, which sees the oppressed shut out of the conversation about their social identity. Of course for the few authors, for example, who manage this ear-garnering feat so well, their intended message is mostly not well grasped, even by the intelligentsia of their lowly classified social location.

The different classes, races, and genders in a society, intermingle and interact, influencing each other, a trafficking of cultural material, as was made mention of in the previous chapter. That cultural products are trafficked across the different segments within a society is both an edifying and deleterious aspect of an inevitable consequence of human mingling. The benefits of incorporating different elements of other cultures are too obvious for us to make further mention of than was done in chapter 1. What's worth fearing about cultural traffic is the incorporation of cultural material to aid in the shaping of marginalizing and harmfully disparaging paradigms. In a patriarchal society, more than black men, black women have borne the grunt of stereotypes that have arisen from cultural traffic gone aryl. Let us for example take up the narrative of the black man's uncontrollable lust for the white women, often said to lead him to raping her. It must be noted that as with describing and characterizing what makes for a man, in white America, the unwanted descriptions of what and who he is not had to be brought to the fore, and then dumped on the unsuspecting victims, white women. In like sense, at the short end of the stick is the black woman. For the myth of the boogieman that is the black man to gain traction within white America, the black woman had to be trampled down, her beauty, internal and external, sidelined to the margins of societal expectations of grace and beauty. The downgrading of black women in America, it seemed, could just not be restricted to the realm of intelligence, culture and politics, but the beauty industry, through the imposition of cultural hegemony also told black women what to do with their own physical appearance. Once more, there is an inescapable irony that is evident when middle class feminists advocate for not being told what to do, or how adorn themselves, while socially pressuring black women towards a Eurocentric envisagement of beauty.

"...it is important to stress that black [female] culture is a highly variegated entity at any historical moment or in any one historical situation...They range from the slave communities of the New World to the rural niches of pre-colonial Africa; from the urban black neighborhoods to the urban native quarters and reserves of colonial Oakland, Nairobi, Kingston, Accra, London, Amsterdam, and Belleville sections of Paris...Hence, when we speak of black cultural traffic, we are always implying the traveling not of whole cultures, but elements- even microelements- from these variegated formations."[47]

It must be noted that although some stereotypes about African American women arise from perversions of truths, most of the notions that spur the noticed group-like behaviors on, are rooted in rational bases. One belief about black women in America that comes to mind is their suspicious attitude towards doctors and hospitals, and their notorious noncompliance with prescription medication. In "The Effect of Patient Race and Socio-Economic Status on Physicians' Perceptions of Patients," in the academic journal Social Science and Medicine, Michelle van Ryn and Jane Burke explore the historical context that accounts for such seemingly irrational behavior.[48] Being that eugenicist and other racial forms of medical procedures are part of a history that most liberal intellectuals in American life are not too proud of, the history of black women can thus not be taken out of context. In a painstaking effort, journalist Harriet Washington shows the long grotesque history of racist experimentation, abuse and deceit carried out on unwilling female slaves. Harriet takes us to the antebellum-era when gynecological experimentations on slaves, and other pervasive practices, such as that of robbing cemeteries in order to procure bodies, black ones, for medical school anatomy classes. Clearly black women are to be given more credit for their undue contributions to the medical field. She retells the appalling Tuskegee experiment. My younger brother James thought of me as a conspiracy theorist, and a sympathizer of black supremacy when I spoke to him of the Tuskegee experiments, not until academic and historical proof was presented to him, did he back down on his neo-liberal belligerent rhetoric toward me. The Tuskegee experiment, as I told it to him, allowed black men to suffer from and fatally succumb to untreated syphilis. Harriet also goes as far as to suggest that professional care of black patients in the US takes place in line with contemporary racial assumptions, which affect the medical care black patients receive.[49]

## Postmodern Feminism: Some of the Theory and its Limitations

My intent is not to demonize nor mock feminism today; the aim rather, of this chapter, as this book, is to point out the apparent heterogeneities wherever they appear in our globalized societies. It is in these lines of fragmentation within society that the true forms of exploitation and inequality are best revealed. The point of critiquing any elements of discourse or behavior, I opine, works towards not intolerant relations between the differing sexes or groups within a sex, but rather the improvement of society according to the ideals we so tout as civilized peoples. Christina Hoff Sommers, in her book Freedom Feminism, attempted to address some of the common concerns facing politically conservative-leaning elements in society. In asking why the term feminism has a lot of negative connotations, and then proceeding to highlight that 70 percent of women when asked if they identified with being a feminist, said "no". Indeed, this does not translate to 70 percent of women being against progress, or the liberation provided by a society that obliges equal rights for both sexes. It of course has a strong correlation with the level of dissatisfaction felt by women about today's form of feminism. Primarily because of her defense of boys and men, according to what she believes are unjust stereotypes, policies and practices levied against them. There's the universal feminist claim that, as in the words of Eve Ensler, who in a 2003 lecture at Harvard said she thought "that the oppression of women is universal. [They] are bonded in every single place of the world. [Thinking] the conditions [as] exactly the same…[and that] the systematic global oppression of women is completely across the globe."[50] On the other extreme, thinkers like Jessica Valenti, a blogger, who once pointed out that, "we have no problem condemning atrocities done to women abroad, yet too many of us in the United States ignore the oppression on our doorstep. We're suffering under the mass delusion that women in America have achieved equality…Part of this unwillingness to see misogyny in America could be self-protection-perhaps the truth is too scary to face."[51] It is, perhaps views by thinkers like both Valenti and Ensler, which helps to account for the public's distaste of the feminist order, yet, there are some truths in both views. The average American woman, however, would not see themselves as "suffering under mass delusion," nor necessarily seem themselves on par with the suffering of women in Saudi Arabia, who didn't choose the life they're in. Sommers, asks for a "reclaiming" of feminism, pointing out its progress. A lot of policies and won court cases by feminist crusaders in the past, can be thanked for a great many universally empowering aspects about western societies in general. These battles that redressed society according to more horizontal orientations than times prior, and brought about concessions on the part of the country's elites, were not without sacrifice and sheer pain. Sommers advocates for a world where the happiness of men and women should not come down to a zero-sum game. Sommers' freedom feminism seems to strike a chord with many more women and men than a great many of the feminist factions today. Although not everything she advocates for is worth agreeing with, her incorporation of a greater section of society, I believe, can be interpreted by many as a more eager willingness to be flexible when needed, in the discourses which shape policy. In doing so, she claims, the freedoms achieved may be preserved and more readily direct us towards exporting such libertarian principles and achievements to parts of the world that are most in need of progress. For Christina Hoff Sommers, freedom feminism amounts to "the moral, social, and legal equality of the sexes" and "the freedom of women to employ their equal status to pursue happiness in their own distinctive ways."[52] In offering forward the concept of "maternal feminist," a traditional form of feminism, mostly relevant during the eighteenth and early nineteenth centuries, Sommers shows the broad spectrum of opinions that feminists should be willing to at least entertain about other women. In her book, Sommers laments how easily forgotten Hannah More is by contemporary feminists and historians, a thinker whom she sees as the founder of feminism.

*"More initiated a humane revolution in the relations of the sexes that was decorous, civilized, and socially cohesive. Above all, it was a feminism that women themselves could comfortably embrace: a feminism that empowered and freed women on their own terms. Indeed if More's name and fame had not been airbrushed out of contemporary women's history, many today might identify with a modernized version of her female-friendly feminism...many of the leading scholars who specialize on the eighteenth and nineteenth century are committed to 'left-wing social ideologies' [causing them to] hate Hannah More because in their eyes she did far too much to stop liberating-French style of political revolution occurring in England."[53]*
Quite visible in the public sphere is this intolerance by modern feminist thinkers of other women, who wish to work within the system, for a form of liberation that calls out most to them, believing that another variation of

feminism will call out to their daughters en mass, and on and on throughout the subsequent generations. This form of change, although not revolutionary, is more inclusive of the vast majority of the country.

In showing the incongruities inherent in third wave feminism, which is, in general, the modern variation of the feminist struggle, one also points out the successes incurred by society's more influential hegemonic forces, to divide and thus to conquer. Prominent feminist philosopher and highly praised intellectual, Linda Alcoff, has on several occasions pointed out the identity crisis within contemporary feminist thought. Her approach was relatively easy, needing only to point out the obvious the cohesion (or lack thereof) of feminist movements in today's western societies. With regard to the more progressive schools of thought, however, Alcoff differs from Sommers, in that she is more accepting of said notions, her views and commentaries more charitable. Alcoff's work has mainly consisted of demonstrating what she considers to be two schools of thought, which she deems as most influential in the current ideologies predominating feminist thought. In so defining these two principle factions of feminism today, Alcoff thus attempts to consolidate or mediate the ideological outlooks of both "cultural feminist" and "poststructuralist feminist" schools of thought. In the case of cultural feminism, Alcoff's description bears vague resemblance to Sommers' maternal feminism, except that the tenets of the principles described by the former are much more radical. For Alcoff, the central issue facing feminism is the notion of woman and what it is that is her essence.

*"It is the central concept for feminists because the concept and category of woman is the necessary point of departure for any feminist theory and feminist politics... [but] the dilemma facing feminist theorists today is that our very self-definition is grounded in a concept that we must deconstruct and de-essentialize in all of its aspects."*[54]

According to Alcoff, it only made sense to reason this way, since, in order for there to be an advocacy for women, and for there to be a promotion of the idea of and the need for feminism, the understanding or definition of what a woman is must first be established. Any attempt, however, to define a woman is subverted and undermined by a discourse and culture that is still very much a reflection of male-dominated constructs of "woman'. In response to this conundrum, more often, the claims by feminists and women have amounted to them having "the exclusive right to describe and evaluate women," or to "reject the possibility of defining woman as such at all."[55] This first response aforementioned is what Alcoff calls cultural feminism, which is the argument that women have allowed themselves to be defined by men for far too long. However, undergirding this belief is that men and women thus have uncomplimentary and opposing views and interests. Furthermore, it postulates that the process of defining woman or man can be reduced to a zero sum game, requiring that every sex fend for itself, that is; if the wish not to suffer at the hands of the other.[56] The second response aforementioned is what Alcoff calls "poststructuralist feminism," which is a school of thought, she believes, is rooted in the linguistic and philosophical principle that all things can be "deconstructed," and that attempts at defining woman, whether by a feminist, man, or woman, or a misogynist, are "politically reactionary and ontologically mistaken."[57] Such notions, grounded in French poststructuralist theory, allows claims by feminist of the second school of thought to claim "that such errors occur because we are in fundamental ways duplicating misogynist strategies when we try to define women, characterize women, or speak for women, even though allowing for a range of differences within the gender. The politics of gender or sexual difference must be replaced with a plurality of difference where gender loses its position of significance."[58] This tenet, effectively thus rids itself of the idea of gender altogether, especially as a centralizing agent, as such, it paradoxically subverts the need for a feminist movement in the first place. Therefore, "transcending these limitations while retaining the theoretical framework from which they emerge is impossible."[59] However, quite similar to Sommers' maternal feminism, cultural feminist view does, to some extent, concede to the more mainstream doctrine that femaleness and femininity can be linked to women's uniquely female anatomy and their biological capacities. What can be deemed as radical about cultural feminism is the standpoint of female liberation, as a counter-culture to the status quo and to male culture. One of Linda Alcoff's sources, Ann Echols, exemplifies this notion, when she, as Alcoff states, "identifies cultural feminist writings by their denigration of masculinity rather than male roles or practices, by the valorization of female traits, and by their commitment to preserve rather than diminish gender differences."[60] Thus, women and men are set at odds, rather than working together towards common human goals.

# Women and Sports: a short excerpt

"...the mass media have become one of the most powerful institutional forces for shaping attitudes and values in American culture. Mass media portray the dominant images or symbolic representations of American society...These images in turn tell audiences who and what is valued and esteemed in our culture...How female athletes are viewed in this culture is both reflected in and created by mass media images. Thus, it becomes critical to examine both the extent and the nature of media coverage given to female athletes."[61]

If there is one method consistently used by scholars to gauge levels of acceptance of women in sports, within society, it is the study of the coverage of female athletes in the media. The year 1996 marked a hallmark year in the attention paid to the performance of women in sports. That 1996 was a year that hosted the Olympic games, and with the successes incurred by United States' female athletes, resulted in a great deal of enthusiastic coverage in America, centered around the lives and accomplishments of these women. In a matter of weeks, the US women's Olympic basketball team was featured on Sports Illustrated, making it on the cover; also making a cover appearance on the New York Times Magazine was Sheryl Swoopes. With Newsweek featuring Olympic gold medalist Gwen Torrence, they proclaimed 1996 the "Year of the woman," reaffirmed by the likes of T.V. Guide, who ran two cover stories about Olympic female athletes.[62] Within this optimistic atmosphere, burgeoned the belief that all female athletes, regardless of marital status, sexual preference, or their view on femininity would finally be afforded full societal acceptance, and a more sincere appreciation of their athletic achievements, rather than the focus on their sex appeal.[63] According to Robert M. Entman, journalists "select some aspect of a perceived reality and make them more salient in a communicating text, in such a way as to promote a particular problem definition, causal interpretation, moral evaluation, and/or treatment recommendation for the item described."[64] As such, news, like art and any other system of communication is propaganda, and can be understood as a narrative with undergirded meanings, of which meanings are imparted through media frames or paradigms. The frame adopted by a media platform is essential to understanding how issues are made relevant or important. As Entman opines, these frames are actually "the imprint of power," in that they often portray a singular or monolithic social identity about a person, which directly translates to transformations in public opinion and discourse.[65] Hertog and Mcleod agree with Entman when they state that "the frame used to interpret an event determines what available information is relevant."[66] Some scholars deem and conceptualize sport as a "system of social practices based on two symbolic assumptions," namely, that the human body is but a tool of power, and also that, "the social construction of the human body is gendered".[67] This line of thinking points to the notion that sport has gifted society a culturally salient mechanism for portraying power relations between men and women, perpetuating misogynistic stereotypes and paradigms. What is observed is that the sports garnering the most media coverage have served to underline men's dominance over women, simply owing to the fact that they are, as in the words of Messner, "organized around the most extreme potentialities of the male body."[68] Furthermore, while women may today enjoy increased media coverage, more often, said coverage emphasizes the "natural" differences between women and men, further deep-setting the ideological hegemony of male superiority. The feminization of women in sports is still rampant, with the manner in which the coverage is framed pivotal to the continuation of the status quo.

*"Female athletes in 'typically male' sports were described regularly using male-to-female comparison and many of the descriptions in the print media focused not on the women's athletic feats, but instead on information that was irrelevant to the athletic even...female Olympic athletes in more typically 'feminine' sports (e.g., gymnastics) did receive more task-relevant coverage, but the coverage was laden with comments reinforcing female stereotypes."*[69]

Although women, like other marginalized groups have a long way until true libertarian standards and equality is seen by them, the problem is not one that is exclusive to single factions of civil rights activist groups. Not until the problems faced by women, and in particular African American women, are paid attention to, exposed and redressed, can authentic and non-hypocritical solutions be offered. White supremacist patriarchal systems of oppression are not the problem as much as they are the symptoms to more underlying incongruities. Power dynamics among the different cultural and socioeconomic classes can't be notwithstanding, in discussions dealing with emancipation for any groups of denigrated persons within society. Western societies, for centuries, have undergone effective divide and conquer techniques, to the extent that we know not anymore our true reasons for revolt.

# Notes

[1] The 1937 novel; "Their eyes were watching God"; Zora Neale Hurston; The protagonist Janie is quoted as saying such.

[2] Joyce Trebilcot, "Dyke Methods," Hypatia 3.2 (Summer 1988): 1. Trebilcot is explaining here her own reasoning for rejecting these practices, but she is not advocating that other women join her in this. Thus, her argument does not fall into a self-referential incoherence.

[3] Trinh T. Minh-ha, Woman, Native, Other: Writing Postcoloniality and Feminism (Bloomington: Indiana University Press, 1989), 65 and 67. For examples of anthropologist's concern with this issue see Writing Culture: The Poetics and Politics of Ethnography ed. James Clifford and George E. Marcus (Berkeley: University of California Press, 1986); James Clifford "On Ethnographic Authority" Representations 1.2: 118-146; Anthropology as Cultural Critique ed. George Marcus and Michael Fischer (Chicago: University of Chicago Press, 1986); Paul Rabinow "Discourse and Power: On the Limits of Ethnographic Texts" Dialectical Anthropology, 10.1 and 2 (July 85): 1-14.

[4] Linda Alcoff; "The Problem of Speaking for Others"; Cultural Critique, No. 20 (Winter, 1991-1992); pp. 5-32; University of Minnesota Press.

[5] Ibid.

[[7]] Alcoff in; "The Problem of Speaking for Others," makes it clear that: The use of the term "Indian" here follows Menchu's use. See her I...Rigoberta Menchu, ed. Elisabeth Burgos-Debray, trans. Ann Wright (London: Verso, 1984).

[8] L. Alcoff, introduction of: "The problem of speaking for others"; 1991.

[9] L. Alcoff, section I: "The problem of speaking for others"; 1991.

[10] Ibid.

[11] Nancy F. Cott; "Historical Perspectives: The Equal Rights Amendment Conflict in the 1920s"; in "Conflicts in Feminism"; edited by Marianne Hirsch and Evelyn Fox Keller; New York: Routledge; 1990; p. 47.

[12] Ibid. p. 49.

[13] Christina Hoff Sommers; "Freedom Feminism: Its Surprising History and Why It Matters Today (Values and Capitalism)"; Washington: AEI Press, 2013.

[14] Nancy F. Cott; "Historical Perspectives: The Equal Rights Amendment Conflict in the 1920s"; in "Conflicts in Feminism"; edited by Marianne Hirsch and Evelyn Fox Keller; New York: Routledge; 1990; p. 48.

[15] Ibid. p. 50.

[16] Christina Hoff Sommers; "Freedom Feminism: Its Surprising History and Why It Matters Today (Values and Capitalism)"; Washington: AEI Press, 2013; p. 49.

[17] Ibid. p. 50.

[18] Ibid.

[19] Ibid. p. 57.

[20] Sara Evans; "Tidal Wave: How Women Changed America at Century's End"; New York: Free Press; 2003; pp. 113.

[21] Ibid. p. 133.

[22] Ibid p. 4.

[23] Ann Snitow; "A Gender Diary"; in "Conflicts in Feminism"; edited by Marianne Hirsch and Evelyn Fox Keller; New York: Routledge; 1990; pp. 33.

[24] Ibid. p. 9.

[25] Ibid. p. 24.

[26] Ibid. p. 28.

[27] Sister Citizen, Melissa V. Harris-Perry, 2011, pp. 16-17.

[28] Anna Julia Cooper, *A Voice from the South* ,1892; New York: Oxford University Press, 1990.

[29] Combahee River Collective, "A Black Feminist Statement", 1977, reprinted in *Words of Fire: An Anthropology of African American Feminist Thought,* ed. Beverly Guy-Sheftall, New York: New Press, 1995.

[30] Sister Citizen, Melissa V. Harris-Perry, 2011, pg 18-19.

[31] Deborah Gray White, "*Ar'n't I a Woman: Female Slaves in the Plantation South*", New York: W.W. Norton, 1985.

[32] Dorothy Roberts, *killing the Black Body: Race, Reproduction, and the Meaning of Liberty;* New York: Vintage, 1998.

[33] Thomas Jefferson, *Notes on the State of Virginia, ed.* Frank Shuffelton, 1785; New York: Penguin Classics, 1998, 145.

[34] Louis Agassiz, as quoted in Harriet A. Washington, *Medical Apartheid: The Dark History of Medical Experimentation on Black Americans from Colonial Times to the Present*, New York: Doubleday, 2006.

[35] Evelyn Brooks Higginbotham, *Righteous Discontent: the Women's Movement in the Black Baptist Church, 1880-1920,* Cambridge, MA: Harvard University Press, 1994.

[36] Tera W. Hunter, *To 'joy My Freedom: Southern Black Women's Lives and Labors After the Civil War,* Cambridge, MA: Harvard University Press, 1997.

[37] Sister Citizen, Melissa V. Harris-Perry, 2011, pp. 32.

[38] Ibid. pp. 34.

[39] See Anita Hill and Emma Coleman Jordan, eds., *Race, Gender, and Power in America: Legacy of the Hill-Thomas Hearings*; New York: Oxford University Press, 1995.

[40] Kimberle Crenshaw, "Whose Story Is It, Anyway? Feminist and Antiracist Appropriations of Anita Hill," in *Race-ing Justice, En-Gendering Power: Essays on Anita Hill, Clarence Thomas, and the Construction of Social Reality,* ed. Toni Morrison; New York: Pantheon Books, 1992, pp. 402-440.

[41] Sister Citizen, Melissa V. Harris-Perry, 2011, pp. 54.

[42] See Aaron Baker and Todd Boyd, eds., *Out of Bounds: Sports, Media and the Politics of Identity;* Bloomington: Indiana University Press, 1997.

[43] Sister Citizen, Melissa V. Harris-Perry, 2011, pp. 55.

[44] Suzanne Lebsock, *The Free Women of Petersburg: Status and Culture in a Southern Town, 1784-1860*; New York: W.W. Norton, 1985.

[45] Deborah Gray White, *Ar'n't I a Woman: Female Slaves in the Plantation South*; New York: W.W. Norton, 1985.

[46] Sister Citizen, Melissa V. Harris-Perry, 2011, pg 55.

[47] "Black Cultural Traffic: Crossroads in Global Performance and Popular Culture"; pp. 19, 2005; University of Michigan Press.

[48] Michelle van Ryn and Jane Burke, "The Effect of Patient Race and Socio-Economic Status on Physicians' Perceptions of Patients," *Social Science and Medicine* 50 (2000): 813-828.

[49] Harriet A. Washington, *Medical Apartheid: The Dark History of Medical Experimentation on Black Americans from Colonial Times to the Present*; New York: Doubleday, 2006.

[50] Christina Hoff Sommers; "Freedom Feminism: Its Surprising History and Why It Matters Today (Values and Capitalism)"; Washington: AEI Press, 2013; p. 3.

[51] Ibid.

[52] Ibid. p. 6.

[53] Christina Hoff Sommers; "Freedom Feminism: Its Surprising History and Why It Matters Today (Values and Capitalism)"; Washington: AEI Press, 2013; p. 24.

[54] Linda Alcoff; "Cultural Feminism Versus Post-Structuralism: The Identity Crisis in Feminist Theory"; in "Feminism and Philosophy: Essential Readings in Theory, Reinterpretation and Application"; ed. Nancy Tuana and Rosemarie Tong; Boulder: San Francisco; 1995; p. 1.

[55] Ibid. p. 2.

[56] Ibid.

[57] Ibid.

[58] Ibid.

[59] Ibid.

[60] ] Linda Alcoff; "Cultural Feminism Versus Post-Structuralism: The Identity Crisis in Feminist Theory"; in "Feminism and Philosophy: Essential Readings in Theory, Reinterpretation and Application"; ed. Nancy Tuana and Rosemarie Tong; Boulder: San Francisco; 1995; p. 5.

[61] Kane, M. J. (1988), Media coverage of the female athlete before, during, and after Title IX: Sports Illustrated revisited. Journal of Sport Management, 2, pp. 89.

[62] Gremillion, J. (1996). Woman-izing sports: Magazine coverage of female athletes. Mediaweek 6 (32), pp. 20-22.

[63] Fink, J. S. (1998). Female athletes and the media: Strides and Stalemates. The Journal of Physical Education, 69 (6), 37-40. & see also; Lopiano, D. (1997). Tomorrow in women's sports: Now is just the tip of the iceberg. Paper presented at the Summit '97 (Women's Sports Foundation national conference), Bloomingdale, IL. & Women's Sports Foundation (1997). Images and words: Protecting your image, respecting her image. Panel discussion at the Summit '97 (Women's Sports Foundation national conference), Bloomingdale, IL.

[64] Entman, R. M. (1993). Framing: Toward clarification of a fractured paradigm. Journal of Communication, 43, pp. 52.

# WALLS

[65] Entman, R. M. (1991). Framing U.S. coverage of international news: contrasts in narratives of the KAL and Iran Air incidents. Journal of Communication, 41, pp. 7.

[66] Hertog, J. & McLeod, D. (1995). Anarchists wreak havoc in downtown Minneapolis: A mutli-level study of media coverage of radical protest. Journalism & Mass Communication Monographs, 151, pp. 4.

[67] Blinde, E., Greendorfer, S., Shanker, R. (1991). Differential media coverage of men's and women's intercollegiate basketball: reflection of gender ideology. Journal of Sport & Social Issues 15 (2), pp. 101.

[68] Messner, M. (1988). Sports and male domination: the female athlete as contested ideological terrain. Sociology of Sport Journal, 5, pp. 206.

[69] Fink, J.S., Kensicki, L.J. (2002) An imperceptible difference: visual and textual constructions of femininity in Sports Illustrated and Sports Illustrated for Women. Mass Communication & Society, 5(3), pp. 317-339.

# 3

# Class

## and

# Class Antagonisms

### ***

*One of the most thriving aspects of capitalism was being able to command the resources of other lands and capitalize, that is to turn into capital, the appropriated resources of elsewhere at home. As such, before the American Civil war of the nineteenth century, the greatest form of capital, slaves, accumulated by the droves. The realization that the creation of this vast structural inequality could lead to unimaginable wealth soon begun to seize the continents of Europe and more especially pre-industrialized Americas.*

Although Native Americans weren't part of the European slave agenda, that didn't exclude them from mistreatment and denigration by white settler. Natives, however, rightly so saw not the problem as relating to matters of race, instead, regarded the newly arrived white settlers, no matter their destructive predilections, as just another group on the land. On several occasions, trade between the two types of communities took hold, with Native Americans sometimes allying themselves with white settlers, so as to fend off other Native American rival tribes. Indeed, the practice of slavery and the slave trade economy that came with it had almost nothing to do with race as it is depicted today. It would be naïve and nonsensical to believe that white supremacy was the reason for the need to have slave to patrons, guiding the primitive African, the often referred to "white man's burden," rather than it being an early form of propaganda, needed to ease the conscience of a supposedly God fearing confederation of peoples. Thus, in order for us to talk about the class antagonisms inherent in society today, we have to lend our focus to the differences in both racial and cultural experiences, and the economic system from which these societal conditions emerge. For capitalism to settle within society, certain conditions needed to first be established. The ability to independently and privately own property as well as the means of production, with a will class of workers, often the cheaper the better; must be guaranteed by the state. A legal framework that is congruent with the efficiency and easy running of business within the state also needs to be part of the infrastructure, needed to encourage a capitalist order. In addition, a physical infrastructure must be erected to allow for the ease of circulation of goods on a macro-scale, with other industries suit on the trail blazed, such as for example, security promotion of these trade roots, for example, soon following suit in a complimentary manner. Agrarian and mercantilist forms of capitalism are the foundations upon which the present manifestations of capitalism delineate from. By the turn of the 16th century in England, the manorial system begun to disintegrate, and the economic foundations of the feudal system gradually shifted evermore substantially. Not unlike in today's society, land and private property concentrated in the hands of fewer patrons, and with time, the estates grew increasingly larger in size. As primitive as life was for serfs under the feudal order, one could argue that they had slightly more power or sway with their landlords, than do the proletariats of today's globalized capitalist system. These medieval peasants at best, saw themselves directly benefit from the produce of their labors, at worst, they would revolt, refusing to lay down their pitchforks, nor accept their mandated starvation. Of course, revolt against the same lords who saw to their shelter, and offered them protection was only resorted to during the most extreme of situations, still, it was one more option I don't imagine the poorest persons in Sri Lanka are entitled to.

Historically speaking, most civilizations in our recorded past, have used the system of exploitation, where the few benefit and the masses suffer under the yoke of relative servitude. Global capitalism, in all its variants, is an economic system that is no different, well rooted in atrocious exploitations. The prevailing economic doctrine of the 16th century, up to the 18th century is commonly referred to as mercantilism, an epoch of discovery, linked to the geographic exploration and exploitation of lands foreign to European merchant traders. These traders were initially predominantly from the Low Countries and England. However some scholars have argued counter to the belief that capitalism originated from merchant forms of exploitative trade, Karl Polanyi being one such advocate for the belief that, capitalism was established only upon the generalization of markets. The markets, according to Polanyi, were standardized for "fictitious commodities", that is; land, labor, and money. According to his line of reasoning, not until 1834, when competitive markets were instated in England, could capitalism be said to have existed. What remains true, however, as aforementioned, is the fact that inequality has always been a preferred socioeconomic system of choice for several past civilizations. As in line with the premise of this book, the exploitation of lower class is maintained beyond their reach and within mysterious social frames. Cultural differences along racial, class and gender lines help to uphold this system of inequality. It is much like a person of significantly little socioeconomic clout going up against a juggernaut in society, the former will be buried and mired in all sorts legal proceedings and litigations before even setting foot in court. In like sense, the different distractions sent our way, racial, class and gender antagonisms, to name a few, are but required circumstances, so as to keep us away from the crux of the matter confronting our globalized world. Along these tectonic lines of fragmentation, cultural variations evidently burgeon. The significance of ideology to keep a system within its element must not be underestimated. White supremacy as an ideology is not necessarily the ardent belief held by global capital accruing elites. However, white supremacy has a significantly pivotal role in the workings of society, the glue that maintains centuries-old entitlements to new land, and the foundations of today's expressions of exploitative economics. These entitlements justified the dispossession of Native American land, and continue to do so, the modern day variant of which would be; the dispossession of other nations' natural resources through cultural hegemony and military predomination. As such it is crucial to understand that, just as the use of racism in contemporary western societies is needed to support an archaic ideology, and thus allow for a certain economic order; so too was slavery tolerated for the greater economic good of those who "mattered". Christianity, for a significant portion of the 400 or so odd years, tolerated slavery and looked down upon it, mostly as an unfortunate situation, much like we in society today perceive the homeless as having arrived to their state of living all on through their own merits. Alluding to the evidence of inequality as a fuel for continued socioeconomic exploitation, today as during the economic system of slavery; is not popular among the respected and rewarded twenty percentile of US society. Economists not wishing to succumb to career suicide, make little mention of the societal dysfunction, ignoring the greed and poor constructions of fiscal policies.

> *"The abysmal state of Black education in the United States and globally is an inhumane situation that calls into question the values and pronouncements of Western 'civilization'"*[1]

The maintaining of the status quo, with mild variations depending on the epoch and the geographic location, requires an educational system that is complimentary to the prevailing economic mode of exploitation. The likes of Raphael and Michael Angelo, in a papal and conservative civilization, could not express themselves too far outside the prevailing cultural paradigm of the day, at least not openly. While the paradigm during a time like the renaissance was stuffed with religiosity, today's cultural frame, in like sense, is made up of a mixture of several inter-related ideologies, which have enjoyed several centuries of molding. Thus, one cannot talk about class antagonism, both in the US and the global community, without speaking of African Americans in US society, and black people in general; who disproportionately constitute the lower classes. Also, with regard to the lower class as a heterogeneous cultural segment within US society, black persons have contributed enormously to the cultural products, through the cultural trafficking of 'blackness' and black cultural material in general. I believe Sylvia Wynter, in an interview, best expressed the thought carried by the premise of this book, as it regards paradigms and genuine knowledge exchange, done outside the hegemonic power and knowledge structures that maintain socioeconomic and political expressions in US society:

> *"...intellectuals and artists who belong to a subordinated group are necessarily going to be educated in the scholarly paradigms of the group who dominates you. But these paradigms, whatever their other emancipatory attributes, must have always already legitimated the subordination of your group...Must have even induced us to accept our subordination through the mediation of their imaginary."*[2]

It is essential that we stray from the narrow, racial or gendered dichotomies of whites/nonwhites or woman/man, since as I've shown, I hope; such single category civil rights movements fail to account for the diversity among women and persons of African descent. When I speak of class differences, however, class refers to the prevalent socioeconomic identity of a particular community. Class structures in the US, like any other society, are, in part, resultant from the social identity of a group, which we said in the preceding chapter, is one way of looking at culture. As such, one would be remiss in not paving allusion to European culture through the framing of it in terms of its significant contribution of "black culture," by the application of socioeconomic and political pressures. One way of defining a class stratum in any society is by picking out which segments have the most access to power, knowledge and the resources of the country, as well as the resources of other countries, appropriated by the governmental state apparatus at the disposal of the elites. Also worth noting as we develop the central ideas of our discussion, is that; that class hierarchies in society are the motivations for racial and gender divides in the lower class segments, does not preclude it from taking a fragmented and hierarchical shape in and of itself. Society's structure as it regards class stratification is a reflection of the surreptitious dynamics of power, or knowledge, or financial accumulation by an exclusive group of individuals. A part of assuring genuine knowledge exchange between the different economic and cultural entities of the global community; is through the guaranteeing of high standards of education, offered to the poorest people of the world. One catch phrase synonymous with western societies is the proclamation that educating women in the developing nations have the right to education, in order to lift them out of poverty, subjugation and ignorance. Thus the control of education and what passes for accurate information, is strongly tied to the interests of the global capitalist elites of our contemporary 21st century and information age of an epoch. Joyce E. King, an expert in pedagogy, in reference to the maintenance of status quo class structures globally and in particular in South Africa, the elites ensured that: "the quality of knowledge the mainstream research establishment produces is implicated in the historical and continuing domination of African people in the United States, the Diaspora and on the African continent as well as in the 'scholarly' justifications of the poverty and other racialized disparities that enslavement and colonial domination has introduced. Besides the "achievement gap", a knowledge gap also exists in terms of the preparedness of Africana researchers, educators, and parents to address the root causes of this crisis."[3] Although our discussion of class antagonisms in this book will in later chapters make further mention of the hegemonic knowledge structures that perpetuate the structure of societies, a quick brushing over of such concepts will do much good, in contextualizing class antagonisms in the US and most of its political state allies by reference to access to knowledge, and power, and resources. The crisis that is Black education, owes itself to the same forces to which sexism, racism, and other forms of marginalization in the world are subjected. As such, society's affinity for exploitation will persist, so long as intellectuals among the marginalized communities are denied intellectual freedom. These aforementioned thinkers must be awarded the liberty to reconstruct education, on foundations relevant to their empowerment, and not necessarily in agreement with the Euro-centric male dominated ideological framework.

The education of persons in society is not limited to scholastic literature, or the schooling system; culture, that is, a group of persons' collective social locations/identities, accompanies economic success, and has political and social ramifications. Therefore, as a result of the globalization of markets and the corporate media, there's evidence of cultural hegemony imposed on developing nations by developed nations in general, and by the US in particular. On a global scale, the United States of America, in a collective sense, is said to have the best universities, its corporations control more of the world's resources than any other nation, and furthermore, lobbyist within the state have access to the world's most influential politicians. What this translates to is: an elite country, it and its western allies, in control of the world's resources, knowledge, and power both military and political. Cultural hegemony thus imparts to the lower classes of society an education central to maintaining the existing order, through "the globalization of markets and the corporate media, people everywhere are being induced to identify with the normative category of the 'whitewardly mobile middle-class'…which now assimilates 'token Blacks and some Chicano/a and Asians as 'honorary Whites' or 'model minorities'."[4] Take for example, an immigrant from a developing nation, of whatever skin color; such a person once in the US has very little incentives for wanting to associate with the values, norms and even speech typical of oppressed segments of US society. The American dream often favors people who comport themselves in accordance with what their racial, or class, or gendered group would consider a betrayal to the collective.

*"The immigrant seeks a form of vertical assimilation to climb from the lowest, darkest echelon on the stepladder of tyranny into the bright whiteness. In U.S. history the Irish, Italians, Jews, and- in small steps with some hesitation on the part of white America- Asians and Latinos have all tried to barter their varied cultural worlds for the privileges of whiteness."[5]*

# Class and the State

It would make little sense to speak of class society without paving allusion to the state apparatus, which fits hand in glove, a necessary coercive force required to secure, maintain and foster private wealth. The disintegration of class society would as such make the state an obsolete apparatus. The state/government is therefore the coercive force wielded by the ruling class in order to maintain its rule over the many. It is easily forgotten, it seems, that for the vast majority of human history, there was no need for a state, this is owed to the fact that during such said a period, there was no need for maintaining a certain class, as, such a notion was of yet inexistent. One thing had in common about American anthropologist Lewis H Morgan and Karl Marx, is that despite the 'debunking' of their claims, their works are heavily relied upon for definitions and as the foundation, for some scholastic societies, of fields in anthropology, economics and philosophy, to name but a few. The nineteenth century was a peculiar time for anthropologists, as it spelled a time when global exploration by Europeans was in full swing, as such the more developed could witness up close the truncated levels of societal progress. While Europeans mastered the craft of warring with one another, long since adapted to the use of gunpowder, they, for example, encountered peoples who were still in the bronze-age of societal development. Taking part in this anthropological gold rush, in nothing short of a significant contribution, is Lewis H. Morgan. Morgan worked among the Native American peoples- in particular the Iroquois tribes- during the mid 19th century. He was among a select few individuals in the world who had a broad knowledge of European and world classical, medieval and modern civilizations. Morgan postulated that and brought forward in writing, the idea that of a law of progression, to which all societies must be subject. He contended that the structure of a society changed with further consolidation into one place, for purposes of ensuring mutual survival, and upon which time technological advances will reinforce said structural changes. When trading was possible, after the collectivization of several tribes on a vast patch of land, in time forming a nation-state; the means of production of goods change. A shift in societal structure often trickles down to the structure of family units, and what such a grouped notion entails for each respective member. Before civilization, Morgan defines the societies formed then as savagery and then barbarism, which are not intended to be used as terms of judgment, but are labels in a grand scheme. The American anthropologist had his appreciations for the values and norms of some of these archaic human societies. He wished to analyze the progression of human society. We know that human kind, approximately 200 000 years ago, the concept of family had an altogether different texture. There were different meanings associated with sexual relations, since, incest was viewed differently, more commonplace, and monogamy was non-existent and possessive jealousy over a woman was much less prevalent, as it made little sense to do so. It's a portrait in which everybody was seen as a parent or a child to everyone else. Among the approaches elected by Morgan, an analysis of the use of language and language progression, for him, revealed elements that exposed the workings of the structure of a society. He puts forward the claim that, language use or the semantics of words in a current society is often that of a previous societal paradigm. He goes on to describe the progression of the most developed of human societies, to better contextualize the emergence of class societies and the state apparatus that maintains it. Morgan described the Mesolithic time period, an age of "barbarism" that saw the invention of arrows, canoes and the like tools. Such human ingenuity, thus, showed a peculiar perceptibility of the environment, a much different in kind to the past era of "savagery." It was also during this lush period, about 12 000 years ago, when pottery was becoming a commoditized household piece of furniture

Another piece of evidence that works towards the central premise of this book, is the principle put forward by Morgan, and much touted by Engels; that women are considered inferior to men is a relatively recent social invention, is seen by the fact that the majority of anthropologist agree to the thought that women played a significant role in the house hold and society. The women had social superiority and clout over men. Women were always seen as the parent of the child, even if the father is recognized. Furthermore, descent was delineated through the female line in gentile society. In this social organization of humans, a tribe amounted to several Gentes grouping together, having each Gens elect two leaders, one for peacetime and his opposite number, for wartime. What was remarkable about the values of societies like the Iroquois in the mid 19th century, is their inclusive political system, where all members in the tribe participate in elections, and also, unanimity was a prerequisite during public discussion between the elected leaders of each Gens; a space that had its doors open to every tribesperson. At this point of human societal progression, monogamy became more apparent, although still not an imposition set in stone, thus, marriage was prohibited within gens. At this stage of development, it is typical of such societies to base societal status according to family ties, who you're related to, being just as important as how you're related to that female member of a Gens. Private property indeed existed, but not in relation to a single person, and more so entailing a collective ownership, where property belonged to a Gens. And inheritance was passed on from the mother, to the next of kin in charge of 'custodianship' of the relatively meager property they had. In a communist societal grouping, the notion of 'free-loaders' amongst the ranks was differently interpreted, the old, physically disabled, and ill were amply looked after as a matter of human responsibility, a commonplace common sense decency.

*"All members of an Iroquois gens were personally free, and they were bound to defend each other's chiefs [war leaders] claiming no superiority; and they were a brotherhood bound together by the ties of kin. Liberty, equality, and fraternity, though never formulated, were cardinal principles of the gens. These facts are material, because the gens was the unit of social and governmental system, the foundation upon which Indian society was organized...It serves to explain that sense of independence and personal dignity universally attribute of Indian character."*[6]

\*\*\*

*"Decisions are taken by those concerned, and in most cases everything has already been settled by the custom of centuries. There cannot be any poor or needy- the communal household and the gens know their responsibilities toward the old, the sick, and those disabled in war. All are equal and free- the women included. There is no place yet for slaves, nor as a rule for the subjugation of other tribes."*[7]

In the case of societies in the Eastern hemisphere, it is widely believed that approximately 8000 years ago, with a surplus of agricultural produce and an abundance of reared or farmed animals, certain practices are shed off, one such being cannibalism. Indeed, with surplus availability of food comes the shunning of the long held practice of eating people, survival has a different meaning to this society than their predecessors. It is around this period of plenty that slaves can be seen within society more prevalently. Slaves, considered property, upon conquest or owing to misfortune in the persons' lives, were delegated to the care of men in the tribe. Initially not much significance was placed on this responsibility. However, this male dominated capital soon heavily influenced the nature of society, at first, ostensibly benign, in the absence of a state apparatus. However, once the state is formed to mitigate newly formed wealth, to alienate and protect elite-class power, this male-dominated sphere of capital gains became deleterious to the rights that women once enjoyed. An economic disparity was made naked, thus necessitating the erection of a state apparatus to mediate tensions within an unequal society. Engels explores the findings and claims made by Morgan, and agrees so far as to explain that, in an attempt to secure their male-only dominated capital accrued, men would sequester the wife, ensuring legitimate children. Monogamy for the sake of hereditary economic interests was strictly imposed, but only as it regards women, men, of course, well, 'men will be men, won't they?' Such patriarchal notions developed as a result of class divisions within a more progressed society. In "The origin of the family, private property and the state", Engels postulates that:

*"The man took control in the home also; the woman was degraded and reduced to servitude; she became the slave of his lust and a mere instrument for the production of children. This degraded position of the woman, especially conspicuous among the Greeks of the heroic period and still more of the classical age, has gradually been palliated and glossed over, and sometimes clothed in a milder form; in no sense has it been abolished"*[8]

The iron age, for the most developed societies of humanity, was approximately 3000 years ago, in Asia Minor, which begun with the smelting of iron and later brought into the era of civilization by inventing writing. At this point in human societal development, the iron ploughshare, for example, led to large-scale agriculture, while the iron axe and spade made possible the mass clearance of forest land for tillage and pasture. Society's advance became exponential from this point onwards, owing to massive increases in both food supply and population. Simply stated, more and closely-knit people on a relatively confined area of land, means a greater ability to learn, and to remember what has been learned. Of course the advent of writing complimented this collective societal learning capacity, since, records about people, places and events lasted longer in the collective psyche. One for the first time in humanity's history had the possibility to amass information from another person, without the need to meet said person. Furthermore, fueling this exponential explosion of civilization is the possibility for labor within the collective to be divided among individuals, allowing others to specialize. An economy of continental trading proportions is formed in such a way. Advanced societies export their expertise and goods to societies abroad, gaining wealth while bestowing a different notion of wealth to the less developed cultures, met along the trade routes. This sort of wealth is the beginning of the undermining of the old natural economy, encouraging further fortified towns, and wars to be waged as instruments of plunder, and not for the sake of survival. A few good examples of societies at this stage of societal evolution, are namely; the Greeks of the heroic age, the tribes of Italy preceding Rome, the Germans of Tacitus, and the Norsemen of the Viking age, to name a few. The Iron Age can also be pointed to in the Eastern Hemisphere, as the age that sparked the evolution of the occasional war leader into a permanent fixture. The transformation of gentile organization resulted in the oppression of neighboring tribes, and domination and oppression of the dispossessed.

**"**...The first class opposition that appears in history coincides with the development of the antagonisms between man and woman in monogamous marriage, and the first class oppression coincides with that of the female sex by male. Monogamous marriage was a great historical step forward; nevertheless, together with slavery and private wealth, it opens the period that has lasted until today in which every step forward is also relatively a step backward, in which prosperity and development for some is won through the misery and frustration of others...**"** [9]

# Class-E Katrina

In order to better understand class conflicts in society, we in the previous section of this chapter, had to contextualize it with regard to the state. However, America and the world's race and gender issues would be almost sinful to omit, when speaking about class or socioeconomic inequality. In accordance with this train of thought, there are thus few better ways, I believe, to critique instances of racial and gender disparity, than the state's response in the aftermath of the storm. As tedious and redundant as speaking about Katrina is turning out to be, it is regardless an excellent example of the poor being left to fend for themselves, and the state only pressed to help during moments of misfortune for the elites, the bailing of incompetent bankers. Upon the contextualization of the state, as an apparatus, having arisen from large socioeconomic disparities within persons in a society, it is my hope that racial, gender and class will be seen as interchangeable antagonisms. Since, one cannot eradicate just one form of moral injustice, and expect the cured crisis to remain at bay and not resurge to retribution, but in a different form. The tree must be uprooted and not merely cut midway along its stem. With such a paradigm in mind, approaching class antagonisms by pointing out the injustices of the state, in failing to effectuate a proper rescue response; it is thus my hope that, thoughts of redundancies by the reader will take a back-seat to the edifying value attached to a broader and more bird's eye-worldview-mindset. I often wondered about the media and nation's affinity towards scenes that depicted the suffering of a class of people. The United States government, the wealthiest in recorded history, of course refused to receive any support from the global community in the way of financial aid. However, as my brother David pointed out, "what good is it to refuse aid, if you're going to still leave your people to suffer. I know that the US has a disaster fund, type, thing…still look at them brothers and sisters suffer." I remember that those were his exact words, since I recorded his spontaneous longwinded moment in the sun of indignation. Indeed, the nation, together with the global community, will always be remembered in history for standing by and watching misery unfold. There were, still more, individual citizens who fund raised and made an effort to contribute to the relief of the human suffering in New Orleans, which, however; is altogether different from the state, and responsible party, opting out of its duties. In the words of David, my sibling, "There's just too many people to save it seems…shame man!" New Orleans, indeed, is a typical example of a relatively wealthy city fuelled by inequality, as is evidenced by the stranded masses of lower classed people, who vastly were persons of color.

> *"Before the storm, New Orleans was a predominantly African American city, and those left in the wake of the hurricane were disproportionately black…Almost exclusively, it was the suffering of black people that was broadcast to a national viewing audience. Poor and black citizens found themselves both more vulnerable to the disaster and less able to recover in its aftermath."*[10]

Representative John Lewis, a senior member of the Congressional Black Caucus, almost pinned the tail on the donkey when he made the assertion that race was the critical basis, in relation to what influenced both media representations of the disaster and governmental response. Indeed, it is as though I postulate that: poising the ocean with radioactive waste would cause all the fish and vegetation to die. This state is true, but does not account for what will happen to the mammals in the ocean. It would be nit-picky of me to object to that statement only because whales and dolphins were left out of the conversation. Ridding this train of thought, Representative Lewis, was as such, speaking about the lower class or poor people of New Orleans, who were predominantly black, but not exclusively. The politician and civil rights leader's reputation acquired a much needed boost, gaining national recognition decades earlier after he had faced a brutal beating for his participatory role in a voting rights march in Selma, Alabama.[11] A demonstration some might remember as the "Bloody Sunday', was the catalytic reagent that led to the passing of the 1965 Voting Rights Act. Resulting from such sacrifices and as an activist in the eye of the civil rights revolutionary storm, Lewis has since then enjoyed a certain moral authority on matters of race. This American of great integrity, as was said of him by John McCain,[12] had his pleas fall on deaf ears when he pointed out the obvious;

that government officials were reacting in an inadequate manner, because of their consideration of the lives of black people as unworthy of resources and action.[13] Because there are more black people than any other race in America in the bottom rung of the socioeconomic ladder, it can seem as though antagonistic matters within society are exclusively tied to race. However, by now, we have expounded on how matters of inheritance, dealing with male-dominated capital, and the need to justify an economic order during the slave society era, in short, socioeconomic gains; were the motivations for the division of society. These chaotic relations in society, once more, work towards the coercion of people so as to maintain a certain economic order, or to preserve the rule of the capital accumulating elites. However, it would also be naïve of me to exclude any mention of the ideology of white supremacy, which, today, works in favor of a certain portrait of society, where race and poverty mingle to justify an exploitative past, and ignore the present ramifications of said past. The action taken in the wake of the hurricane, or rather, the lack of any meaningful action, was an issue that brought to the fore, US society's (mis)treatment of the poor.

*"Still, the alchemy of race and disaster produced a powerful image of chaos and crime that dominated the first news reports. In this way, Hurricane Katrina became more than an object lesson for preparing for natural disasters...[through] its distinctive racial and political character, the debacle became a site for the contestation of black citizenship"*[14]

When speaking about class, one must understand, and as mentioned much earlier; class refers to the first and second-class citizenry in the US, while also alluding to the fact that some cultural values (European) are view as superior to others (African and Asian, e.t.c.), and the most obvious mention of class in terms of socioeconomic status. Black people, whom for the most part are universally considered poor, either materially or culturally, or both, together with all poor people; are often considered second class citizens, not just in America, but the world around. We are quick to judge the poor, and to blame their misfortune as unequivocally their fault. The poor, as well as black people, woke up to the vivid realization of their marginalization and their second class citizenry status in the wake of the storm in New Orleans in August of 2005. Parnell Herbet, a survivor of the storms unforgiving strike, had his story recorded in, "Overcoming Katrina: African American Voices from the Crescent City and Beyond," where he asks us to pay attention to the displays of black Americans laying claim to their rights as citizens:

*"Something that really surprised me was the number of African Americans in New Orleans who had large American flags in their homes. Were they flags that once draped a loved one's casket? Why did the survivors begging for help from the US military forces feel it necessary to wave the American flag, as opposed to a white sheet or blood stained towels?"*[15****]

Herbert's observation is to us a reminder of people of African ancestry, and poor people in general (e.g: the Irish at one point in American history), constantly needing to show that they belong, and to lay claim to their citizenship. As such, in many ways, Hurricane Katrina can be interpreted as race and class hierarchies, structuring the consequences of a natural disaster, and the madness that ensues among black persons after the ruling and predominantly white institutions ignore their suffering.

***

"The social contract is the basis of the democratic citizenship…The social contract of democratic governments assumes that governing authority is derived from consent of the governed rather than from divine command, hereditary connection, or armed capacity. American founding documents draw heavily and explicitly on Enlightenment traditions steeped in the idea of a social contract in which recognition plays a central role. For example, the Declaration of Independence assets citizens' collective right and responsibility to draft a social contract that allows not only safety and freedom but also the pursuit of happiness."[16]

## Cultured Class

In western society, generally speaking, and hoping to not fall in the traps that come with such generalizations; one is said to be cultured when he or she is well acquainted with Beethoven or Verdi, but the likes of Rumi or Achebe or not as highly considered. This is only natural, of course, and will be discussed in the next chapter, when discussion cultural hegemony. The heritage of the most influential and well situated individuals in society is predominantly European. As a civilization that was advanced enough to explore and colonize lands worldwide, presupposing European civilization as under a collective umbrella; they exported and imposed their culture on the conquered. Indeed European and American civilizations have offered much to humanity, but it is also part of the problem, in that, refusing to change their societies in an ameliorating direction, is partially to blame for the perpetuation of global class antagonisms. Despite the disparagement by elite and the bourgeois classes, of the lower classes and their cultures, among which are both poor white and nonwhite persons; cultural material transfer is a spontaneous phenomenon with no equal, and thus is at work despite conscious efforts to denigrate one class culture. The various cultures attached to every class further differ and fragment along racial and gender lines, further hinting at the intricate and intermingled web social relations along these divisive social constructions. One example of what I mean by this can be seen among black people in US society, whereby elite and bourgeois and quasi-proletariat classes of people adhere to different norms and practices. Such cases are emblematic of any racial category in both the US and global societies in general. I need not mention once more the divides and differences in experience, undergone by women in society; fragmented along racial and socioeconomic lines. Still, accounting for all the diversity, there is a constant interchange of cultural material, across the boundaries delineating these several societal fragmentations. One problem with cultural material transfer is that it can be subject to stereotypes and other such antagonistic manifestations, when carried on to another culture. That poor whites and nonwhites have differing cultural practices is evident, and not surprising, but that there are significant commonalities in their experiences, as compared to the experiences between the poorest black persons and middle-class black people, is less recognized in several scholastic endeavors. Taking a socioeconomic approach is less rewarding than undertaking a study that exposes racial disparities. I wish to distance myself from such reservations and restrictions when exploring and discussing elements central to societal malaises. Hence, as before, going forward, it is important to understand that when referring to black culture in the proceeding passages, I do not ignore the complex heterogeneity of this categorization. I simply wish to simplify already complex aspects about society, since a broader view point is what I am at extrapolating, leaving the reader to further the discussion through other research means. That I will speak about black cultural trafficking of material does not mean it is a phenomenon that is exclusively linked to 'blackness', or to 'black culture'. What's of some importance about the proceeding exposition on black cultural traffic, and what I wish to successfully show; is the extent to which cultures/ social locales or identities inter-influence one another, in a web like manner of interaction.

Instances of cultural traffic are abundantly evident and forthcoming within society, and come in large, medium, and small episodes. One example of a large episode of cultural traffic in western society's short history is the emergence of jazz in early twentieth century New Orleans. African-, Cuban-American, Parisian, Martinican, and Iberian musical influences were rampart in the streets of this multi-ethnic, multi-cultural city. New Orleans was a carnival city that was mixing cultural practices in almost an unprecedented fashion. Combining his trumpet experiments with scat singing, the casual delivery, and unique solo accenting, Louis Armstrong's first highly original recordings of 1925-28, was unconsciously drawn from elements within the aforementioned diverse musical corpus.[17] An example of a small-scale episode of cultural traffic can be observed in places as foreign and disparate as West Africa, namely; Uganda and central Africa. In these aforementioned regions, postcolonial female garb for special occasion could be seen to blend several local dress styles, while spicing it up with Victorian English dress flavors. What was created was a unique and beautiful example of authentic cultural exchange, the product: an Afro-Victorian dress genre had emerged, bustles and all. "Misisi" was one reference of such skirts among some social groups in central Africa.[18] These new editions to cultural expression, often became the source of great pride, and in the years that proceeded after 'independence', considered as "distinctive national dress," when traditional cultural revival was a nationalist goal. Limitedness of the idea of "hybridity", as is perceived in the field of biology, to superimpose upon culture as a way of understanding and conceptualizing the fusing of cultural elements, is too mechanical, so to speak, and too easy an explanation. This is a concept spoken of by scholars like Sabine Mabardi, in "Encounters of a Heterogeneous kind: Hybridity in Cultural Theory". Cultural traffic is much more fluid and complex, and still not well understood or fully accounted for in both contemporary and historic accounts.[19]

Class antagonisms are exposed, for example, when lending attention to jazz's reception, both reviled and desired by many, regardless of racial identity, and only because it was seen as having had emerged from form the lower abysses of black experience, sometimes alluded to as a form of primitivism. As such, marginality of black cultural material is evident among whites as much as it is among communities of black persons. Undergoing such skeptical reception are musical art forms of both jazz and early rhythm and blues, simply owing to their origins from the poorest classes of society. It was therefore not unusual to see black musicians playfully engaging in the notion of "junglefying" their club, or the early films, and recording appearances. A typical embodiment of the need by outsiders, white and black patrons, to make the production fit in to their preconceived world view, and as such further intensifying societal antagonism, through stereotypes. Outsiders watch marginalized culture from a distance, with the mainstream media of the day, chief in the propagation of such conceptual societal dilapidations; making lower class whites and middle class blacks feel better about their location in society.[20] However, with time emerged all-white performances, which projected a faux 'black culture' of the minstrel variety, vastly outpacing black entertainment, and the opportunity for these entertainers to gain some socioeconomic relevance. For many audiences, soon after seemed, minstrelsy as black life. Some authors suggest that "after slavery ended in 1865, black entertainment challenged the hegemony of white minstrelsy, by often "corking-up," too, and following the minstrel themes."[21] For the sake of economic gain, and as a show of independent defiance, these entertainers went along with the notion of giving the people what they wanted, in a period when blacks had little alternatives for earning a living.

Class antagonisms within society are prevalent and complexly mingled, as such; it would be a difficult, to say the least, to portray every intricate brunch and its relation to the fragmentized segments of segments within a society. To simplify matters, I wish to proceed with the discussion in a manner that fixes only one antagonistic variable, race, and thus speak further of class within the societal division that is race. I prefer to analyze the class antagonisms within the African American and black communities in the US, since, for one; black persons are disproportionately represented in the lower classes, and would go amiss in a discussion on socioeconomic inequality. Since class is as a result of socioeconomic disparities, its manifestations can be perceived to permeate every nuanced element within a national or international society. By this I mean to say that, an analogy between a nation and an individual can be created, in that, the nation bespeaks the sentiments of the collective, or at least in principle is supposed to; and the state can viewed as pursuant of a collective set of interests as a global actor. Considering thus a state as an individual is important in contextualizing it as an actor among many others within a global community. These simplifications aid us to make mention of socioeconomic disparities between states, and the need for hegemony; as seen on a micro-scale within the workings of national society. However, I digress. As it regards looking at class through one racial telescope, and since class disparities can be viewed through the lens of culture, or state actors, or the several other devices; the antagonisms in cultural trafficking show, I think, the evidence of class and the power tug-of-war explicit in the black community. One of the most vivid embodiments of resistance to cultural material from the lower classes came in the way of a poem. Chicago-based Margaret Danner in, "The Convert," explains how she at first disliked greatly an African nude sculpture. The art piece was gifted to her by the actress and art-lover Etta Moten, or rather to her Chicago Art Study Group. Imagine a period when one might expect art from "mother-land" Africa to be of some value among literary and artistic urban black middle classes. This, however, was not the case, at first. Moten's poem begins as such:

"Parisian-poised and as smart as a chrome toned page/from Harper's Bazaar, gave/my shocked/ guests this hideous African nude, I could have cried."

For Danner, every feature of the black bodied sculpture was profuse with an aesthetic of exaggeration. Her sentiments of the African art would later change of course, and no longer had the "tea" devoted to "art study" been upset. She would come to find that with "the turn of calendar pages," her "eyes would skim/ the figure…/ until, finally, I saw on its/ ebony face…a radiance." She was well on her way to a new aesthetic middle class envisagement of art.[22]

As a confessional, Danner's poem offers to us a peculiar and invaluable insight into the frictions, and hesitancies which made for black people's approach to African artistic performance. In recent years Pan-Africanist cultural agendas have, however, made it seem like this expression of lower class 'black-culture,' has always been a welcome edition. Part and parcel of the reason for the aforementioned hesitancies of black people in America, to adopt anything African, in 1937, could stem from the fact that, it seemed to their advantage not to adopt anything African. Original African artifacts were at that time, often deemed savage imagery. The pursuit of a new identity was still well entrenched in the black American culture, along the way influenced by class and racial antagonisms, sought the acceptance of their white-supremacist environment. After the civil rights era, black people were still in search for this fleeting identity that would rebalance society, and in the 60s and 70s, being African was fashionable among youths in America, just as being American was fashionable among the youths of Africa (Bamako, for example). There was more trafficking of African (thus predominantly poor and black) and the African Diasporia's cultural material the world around.[23] The colonial period was a watershed in expanding and intensifying significant flows of African cultural material into the world. Colonials would collect large amounts of African art, often to be exhibited in the museums of Europe, and the local curio shops, as well as for purposes of other economic gains. At this stage in time, African performers were not directly involved, instead; the artifacts became an inspiration, around 1905, for the early variant of European and American cubisms. In western society, black American painters and sculptors became significant contributors to the art and culture. The cultural meshing was intoxicating, revitalizing and, in the words of Gertrude Stein, avant-garde cultural promoter, "a veritable cataclysm."[24] Stein considered it as such because African art had altered the mental framework for representations of the human body in the West, with the next expansion following suit after World War I. It is from this brew that the Harlem Renaissance fermented, one of only several black renaissances taking form in places like Havana, Paris, London, Germany, Accra, Lago, and South Africa, to name but a few.[25] Making possible such expressions of poor black culture was the advent of recorded music. Musicians like Bessie Smith, burgeoning from humble origins, released her first recording, "Gulf Coast Blues" and "Downhearted Blues," selling over 750 000 copies.[26] The ascendancy of appreciation for poor black cultural material was a global phenomenon, the effects of a post-World War I global community's search to redefine what it meant to be human, and the questioning of the importance of said life. Singer Siti binti Saad from Zanzibar (Tanzania) went on to sell 75 000 of her copies, along the

East African coast and Indian Ocean rim.[27] The 1920s could be considered as the beginnings of a period of globalization, and the rise of international elites, and their corporate machinery. It was also a period when international travel was coming into its own, when African cultural performers could manage the better option of flying abroad. An example of this was Asadata DaFora, the Sierra Leonean. DaFora taught dance in Berlin and Dresden, but would be remembered more for her touring company, which traveled and performed in Europe, Canada, and the United States. She settled in New York for the final stages of her life.[28]

"*Black cultural productivity was so vast during the 1920s that one sometimes overlooks the place of black renaissances within wider cultural upsurges in places like Vienna, Prague, Moscow, London, Paris, and Berlin. Black cultural traffic was advanced by, and influenced, the voltage behind a worldwide attempt to reshape culture after the disastrous European war* (Alfred Appel, Jr., Jazz Modernism: From Ellington and Armstrong to Matisse and Joyce (New York: Knopf, 2002), 7-84.). A war-weary world yearned for cultural revivification.)"[29]

That cultural material from the most marginalized segments of global society took hold, is symptomatic of the fluidity of human relations. Culture, as a social identity/location, is in constant flux, and cultural notions or the social constructs, which emerge from a certain class, will always be influenced by its social environment. Initially, as with the poet Margaret Danner, cultural products from the lowest rungs of society are regarded with distaste. This resistance from a select number of elite social individuals and organizations, mostly, arises from the fear that small changes may result in big consequences. With time, however, efforts to suppress the incorporation of foreign, low-class cultural material tends to amount to little success. Cultural and societal constructs, as having had arisen from mental fabrications, take up a different nature and, adapting a peculiar behavior. The manifest development of some elements of cultural material is independent of external coercion. The period after the Second World War, not surprisingly, induced questions not unlike those posed in the wake of the First World War. Let us venture to the mid-1940s, and traversing to a period just after Ghana's national sovereignty was declared to the world, 1957, and even into the early 1960s. Amidst a plethora of cultural material exchange, in an intricate and web-like entangling of social relations, the disparate Gold Coast (Ghana) personified the significant contribution of cultural material, by the socioeconomically subjugated masses of the world. Post-'independence'

Ghana was one of the centers where one would have found vibrant, and authentic political and cultural traffic in the black world, were said person walking down the streets of 1960s Accra, of course. The ideas and cultural products leaving Ghana, was globally received amongst not just members of the intelligentsia of the African Diaspora, but also by the European liberal leftists and Asian de-colonizers. Ghana was an intellectual hub, a shelter which fostered and supported the talents of persons economically inferior to most in the world, let alone the West.[30] It is important, as we cite Ghana, and its role as the focal point of the cultural flux in Africa, to recognize the defiant form of black cultural traffic, with which national, regional, and linguistic groupings were imbued with. The defiance depicted within the annals of black cultural materiality, can best be seen in some of the jazz-variants produced in this era, by musicians of likes of Randy Weston, or Mongo Santamaria. E.T. Mensah, the Ghanaian, in his "Ghana Freedom" album, or typical South African township jazz, show a blended jazz style, which sought to redefine a society into a different, yet original expression of the needs of the masses.[31]

*"It was to be a music inspiring to capture this unprecedented moment of black quests for freedom. For this period of the 1940s through the 1960s, we can also see in the photographs of Mali's youth and young adults in and around the capital city of Bamako made by the West African Malick Sidibe, [as] other ways in which black cultural traffic defied previous boundaries. His party photographs show young Africans dancing to Chubby Checker and James Brown in the early 1960s and preening in the dress and hairstyles of the era..."*[32]

According to commentators like Manthia Diawara, who insisted that what seemed as Malian-youth imitation and cultural appropriation of US 'black culture', was in fact a renegotiation of their social contract. The bell-bottoms and manicured Afros, and album covers that were prominently displayed at dances, as with the Malian-youth's use of music and dress; were all an attempt to renegotiate the heavy French colonial influence that lingered after their so-called independence. A new culture and direction for the Malian society was what the young segment of the population of Bamako was aiming towards. "The youth were assembling a new cultural presentation of self, partly African American and partly new Malian."[33] For Diawara, these new cultural personas was a discursive or communicative space created, beginning with the youth but ultimately radiating outwards to affect the collective society. The aforementioned communicative platform aimed, and to some extent succeeded in transcending the former dualistic paradigm of divisiveness, Malian and French, or colonized and colonial overlord, or of

African and European, just like the dichotomy of "noir" and "blanche".[34] Could dress and music, and dancing and partying, achieve the socioeconomic, and cultural liberation needed by Bamako's youth? I highly doubt so. However, these performances, as with the promise showed during the 1970s in American society, post-civil rights intensifications of the mid-60s, were an aspiration, and held open the possibility for change. The crossing of old boundaries, and creation of modes of black performances, in the middle decades of the twentieth century; demonstrate the vitality of the free-roaming expressions of self, among Malian youths, in conjuncture with young people globally.

Further evidence of the class antagonisms, as seen within the African communitarian discursive realm, and expressed through cultural art forms, appears in Karin Barber's concerted efforts to explore Nigerian popular theater. More particularly, in relation to Karin Barber's critique of "petro-naira", a production that portrays a discontent, brewed among the middle and lower-class people within Nigerian civilization. In the case of this cultural production, a reaction emerges from among several intelligent voices in Nigerian society, in reflection of their acknowledgement and detestation of the misappropriation of state funds by local elites, in collaboration with a global hegemonic order. Vast sums of money, during the late 1970s oil boom days, had flooded the Nigerian society.[35] Yet, typical of any civilization built on exploitation, as is evidently practiced and observed in pre- and post-independence Nigeria; the masses, or insignificant and poor persons, see little to no benefit arising from the finances acquired through such trade. In the aforementioned case, cultural material circulation had less to do with leverage against the state, as commentary on a new moneyed class. This message struck a note among the majority, the poor, the many who packed the theater that hosted this cultural performance. The large audience was a mélange of "not elite but farmers, workers, petty traders, minor public servants, drivers, school children".[36] The fervent reaction, and warm reception of such a theatrical production may be attributed to, what to Nigerians seemed as the subversion of the traditional conceptions of wealth, and its means of and rate of acquisition. For many poor Nigerians, and rightly so, the feeling was parallel, in many respects, to the embittered taste of having been swindled out of their inheritance.

"…we are reminded that the critiquing power of popular culture can be a source of its momentum and mobility."[37]

As jazz was to the post- First World War, so is hip-hop to, not only the contemporary self-depictions of lower class and black cultural material, but the collaborative effects of the depictions of Black identity, by external class and cultural elements. As a musical art form, hip-hop it is thus of no surprise to find hip-hop as the launch-pad from many an academic social commentary on "Black culture". The reason, I feel, to threat over hip-hop centric studies owes itself mostly to the fact that they focus primarily on African American cultural products, and often, maybe not intentionally, may cause us to disregard or overlook other forms of Black cultural dispersion and affinity for dissemination. One must not forget the Caribbean and African and even European cultural elements, which contributed to the formation of the hip-hop musical form. In Africa, this musical form, although the cause of what some see as an erosion of societal morality, has just as well been used as a tool, a powerful platform upon which black mass cultural material is used as populist weaponry in contestation with the respective states. Kenyan writer Ngugi wa Thiong'o's experience best bespeaks of the state's hegemonic control, needless to say, in pursuit of global elites' interests (a few of whom are Kenyans) in conjunction with the predominantly local elites' interests. In 1977 Thiong'o's entertained his most startling revelations, which he revealed years later, realizing that the colonial and post-colonial state saw "the entire territory as its performance area…the nation-state performs its own being relentlessly."[38] He said this due to his failed attempts to mount theatrical productions containing political commentary, skeptical towards the state's role in his society, he believed then that popular theater material enters a realm where "enactments of power" subsist and operate. As a visionary and relentless individual, he launched his Kamiruthu People's Theater in Kenya. The theater was an open air edifice, built by locals, and during its inaugural launch put on "I will Marry When I Want, for thousands of people to witness. Ten performances later, seemed to be ten performances too much in the eyes of the Kenyan government, which shut down and destroyed a communitarian effort. The threat to the socioeconomic order, both on a local and global order, the threat playing a less significant role in the latter; would later translate to the destruction of concerted work done by the women of the village. These women were theater builders as well the actors, allies through the confrontations with the state's minor nudges, in any direction away from cultural material production that criticized the civil society.[39]

Culture, as a social location or identity, deals with interlocked and interacting mental elements, and depictions of self, as well as the depictions of the surrounding social and cultural locations. "Blackness," or the notion of someone as a "coconut" or "Oreo," I'm sure, is not foreign to some readers. Such a term as Blackness or being or acting black, has successfully and readily supplanted some of the terms used to refer to poor people or "barbarians," if you will. The aforementioned term, rarely is used to describe an educated middle or upper class black individual, at least, he too ensures that his mannerisms correspond to the Euro-centric ideals. Blackness is not a phenomenon that belongs to any particular individual or group, but rather what is observable is the appropriation of said concept by individuals and groups. Appropriation happens in order to circumscribe its boundaries, excluding and including as it evolves. The media, as a gem in the toolbox of elite tools, in manipulation of society, propagates and is among the influential societal forces, which influence some of the external pressure to be directed towards the constitution of blackness and black life. When blackness is appropriated for exclusivity's sake, social identity turns political. Since blackness lacks essence, "black authority is [predominantly]...contingent on the historical, social, and political terms of its production."[40] Moreover:

*"The notion of authenticity implies the existence of its opposite, the fake, and this dichotomous construct is at the heart of what makes authenticity problematic."*[41]

It is thus not too far a leap in perspective, to attribute black authenticity, or blackness as yet another trope manipulated for purposes of cultural capital gain. Having made that known, I, however wish not to attach value judgment on the notion of authenticity, as, there are several ways in which authenticating discourse permits disparaged segments within society to run counter to oppressive representations of themselves. What is of importance in our discussion is the cognizance of the arbitrariness associated with authenticity, and the dormant dangers of impeding the possibility of genuine cultural exchange and understanding. Or, in the much better words of Henry Louise Gates Jr.; "now human culture is inaccessible to someone who makes the effort to understand, to learn, to inhabit another world."[42] It is a headache, for the libertarian intellectual, knowing that the reality of living in a racist, white supremacist, and capitalist global society, means that cultural appropriations have social, cultural, and political consequences. Historically speaking, the elites, predominantly Whites for the past several centuries, and even now; have demonstrated their affinity for cultural usurpation, in relation to art forms not their own. Bell hooks terms this aforementioned affinity as "eating the other," referring to the many instances of observable exoticization or fetish of blackness by Whites.[43]

*"Thus, when white-identified subjects perform "black signifiers"-normative or otherwise- the effect is always already entangled in the discourse of Otherness; the historical weight of white skin privilege necessarily engenders a tense relationship with its "others."*[44]

This reality withstanding, humans, as social animals, necessarily assimilate and adopt cultural aspects of the other. That said; every form of cross-cultural appropriation spells out an instance of colonization and marginalization and subjugation. Among the vast amount of appropriations that take place, some of said instances are moments of genuine interchange of dialogic performance. Said moments provide fertile soil, upon which to sow and nurture new epistemologies of self and of other.

"The Nixon campaign in 1968 and the Nixon White House after that, had two enemies: the anti-war left and black people. You understand what I'm saying? We knew we couldn't make it illegal to be either against the war or black…but by getting the public to associate the hippies with marijuana and blacks with heroin, and then criminalizing both heavily, we could disrupt those communities. We could arrest their leaders, raid their homes, break up their meetings, and vilify them night after night on the evening news. Did we know we were lying about the drugs? Of course we did." - John Ehrlichman (Nixon Advisor)

Some authors (e.g. Cox, 1948), have considered the pervasive exploitation of dark-skinned workers, as rooted in the imperialistic expansion of Western European capitalism. For them, the dilemma boils down to something much more simplistic, along the lines of Europe colonizing the world in order to continue its accumulation of capital, in a much more effective, and fast-flowing, steady-stream manner. As hinted to above, a multi-ethnic society, perversely exploited, serves to uphold the interests of the capitalist elite class; people who can be used almost as a reserve army of labor, allowing for manageable business cycles (Baran and Sweezy, 1966). Employers, the middle and upper classes within the society, have more leeway, and diverse labor needs can be filled by the "useless" class. Class antagonisms are phenomena that are evidenced in society, even if our gaze were to be shifted away from the national sphere to a more global perspective. Nation-states, like cultural identities assumed by individuals, are a fiction of society. As a social construct, the nation, with inherent antagonistic properties, is imagined as having an identity and a set of interests. Such aforementioned interests, as well as a nation's identity, are less reflective of the needs and interests of its heterogeneous masses, and adheres more to the sum of interests of the elite class within the nation-state. It is often the observable case that, some corporations or organizations, upon which elites stand; have their interests moving at countercurrent to other factions or corporations within the nation. Thus, pointed out on several occasions, antagonism, as with race, or gender, exist even within the same class, as inequality is also still a thing of concern. Within the top 1%, of the wealthiest individuals in the world, the 0.1% wealthiest persons would be considered the crème de la crème, the elite among the elite, in socioeconomic terms. The exploitation of some states by others is as much the case globally, as it is evidenced in US society. There are constant power struggles taking place, a hegemonic form of dominion, something that has since been witness, dating back to the advent of written history. In our modern era, the global class antagonisms, or power struggle/sharing that ensues between the various states, is the embodiment of past colonial present imperial regimes. Since alluded to much less than issues that are exclusively centered on racism or sexism; the state as one of several apparatuses used by the elite class, is always blamed, independent of those individuals who truly control it. An example of what I mean by this comes in the form of the US' decision to invade Iraq in 2003. The state is thus the buffer that subsists between the lower classes, the masses of the disenfranchised, and the elite or ruling class. Although we initially react appropriately upon being swindled, by bankers, out of our pensions and funds, towards the end of the first decade of the century, it soon became incumbent upon the media and the state to stave off the blame from their masters. We went about our lives, having personal concerns of our own, if not directly affected by the banking rip-off, and soon forgot about the use of our tax funds to bail out incompetent acting corporations. The blame was projected, instead, onto other local, national, or global issues, and toward the state itself, with often at least one of the two political parties absorbing most of the pressures from the masses. If, however, at every instance that the State is made mention of, we mentally label this tool as belonging to the ruling-class' toolbox, then, it goes without saying that we would see state-sponsored belligerence and state neglect under a different light. The demonization of the economically subjugated was used as a justification for the mistreatment of the poor classes, during slavery, for example, and in like sense, today; a parallel can be drawn about the global hegemonic practices of the US and its European allies. After Hurricane Katrina made landfall, the poor and desolate people of New Orleans were demonized, as thugs and rapists and more. Today, Arab-Muslims are demonized as "terrorists", taking away from the effectiveness of human rights activists' denouncements of state-sponsored, or capitalist-elite supported belligerence towards, and neglect of, the voiceless and poor masses within several Middle-Eastern societies.

Failed states, like the Congo (DRC), home of the poorest people on the planet, if in a just society, would have been among the wealthiest nations of the world. Is the plight of this country owed exclusively and unequivocally to the local elite's (mis)management of state affairs, independent of external state and corporate forces? As was pointed out to earlier, regarding the need for a chaotic or antagonistic state of affairs, a failed state, such as the DR Congo, is well incorporated and situated in the globalized economic order. In fact, incorporation and situation of such a failed state into the workings of the global economic system, is more entrenched than most in the West have considered. With such wealth in resources, found within the borders of a single country, exploitation is rendered convenient.

# Hearts of Darkness

## (or: Where Does My Smart Phone come from?)

Known today as the Democratic Republic of the Congo (DRC), is home to one of the most multilingual nations in not only Africa, but the world. The conservative estimates tell us that there are 214 living indigenous languages or ethnic groups (Ethnologue 2005). However, due to the state's willing inability to garner the relatively meager resources needed to carry out a census, inclusive of a linguistic component, we have no idea what this partially unchartered terrain has installed for us. Still more, to this known number must be added French, Lingala, KiKongo, and KiSwahili, the country's four official languages. Before even paving allusion to the extremely abundant wealth in mineral resources or the lush wildlife, the abode to the equatorial rainforest, a vast jungle sheltering many an endangered species; its ethnic wealth is one worth of mention. The nation's history is wrought with ethnic antagonisms; to say that these ethnic groups have behaved belligerently towards one another would be an understatement. In a nation where Lebanese Arabic, English, Greek, Hindi, Portuguese, and Wolof, among many others are spoken; it is bespeaking of a global ruling class' divide and conquer tactic that more lives have been taken by wars since the gaining of independence, than in the Second World War. With twenty one languages spoken by at least five hundred thousand people each, some may say that it is no wonder that antagonisms exist, as with a nation recently out of an incessant tribal conflict era, and with a disorganized state apparatus, how can one expect there to be unanimous satisfaction. Still more, it is my claim, of which I will proceed to expound upon, that it is as much the locals' faults as it is the international community that the Congo is found in the state it is in today. That, however, the colonial masters were in it for civilizing effects, and proselytizing missions, out of pure benevolence, the old "white man's burden" excreted jargon; is a fallacy long ago disproven in rhetoric, yet the actions of the ruling class, following newer justificatory ideologies remains parallel to the pre-'independence' era. Having had invested several billions of dollars in mines in the Congo, especially the Katanga region, it should be of no bewilderment that the wealthy individual capitalist investors and the various assortment of corporations would subsist, and refuse to simply pack up and go. There's a mass pillaging going on in the Congo, and those undertaking the harassing and superior stance, have been at it for more than is morally acceptable. As with most of Africa, so-called 'collapsed states' are extreme cases of the complex, and even contradictory processes of state making and unmaking, which ravaged these countries post-'independence'. As is ever more apparent with the ease of communications, the world around, beneath the veneer of sovereignty, these shells were what one could refer to as shell states. One of two eventualities were ostensibly observed, either self-destruction (state collapse) or the attempt to fill the shell with institutional content (state making), some of which content arises from international coercive forces. These poor states, throughout Africa, are purposely kept that way through the stripping of agency from the masses, the average Congolese, by both the local ruling class and the international profit seekers, also tactics as the divide and conquer method, do more to aid this exploitation. Some key external factors undermining the state or building project are private military interventions. This militarism can either be dressed in the traditional 'soldier for fortune' garb, or be cloaked in the corporate attire; the privatization of security, needless to say, has an inflammatory effect on the governance process in weak states. What is clear is that, since independence, the populations of Africa, the second class citizens of a globalized world, have been subject to structural violence, which indeed has highlighted force and de-emphasized the need for human security, as the foundation of governance. What all this exploitation of the majority of Congolese peoples by the local and international ruling class amounts to, is a collusion of wealthier state entities to maintain said class or hegemonic global rule by these said state entities. What it also amounts to is the suffering of a vast range of a great mass of people, for the benefit of the relative few.

# Class Antagonisms
## (The Economics of Civil War in the DRC)

Léonce Ndikumana of the Department of Economics at the University of Massachusetts, and Kisangani Emizet of the Department of Political Science at Kansas State University, undertook a study on the Economics of civil war in the Congo and came up with five conclusions. Before venturing on to discuss the methods of their study, and the relations these discoveries elucidate about the socioeconomic antagonisms, inherent in the Congo; I wish to list out their findings. The claims bespoken of and the conclusions drawn by Ndikumana and Emizet in their study are:

*Conclusion one:* The level of income and its growth rate show a reduction in the cost of organizing rebellions, but to that effect, and to a limited extent, it also reduces the government's ability to countervail said rebellions.

*Conclusion two:* That regional ethnic inequality served as a basis for the burgeoning of war is true; however, these ethnic antagonisms were often seen to be an obstacle to the expansion of these wars beyond the province of their origin.

*Conclusion three:* Natural resource dependence was a major factor in the mobilization of civil wars in the DRC. But to stop there would be somewhat inconsiderate of, and may lead to the incognizance of, the role played by the geographic concentration of mineral resources, more so than wildlife, and the unequal distribution of the wealth assumed from these minerals.

*Conclusion four:* International military intervention and support, instead of the governments own economic and military capabilities were used for the quashing of most rebellions.

*Conclusion five:* Discriminatory laws, as it regards nationality, and what was referred to as being 'authentically Congolese', upon changing the country's name from the Congo to Zaire; caused significant disruptions in the ethnic balance of the eastern Congo region, the laws being a direct reaction to the influx of Rwandan Hutu refugees in 1994. That there was shared ethnicity between rebels and neighboring regimes did not help, as this, instead of state intervention, shifted the tide of in the direction of some marginalized groups, making for a bloody affair throughout the 1990s.

The two researchers relied on a model constructed and established by Collier and Hoeffler. Collier and Hoeffler applied their econometric model to analyze civil wars in sub-Saharan Africa. Their observations showed that Africa, with some minor exceptions, is in line with a global pattern of conditions, and a socioeconomic environment as that seen in other developing regions. However, they assert that the form or structure of risk differs significantly from other regions. Africa is extremely vulnerable to conflict, but offsetting this high risk factor and propensity for war is the uniquely and culturally and traditionally rooted societal practices, making it atypically safe. In their study, Paul Collier and Anke Hoeffler went so far "to analyze the contrasting trends of conflict: rising in Africa and declining in other regions. Also, they went on to "show that these trends are predicted by [their] model." They posit that the intensification of conflict in Africa is resultant to its "atypically poor economic performance".[45]

Superimposing the case of the Congo onto the Collier-Hoeffler model, using a sample of 161 countries for comparative purposes, Ndikumana and Emizet, with the aid of the Collier-Hoeffler research, estimate the risk of an outbreak of war. The Collier-Hoeffler model establishes proxies of greed and grievance, dependant on the society, as explanatory factors to judge the levels or the point when the need for conflict is piqued. In one model, for example, the Collier and Hoeffler "core model" is inclusive of the rate of high school enrollment of males, as a predictor or explanatory variable. In an "alternative model", however, this 'predictor'/variable is substituted by the initial per capita income. The Congo's case, according to the precepts outlined by the Collier-Hoeffler research, is replete with the three main economic greed factors, namely; the initial income level, growth rate of income, and the shared distribution of primary commodity exports to the rest of the population, out of the total exports. The aforementioned economic greed factors, in "The Economics of Civil War: The case of the DRC", were ostensibly poor and verging on a tipping point.[46] These grievance factors, or the intense subjugation of a socioeconomically minority group, are resultant from the pre-colonial feuds that existed, but would, of course later be exacerbated upon European interaction. According to Ndikumana and Emizet, these aforementioned grievance factors were, however, found to play a less significant role in the prediction of civil war in the Congo.

*"The probability of war in the DRC ranges from 8% in the 1975-79 period to 77% in the 1995-99 period compared to an average of 7% for the sample. However, the Collier-Hoeffler model does not account for regional distribution of mineral resources as a mechanism through which mineral resources cause conflict...it is regional concentration of mineral resources more than resource dependence per se that has made the DRC particularly prone to conflict."*[47]

War, in part, arises at that threshold where class antagonisms, due to the uneven distribution of wealth, and much like a volcano, violently gushes out in relief from the periods of mounting pressures. The Collier and Hoeffler model helps to establish an estimate, or portrait of class antagonisms through quantitative means. When the secession of the Katanga region from the rest of the country was undertaken, although unsuccessful in the long run, was nonetheless an emblematic illustration of the greed involved in the amassing of wealth, by a minority of mining investors, among others, who weren't even nearly as entitled to the benefits as the average local. In relation to the socioeconomic status of other states globally, the DRC counts among the number of those considered untouchable, if you will, the lowest class, the poor, and disenfranchised and developing countries of the Global South. To better grasp how a failed state as the Democratic Republic of the Congo finds itself among the lowest ranked countries in the world, and yet be pivotal to, and well integrated into the economic system, we must understand more about the myths that went into creating the Congo. The heart of darkness, inhabited by dark hearts, it was told, was the Kongo; an uncivilized dispersed and de-centralized assortment of constantly warring societies. Myths, as hinted to a priori, play an important role in that they afford us a set mental structure, on which to start from whenever a concept, in our case the Congo, is blurted out. There are few places in the world where deaths go ignored by the international community, as to the extent in which it is done in the Congo, in the sense that; pre-independence violence notwithstanding, this impoverished country has known more deaths than the collective world during the Second World War. That there just isn't much information on the matter is a fallacy, but rather, it would be more accurate to suggest that myths, as for example, of the Congo's affinity towards ethnic antagonisms, or the need for paternal guidance from external forces, are partly to blame for the laissez-faire attitude the international community has vis-à-vis the Congo. It is much the same reasons as for why a significant number of people I've talked to, of relative wealth and socioeconomic standing; disparage the homeless or the poor, believing it to be fully their responsibility. It is the choices we make and the actions we take, people reason, that the destitute find themselves faced with such hardships. However, to say that such a line of reasoning is wrong, would not be fair either, it however, I believe, simply an unfinished description of such an evidenced reality. By now, at this stage of the book, I need little by way of explanation, to reiterate the conveying of the notion of class antagonisms, how this has a significant role, together with a person's agency, in the shaping said person's life. Therefore, it behooves me to expound further on the Myths that led the world down a road of nonchalance, as it regards their attitude towards the mass murder, and poignant affliction of the human beings of the Congo.

Thus, it is my view that deconstructing some of the myths that led to the image of the Congo as is globally perceived, contemporarily, is a needed segue that will help encapsulate the discussion on Hegemony, both cultural and military, and the profitability of war. As it is only until we question all aspects of all social constructions, can we claim to be on a level of civilization that pragmatically sets the course of its future, for the benefit of the race; humanity.

# Myths of the Congo:
(Deconstructing Euro-centrism in a People's History)

Dominating the realm of mythology, as it regards historical narration of central Africa, as is the case with almost every other sub-Saharan African society, entails early European contact with these 'primitive' ethnic groups. The story of the aforementioned contact with Europeans, is often told along the lines of early subversion of these primitive societies, and their domination by Europe. Central to the theme of this section, the Kingdom of the Kongo, for instance, was said to have been dismantled and subverted by the sixteenth century, upon establishing contact and a line of communication with the Portuguese some decades prior. The origins of such myths about the Kingdom of Kongo, in the mainstream of contemporary history, can be traced backed to 1959, with James Duffy. Echoing Duffy, and peddling myths that would justify some of the brutalities levied against the simple Congolese people, only a couple of years after the publications of Duffy's "Portuguese Africa", was Basil Davidson's "Black Mother".[48] According to this argument laid down by Duffy and Davidson, amended and altered through the years, however, still retaining its main core; the Portuguese were said to have found a well-established and developed Kingdom of the Kongo. They reached the Zaire River in 1483, forming an alliance with the ruler, who at first contact was king Nzinga a Nkuwu, whose name was subsequently changed to Joao I in 1491, upon his acceptance of the Christian faith that the Portuguese missionaries had imported. The next generation was just as open to trade and consolidating the already well entrenched partnership between the two kingdoms. Mvemba a Nzinga, the son of the aforementioned king Joao I, or better known as Afonso I (ruled A.D. 1506-1543), had a different relationship with the Portuguese, not too dissimilar from that had between the US and Japan today. Afonso I's partnership with the Portuguese, some maybe saw as progressive, afforded the Europeans to settle in Kongo, providing technological and military expertise and assistance, in exchange for trade, mostly in the form of slaves. During this time period the Kongo had adopted

Christianity as the kingdom's faith, no longer pagan (worship of multiple deities), thus King Afonso I and his European counterpart always referred to one another as "Brother". According to the consensus, a narrative adopted and developed from the Duffy and Davidson days; it is suggested that despite the benevolent start of relations between the two kingdoms, the settlers' greed soon became an upsetting factor. The Portuguese, it thus goes, had always conceived of the relationship as an opening for quick wealth-gain through the instating of a slave trade/economy. The pressure was mounting for the Lisbon bureaucrats of the Portuguese court, with its high aspirations, it seemed, was unable to control the settlers in Kongo or Sao Tome. In a couple of generations, the benefiting of the more technologically developed of the two kingdoms, resulted in the exploitation of the other. Unequal sharing of resources among the population, and exploitation of the newly marginalized, as is premised throughout this discussion, is the cause for antagonisms, be it class (socioeconomic), or ethnic, any other forms of antagonisms between different social identities/locales. In a nutshell, the Portuguese abandoned Kongo after deeply meddling in local affairs, establishing a colony in Angola instead, with Kongo, the semi-colony, left in ruins, to gradually sink into chaos. This is the Kongo myth that epitomizes a legacy of justifications. The myth that persists in our collective, features ideologies as "the white man's burden" to civilize, or the inferiority of the lower classes, in general, and black people in particular, a form of social Darwinism, if you will permit me.

However, we would be amiss if lacking in the mention of the backlash and resistance evidenced, especially from 'Africanists'. Proponents of a less patronizing and disparaging view articulated their opposition. Among the outspoken was Jan Vansina, who in 1965, as it regarded the history of Kongo, pointed out that, far from crumbling and disintegrating under Portuguese contact; Kongo continued more or less as before, at least in reference to the bureaucrats' capacity for imposing an organizational structure.[49] Well into the seventeenth century, evidence of a civilized, centralized and organized society was uncovered and further analyzed. There's ample documentation illustrating a sturdy, centralized, and independent monarchy. Of notability, and further attesting to a more balanced state of affairs, between the two kingdoms, is David Birmingham.[50] As it is with Vansina, so with Birmingham who refused to succumb to the predominant relevant ideologies, which speaks on behalf of the economic order of their day.

*"Whatever the Portuguese motives might have been, and no matter how much they had tried to interfere in Kongo or create a puppet king, in the long run they had not succeeded in doing so."*[51]

However overwhelming the evidence, and regardless of the tenacious resistance coming from scholars, among others, the myth on the Congo, its history, and reasons for the evidenced perilous well-being of the average local, still lingers, persists and subsists.[52] What has tended to happen, the extensive exploration into the African side of the historical narrative, has relegated the more documented, and physically evidence-ridden Portuguese side of the tale. As a springboard towards the acquisition and subsequent expression of the truth, more neutral authors as Vansina or Birmingham, strayed not too far from the template-narrative instituted by Duffy and Davidson. Instead, these afore referred to neutral authors countered the disparaging effects of Euro-centric interpretations, by correcting the false claims laid about the Kongo's state of affairs through heavy reliance on and the careful use of the documents regarding the Kongo Kingdom throughout the sixteenth and the better part of the seventeenth century. The claims that wish to subvert the Euro-centric interpretation, a consolidated and reaffirmed interpretation, during the years that proceeded the civil rights era of the 1960s; are subversive assertions that pave allusion to the intactness and centralization of the Congolese societies, prior to the scramble for Africa. Of course, the scramble for Africa, I opine, afforded Europeans, particularly Belgium, little resistance from the ethnically antagonized and decentralized multitudinous ethnic groups. Walking along the same path, is the premised narrative of both old and new interpretations of the events in Kongo, post-European encounter. According to both views of the Kongo-Portugal relations, the contact between the societies of concern was replete with tales of Lisbon's control, or lack thereof of the profiteers abroad, and their anxiety for fortune making in the Kongo. Despite the recognition of good and smooth sailing relations between the two kingdoms, both viewpoints attest to the dissolute lives had by the Portuguese in Kongo, with trickery in their political engagement never to be put past them. However, where 'Africanists' and Euro-centrists diverge is the end result, with the former demonstrating a semblance of the continuation of status quo affairs, while the latter, adamant about the disastrous and almost instant dilapidation of the Kingdom.

*"While later historians have relied heavily on Duffy or Davidson for their understanding of Portuguese motivation and behavior, they have failed to see that neither of these writers gave the sixteenth-century Portuguese documentation the kind of systematic reading necessary to document the period properly... Both had thus begun from the perspective of modern African and had projected those relations back into earlier centuries... In fact I believe that Portuguese and Kongolese society were much more similar to each other than many students of Kongolese history believe, at least similar enough to*

*allow us to abandon the idea of economic domination (translated into political domination) of Kongo by Portugal in the sixteenth century.*"[53]

John Thornton, in "Early Kongo-Portuguese Relations", elaborates on his disapproval as it regards the contention that, the fact that Portugal possessed more developed marine technology, firearms, and building technology, translated to "a decisive structural advantage over Kongo". Instead, Thornton supported his argument, with the appropriate documentation and a keen scholarly examination of sixteenth century Portuguese society, and its misconceptions today, and what effect that incurs upon contemporary Congolese historical, and as such cultural descriptions. Indeed, abundant is the evidence and historical documentation that depicts the starkly similarities between Portuguese and Kongolese societies. Both were monarchies, under the rule of kings and a class stratum of nobles, as a system of relations of kinship, patronage (clientage), and socioeconomic clout dominated the airstreams of political life.[54] In spite of the highly attained levels of political centralization, the rural settlements, for both Portugal and Kongo moseyed along as was customary in centuries past.[55] Productivity in Kongo, according to the tales expressed by European visitors to exotic kingdom, portrays an order of equal or higher levels of said productivity, in comparison to most of Europe. However, it must be noted that due to Europe's low levels of agricultural production in the sixteenth century, the productivity, though high, were nowhere near today's imaginings, and should thus be read only in a context of relativity.[56] As for famine and pestilence, as in Portugal in the sixteenth century, so in Kongo, during the same epoch.[57] However, as with the analyzing of any inter-societal relationship, the crux of the exploration tends to place importance on the economic relations and dynamics of commercialism, and rightly so. The aphorism, follow the money is poignant for such like reasons. However, the historical documentation, when comparing Portugal with Kongo, and as has been further explored by authors nearer to our contemporary era; demonstrates little distinction in the way of economic performance. As an example, it is readily apparent that both kingdoms had in-place 'general-purpose monies'; that is, gold and silver in Portugal and monetary cloth and nzimbu shells in Kongo. Still more, the modern rendition of 'money', in the general written use of the term in economic or anthropological spheres, was nonexistent for both societies.[58] That gold and silver, however, were often readily acceptable around the globe, made for an easy international monetary language, and both countries were in possession of such mineral resources, not least Kongo. Although, cowrie shells, in spite of the lack of global reach compared to gold and silver, still more widely circulated in Kongo, most of Africa and parts of Asia.[59]

*"The two countries [(Portugal and Kongo)] solved the problem of the non-convertibility of their currencies by evolving a rather complex system of currency exchanges and credits."*[60]

The manner in which trade relations were endeavored can be evidenced from a "letter of credit", in whose possession was Manuel, Afonso I's brother, travelling to Rome and embodying the role of ambassador in 1540. The letter made known to its reader, the request laid down by king Afonso, where he asked for a grant of 5 000 cruzados, creating a system of reciprocity by in turn instating a credit of 150 kofu of nzimbu in Congo, to be used at the discretion of the king of Portugal.[61] Of course, there were no flights to Lisbon at the time, and as such asking of Manuel to depart from city to city the instant he arrives, would be too taxing, and nonsensical, and that's where Antonio Vereira, a noble Kongolese comes into play. Antonio Vereira, needless to say, a Christian convert, was the representative of King Afonso for matters on money and the economy, and a resident of Portugal for approximately fifteen years.[62] Indeed, 'the sixteenth century', the mere pronouncement of such a statement is often to the effect of disparateness, of an epoch inaccessible the average Josh. However, following Newton, as it regards the belief in standing on the shoulders of giants, or already established and notable scholars of integrity; a semblance of the lives led by Europeans and Africans, during such an ostensibly unknown dark past, may be easily attained. For example, some scholars, with the aid of well documented archives, have shown how the flow of gold from the Gold Coast (Ghana) to Portugal, was not restricted to a bilateral trade. Gold from the Gold Coast to Portugal was, in part, made possible or subsidized by the exchanging of cooper bought in Kongo, for slaves in Benin, which, in turn, were sold to Akan traders for the much desired gold. It may have even been possible that some of the copper from Kongo was purchased with cowries, the very ones obtained in the Maldives, only to be imported by western and central African societies since the beginning of the sixteenth century.[63] Much to the chagrin of later Kongo kings, however, and parallel to the Spaniards' influx of silver in sixteenth-century Europe; foreign shells circulated Kongo, and thus reduced the revenues of the Kongolese kings who were to later follow in Afonso I's footsteps, as rulers of a politically centralized, yet heterogeneous society. Hence, much like the manipulation of the silver market of the northern hemisphere by Spain, so too, was there seen to be a manipulation of the 'money' market of the southern hemisphere by the Portuguese.[64] Therefore, the I maintain that the myth of the Congo evolved from a place of subverting the legacy of a people, so as to fit a narrative or ideology beholden to white supremacy and continual antagonistic relations between poor black and white persons. Apart from the economic basis for the slave trade, and a system centered around the treatment of other humans as capital, slavery, for the Congo, and as such, for Africa, had the effect not only of depopulation, but more pertinently, of undermining of the royal prestige of the Kongolese society. Slavery and its effect on Kongo must be read through the appropriate lenses circumspect by historical context. The main drive for Kongo's political centralization, it seemed, was the forced movement of goods and services, and more importantly people (human labor) "from neighboring and peripheral areas of the kingdom to the center and capital of Mbanza Kongo…".[65] It thus holds that, for the centralized state of affairs to persist, Kongo, at some point, necessarily had to cut its ties to the slave trade route.

"…once Kongo had developed fully toward the end of the sixteenth century, it was no longer a center of the slave trade, and seventeenth-century sources stress that slaves were rarely obtained in Kongo. In this respect Kongo resembled Benin, which had also acquired slaves and sold them to the Portuguese in exchange for military assistance during their wars of expansion…Kongo made most of her exchange with the Portuguese in cloth, which the Portuguese re-exported to other parts of Africa in order to acquire slaves. [In this regard,] Kongo thus had complete political control over its own development, and trade considerations were always secondary to the main logic of this development…dictated by internal need and not by external pressures from trading partners."[66]

Hence, the effective propagated myth of a failed state as the Democratic Republic of the Congo, affords a lesser inquisition of whether other external and internal elements, a priori dismissed with little thought, play a role in the nation's plight. If, however, the aforementioned elements or influences are uncovered, then, the extent of involvement by said forces must further be plowed into, if, that is, an approximation to the truth, and a rebalancing of the discursive socioeconomic scales is the sought after result. Since the DR of the Congo is the shanty town or ghetto on the peripheral of our wealthy Western communities/societies, human rights abuses are seldom punished, and often, almost no Western society-linked perpetrators are brought to answer for any misdeed. Before concluding on what I hope was a brief and schematic portrayal, a conversation starter if you will, of socioeconomic antagonisms in both the US and on a more global yet circumspect platform; I wish to discuss and bring to the fore the notion of existing atrocities committed by human rights groups, or the UN in particular, as well as share a testimony or two from survivors of such injustices, of which are undertaken in an ignored community of human legacy.

# Keepers of Peace and Leavers of Pieces

The year was 1999 and the United Nations Security Council authorized the resources at their disposal to be poured into the Congo, in the form of peace keeping, or arm bearing forces. The U.N. Mission in the Democratic Republic of the Congo ("MONUC") was established, and of course welcomed in those parts of the eastern Congo, as, there, a weary and insecure and desolate atmosphere reigned supreme, an ever more everyday tale of menace for the locals. In conclusion to a chapter that has propagated and added a unique perspective, or at least tried; to the already and much undertaken literature, as it regards socioeconomic or class antagonisms. The following concluding section is not an outright condemnation of the United Nations, or its MONUC forces in the DRC, rather, not wishing to toss the baby out with the bath water, I wish simply to do a bit of my bit of due diligence, as a global citizen, in adding to the collective sociopolitical checks and balancing pressures, needed for all organized entities. Not all is bad with the UN, however, neither is all smooth sailing, and that is to be expected, but the effort put into resolving internal discrepancies, as an international body acting in a sovereign state, must be in equilibrium with your attested benevolent mission. For the most part, the majority of peacekeepers are ostensibly strictly performing their duty, honestly and sometimes, it seems, out of genuine goodwill. Most peace keeping forces appear to be professional in regards to their attitude towards the tasked duties. Some of the UN peace keepers, coming from around the world, have lost their lives, as they're intended purpose is to act as that intermediary buffering force, between rebel insurrectionary forces, and the globally disenfranchised citizens of both the world and the Democratic Republic of the Congo. However, as for the rotten apples amidst the fresh plump bunch, their actions have led to a spate of academic journals and newspaper articles in 2004 and 2005. The themes ranged in coverage, from rape to torture, to fathering what has become known as "peacekeeper babies", and even gone so far as to perpetrate more heinous acts, as their recent activities, which entailed, capturing Congolese women and children on tape, as they proceed to the enactment of misdeeds. They, of course, subsequently deserted their ranks.[67] Indeed, a report, conducted by the UN Office of Internal Oversight Services ("OIOS"), in March of 2005, set about to chronicle the owl-eye raising discoveries. The a priori mentioned report yielded a wave of criticism and reform, although, this reform came into proper effect at an ebb and flow pace.[68] As for the United States' response, however, members of the 109th Congress, in counteracting manner, set into motion bills in that same month of March of 2005. The Congress, and as such the American government, urged that the UN suspend payment of peacekeeping funds. Subsequently, the US withheld military assistance to countries, as the Congo, where evidences of abuses were reported, especially where there was seen to be a failure to investigate, and subsequently effectuate apt punitive measures in recompense of the misconducts.[69]

In the case of the DRC, as all concerned parties must save face, the government requested from the International Criminal Court (ICC), that it undertakes an investigation of the apparent crimes inflicted to the vulnerable, by the UN peacekeeping forces, during the course of the war.[70] The DRC, being party to the Rome statute, at the heart of the creation of the ICC, thus affording the court with jurisdiction over genocide, war crimes, as well as crimes against humanity, committed after July 1, 2002. The aforementioned date marks the period when the ICC's temporal jurisdiction went into effect. As such, it is important to note that some UN peacekeeping members' atrocities, went unpunished, due to the misdeeds having taken place before the temporary jurisdiction had kicked into effect.

As it regards the UN, there mandate in the DRC was renewed, the MONUC was there to stay, and for the most part, that was a more than welcome influence, for the disparate and vulnerable in those parts. Having renewed the prior mandate, the UN increased the number of soldiers, and complimentary associates, installing what is the largest peacekeeping mission in the world, in the Congo, with 16 047 soldiers, and over two thousand employees of a civilian nature.[71] The indispensability of peacekeeping forces in the Congo is not in question. That said keepers of peace protect civilian employees and local civilians alike, sheltering and hindering rapes from being inflicted upon civilians, and so too prevention of murders, and looting of armed militia groups; is widely known, and in fact appreciated. Putting their live on the line, these UN peacekeepers forcibly engage in the disarmament of militia factions, who incessantly terrorize the local people, more especially in the eastern Congo, near to the shared bored with Rwanda.[72]

*"[m]ilitias have been attacking civilians, and if MONUC was not protecting the people there would be no one to rely on. They'd be at the mercy of the armed men, who have been raping and killing and burning villages."*[73] What sticks out about the UN forces' stance on confronting and disarming militia men, while at risk, is the relatively newly adopted mandate for belligerency and retaliatory firmness, rather than the more peaceful, passive aggressive, and non-confrontational, 'only fire when fired upon' approach.[74] However, through, and amidst all this good, the rotten bunch, as is customary of any grouping, organization or community; went on unimpeded by the lax reforms and regulations the UN imposed on its lower ranked forces, with the higher ups receiving inadequate formation on how to deal with those over whom they hold charge and responsibility.

**Yvette:**

Claims and reports by girls in the eastern Congo, surfaced, chronicling the sexual relations had with UN peacekeepers. Girls in this part of the world are vulnerable, since, starvation and desperation are the constant and everyday state of affairs. Some of these girls engage in risky behavior, not to supplement their household's meager income, but as a result of their homelessness; having been kicked out of their home, for reasons ranging from religiosity to superstitious approbations of that the girls are involved in the practice of witchcraft. Some of these aforementioned girls are as young as ten years old, needing to sexually offer up their bodies and souls for as little as, a cup of milk, one hand full of eggs, peanut butter, or otherwise, for a dollar. Yvette is one such girl, a fourteen year old from a village called Bunia. In said community, she is widely known, and in fact commonly referred to as "one-dollar girl" or the "kidogo usharati", meaning "the little prostitute". Everybody was aware; it seemed, of her activities and how much she charged UN peacekeepers, in UN cars, or at peacekeeper camps.[75] Yvette's story goes much deeper in fact, her past spurred her to where she was, at the age of ten, she was raped by a militiaman. Hence, at ten years old, Yvette was told that no man would be willing to take her as a bride, being a woman in the 'third world' and to some extent neglected by 'first world' feminists, marriage was her only way out. As it regards having sex with peacekeepers, Yvette told the global community which so ignores her suffering, that:

*"I'm sad about it. But I needed the dollar. I can't go farm because of the militias. Who will feed me?...sometimes it happens in U.N. cars, other times at the camp. But at least they paid us. I was worthless anyhow. My honor was lost."*[76]

Yvette's friend, Francine, found herself in a similar predicament in the past, in her case, much like Yvette's, Francine was raped by a militiaman. Francine was raped at least twice; on the first occasion, when gleaning food at the field, she was attacked by the militiaman, and subsequently, with prostitution the only recourse, she was once more raped by Moroccan peacekeepers. The sixteen year old Francine described the souring encounter with Moroccan peacekeepers, when upon receiving compensation from one soldier, five soldiers appeared, intervened, and raped her. Francine later expressed that;

*"I feel bad about what I did. I don't want to go through that again."*[77]

That the report from the OIOS, on behalf of the UN organization, was written up, and went so far as to address particular instances of atrocities, committed by peacekeepers, even undertaking an investigation in Bunia, was,

# WALLS

and still is not  sufficient enough as to quell occurrences of misconduct. The fact remains; the Congo, like other impoverished nations, is not subject to the attention afforded the wealthy communities in the globalized order. As such, in spite of written reports and media outrage, attention given to these downtrodden folk, both the rhetorical hype and the subsequent reforms which follow, persist not, or, as in the case of the UN's higher-ups, are inaptly executed.

Therefore it is not so much the evidence of action taken, but rather, the absence of the evidence of the pursuit of justice, as is seen in the Western world, when happening to wealthier, and often white women and men. The notion that, "that's just Africa," or "what do you expect of the middle east," with little to no enthusiasm in, or genuine pursuit for justice owed, is the very lulled into, unquestioning state, which aids to propagate socioeconomic norms and perceptions, the patriarchal, white supremacist and capitalist elitist, social construction in which every day we have to live.

# Notes

[1] Joyce E. King, "Black Education: A Transformative Research and Action Agenda for the New Century", 2005, pp. 3.

[2] Cited by Scott, D., September 2000, in "The Re-enchantment of humanism: An Interview with Sylvia Wynter. *Small Axe, 8*, pp. 119-207.

[3] Joyce E. King, "Black Education: A Transformative Research and Action Agenda for the New Century", 2005, pp. 8.

[4] Ideas by Chafets, Z., March 25, in "Changing races," New York Daily News, p. 4; mentioned by Joyce E. King in "Black Education: A Transformative Research and Action Agenda for the New Century", 2005, pp. 9.

[5] "A Transformative Vision of Black Education for Human Freedom," Georgia State University, in "Black Education: A Transformative Research and Action Agenda for the New Century", Joyce E. King, 2005, pp. 10.

[6] "League of the Iroquois," Lewis H. Morgan, 1851, Citadel Press, Secaucus, NJ.

[7] "The origin of the family, private property and the state," Friedrich Engels, 1884.

[8] Ibid.

[9] Ibid.

[10] "Sister Citizen," Melissa V. Harris-Perry, 2011, pp. 9.

[11] For more, see: John Lewis and Michael D'Orso, Walking with the Wind: A memoir of the Movement; New York, Mariner Books, 1999.

[12] John McCain with Mark Salter, "Why Courage Matters: The way to a Braver Life", New York: Random House, 2004.

[13] Michael Eric Dyson, "Come hell or high water: Hurricane Katrina and the color of Disaster", New York: Basic Civitas, 2006.

[14] Sister Citizen, Melissa V. Harris-Perry, 2011, pg 14.

[15] Penner and Ferdinand, "Overcoming Katrina: African American Voices from the Crescent City and Beyond."

[16] "Sister Citizen", Melissa V. Harris-Perry, 2011, pg 36.

[17] "Louis Armstrong in His Own Words," ed. Thomas Brothers, New York: Oxford University Press, 1999, 82-110, contains his writings, often detailing his musical contexts, from 1918 to 1931. An excellent view of Armstrong's synthesis of vast musical material and its extension through his own powerful will to innovate is presented by Laurence Bergreen, Louis Armstrong: An extravagant Life (New York: Broadway Books, 1997), 143-235.), cited in: "Black Cultural Traffic: Crossroads in Global Performance and Popular Culture", 2005; University of Michigan Press.

[18] David Kerr, "Dance, Media-Entertainment, and Popular Performance in South East Africa", Bayreuth: E. Breitinger, 1998, pp. 31.

[19] "Black Cultural Traffic: Crossroads in Global Performance and Popular Culture", pp. 18, 2005; University of Michigan Press.

[20] For more on African cultural traffic, see: Michael A. Gomez," *Exchanging Our Country Marks: The Transformation of African Identities in the Colonial and Antebellum South"* (Chapel Hill: University of North Carolina Press, 1998) records the time before the 1840s in which African customs and cultural practices were brought to the Americas by Africans caught in the Atlantic trade in humans. Under "Festivities and Pastimes," A.C. Saunders's *Social History of Black Slaves and Freedmen in Portugal: 1441-1555* (New York: Cambridge University Press, 1982) writes of dances (one called the *guinea,* no doubt after West Africa's Guinea coast) and singing by blacks as well as comments on their drumming and flute playing at public festivals. Blacks also held parties of their own, one the *festa dos negros* where they elected a king. Al black gatherings were outlawed in Lisbon in 1559.).

[21] "Black Cultural Traffic: Crossroads in Global Performance and Popular Culture", pp. 20, 2005; University of Michigan Press.

[22] Margaret Danner, "The Convert," in *A Broadside Treasury,* ed. Gwendolyn Brooks (Detroit: Broadside Press, 1971), pp. 40-42. Cf. Also her "Her Small Bells of Benin," pp. 39, and "Etta Moten Barnett's Attic," pp. 39.

[23] "Black Cultural Traffic: Crossroads in Global Performance and Popular Culture", pp. 15-16, 2005; University of Michigan Press.

[24] Gertrude Stein, "Picasso", Paris: Floury, 1938, pp. 64.

[25] Abiola Irele, "Negritude or Black Cultural Nationalism," Journal of Modern African Studies 3, no. 3 (1965): pp. 321-48, especially pp. 330-38 on multiple renaissances. The companion essay, also pioneering, is Abiola Irele, "Negritude-Ideology and Literature," Journal of Modern African Studies 3, no. 4 (1965):pp. 499-526.

[26] Lawrence Cohn, "Nothing but the Blues: The Mucsic and the Musicians", New York: Abbeville Press, 1993, pp. 90-91.

[27] Laura Fair, "Pastimes and Politics: Culture, community, and Identity in Post-abolition Urban Zanzibar, 1890-1945", Athens: Ohio University Press; Oxford: J. Currey, 2001, p. 3.

[28] Bruce Kellner, "The Harlem Renaissance: A Historical Dictionary for the Era", New York: Methuen, 1984, 93-94.

[29] "Black Cultural Traffic: Crossroads in Global Performance and Popular Culture", 2005; University of Michigan Press.

[30] Two of the latest entrants in the story of Ghana's magnetism are Gerald Horne, "Race Woman: The Lives of Shirley Graham DuBois", New York: New York University Press, 2000; and Doran H. Ross, ed. "Wrapped in Pride: Ghanaian Kente and African American Identity", Los Angeles: UCLA Fowler Museum of Cultural History, 1998.

[31] Robin D. G. Kelley, "Jazz Folk Here and There: A Transatlantic Conversation," St. Clair Drake Memorial Lecture, Stanford University, May 23, 2003.

[32] Cited in: "Black Cultural Traffic: Crossroads in Global Performance and Popular Culture", 2005; University of Michigan Press.

[33] Ibid.

[34] Diawara, "In search of Africa," pp. 101: Diawara discusses how the speaking of English by Malian youth was an innovation in a "Francophone country, where one acquired subjecthood through Francite-that is, thinking via French grammar and logic." Diawara spoke English to a traveling African American musician in Junior Well's band and became an overnight sensation in Bamako. The youth dream then has been to "be as adept at Francite as Senghor, who spoke French better than the French.".

[35] Karin Barber, "Popular Reactions to the Petro-Naira," in Barber, Readings, 91-98.

[36] Ibid. p. 92.

[37] "Black Cultural Traffic: Crossroads in Global Performance and Popular Culture", 2005; University of Michigan Press.

[38] Ngugi wa Thiong'o, "Enactments of Power: The Politics of Performance Space," Dance Review, 41 (fall 1997): pp. 13.

[39] Ngugi wa Thiong'o, "Women in Cultural Work: The Fate of the Kamiruthu People's Theater in Kenya," in Reading in African Popular Culture, ed. Karin Barber (Bloomington: Indiana University Press, 1997), pp. 131-137.

[40] Cultural Traffic: Crossroads in Global Performance and Popular Culture", 2005; University of Michigan Press.

[41] Regina Bendix, "In Search of Authenticity: The Formation of Folklore Studies"; Madison: Wisconsin University Press, 1997, p. 7.

[42] Henry Louise Gates, Jr., " 'Authenticity,' or the Lesson of Little Tree," New York Times Book Review, November 24, 1991, p. 26.

[43] Bell Hooks, "Black Looks: Race and Representation", Boston: South End Press, 1992, pp. 21-40.

[44] "Black Cultural Traffic: Crossroads in Global Performance and Popular Culture", 2005; University of Michigan Press.

[45] Paul Collier and Anke Hoeffler; "On the Incidence of Civil War in Africa"; 2000; Center for the Study of African Economies; University of Oxford.

[46] "The Economics of Civil War: The Case of the Democratic Republic of Congo"; July 1; 2003; Léonce Ndikumana, Department of Economics, University of Massachusetts; & Kisangani Emizet, Department of Political Science, Kansas State University.

[47] Ibid.

[48] James Duffy; "Portuguese Africa"; London; 1959; pp. 49-58; & Basil Davidson: "Black Mother"; London, 1961; pp. 116-50; & Basil Davidson: "Angola's People: In the Eye of the Storm"; London; 1972; pp. 80-92.

[49] Jan Vansina; "Kingdoms of the Savanna"; Madison; 1966; pp. 37-70.

[50] David Birmingham; "Trade and Conquest in Angola" London; 1966; pp. 23-32; & his more recent contributions to vols. 2 and 3 of the Cambridge History of Africa.

[51] "Early Kongo-Portuguese Relations: A New Interpretation"; John Thornton; Source: History in Africa, Vol. 8 (1981); pp. 183-204; Published by: Cambridge University Press.

[52] Text books such as: is J.D. Fage; "African History"; New York; 1978; pp. 238-40. Also: Davidson's "A History of East and Central Africa to the Late Nineteenth Century"; London; 1967.

[53] "Early Kongo-Portuguese Relations: A New Interpretation"; John Thornton; Source: History in Africa, Vol. 8 (1981); pp. 183-204; Published by: Cambridge University Press.

[54] For further reading on Portuguese life at the time, see: Jose Hermano Saraiva; "Historia Concisa de Portugal"; 3rd ed.; Lisbon; 1979; pp. 102-04, 124-27, 139-46. & further reading on historical Kongolese life see: John Thornton, "The Kingdom of Kongo, ca 1390-1678: History of an African Social Formation," Cahiers d'e'tudes africaines. Also; Jan Vansina; "Kingdoms of the Savanna"; Madison; 1966; pp. 41-45.

[55] For rural living in Kongo, see: John Thornton, "Kingdom of Kongo," Chapter 3. & for rural living in Portugal see: Jose Gentil da Silva; "L'Autoconsummation au Portugal"; in Annates: Economies, Societes, Civilisations; 24(1969); pp. 250-88.

[56] John Thornton; "Kingdom of Kongo"; pp. 105; where he compares observations of European by observers, with modern descriptions of seventeenth-century European agriculture.

[57] For the expounding of Kongo's demography see: John Thornton, "Demography and History in the Kingdom of Kongo, 1550-1750"; JAH; 18(1977), pp. 507-30.

[58] The working definition of primitive money, as is widely accepted by students of monetary history; see: Paul Einzig; "Primitive Money"; London; 1949. Since, however, European money during the course of the sixteenth century circulated by weight only ( with no face values attached, and nor was there a concept of fiduciary value), then, they must be counted as primitive, alongside shells, beads, hoes, salt blocks, and the like resources.

[59] For more on cowrie currencies see: Marion Johnson; "The Cowrie Currencies of West Africa"; JAH; 11(1970); pp. 17-49, 331-53.

[60] "Early Kongo-Portuguese Relations: A New Interpretation"; John Thornton; Source: History in Africa, Vol. 8 (1981); pp. 183-204; Published by: Cambridge University Press.

[61] Afonso I to Joao III; 4 December 1540; MMA; 2:102.

[62] Diogo I to Diogo Gomes; 15 August 1546; MM4; 2:149.

[63] Duarte Pacheco Pereira; "Esmeraldo de Situ Orbis"; London; 1954; pp. 172.

[64] For more on the manner of trade, see: Walter Rodney, "Gold and Slaves on the Gold Coast," Transactions of the Historical Society of Ghana, 10(1969), pp. 13-28. Also: Alan F.C. Ryder," Benin and the Europeans", London, 1969, pp. 35-75. On the sale of copper from Kongo, Afonso to Manuel I, 14 October 1514, MM4, 1:295-304, passim.
As it regards the complaints of the Kongolese kings, the First complaint: Afonso's letter to Joao III, reflected in Joao III's answer: MMA, 1:528. As it regards the flooding of "Spanish Silver" into Europe see: for example; Fernand Braudel; "The Mediterranean and the Mediterranean World in the Age of Phillip II"; 2 vols.; New York; 1972; 1:476-515.

[65] "Early Kongo-Portuguese Relations: A New Interpretation"; John Thornton; Source: History in Africa, Vol. 8 (1981); pp. 183-204; Published by: Cambridge University Press.

[66] Ibid.

[67] See: Marc Lacey; "In Congo War, Even Peacekeepers Add to Horror"; N.Y. TIMES; Dec. 18, 2004; at A1. & also: Colum Lynch; "U.N. Sexual Abuse Alleged in Congo"; WASH. POST; Dec. 16, 2004, at A16.

[68] See: UN Report on Abuse; supra note 12; where they note that U.N. Secretary General Kofi Annan requested an investigation into the abuses alleged in the DRC.

[69] See: "Protection of Vulnerable Populations During Humanitarian Emergencies Act"; S. 559, 109th Cong. § 305 (2005). & also: "Women and Children in Crisis and Conflict Protection Act"; H.R. 1413, 109th Cong. § 305 (2005).

[70] Marc Lacey; "Novelty in Congo: U.N. Investigates a Massacre"; N.Y. TIMES, Dec. 24, 2004; at A13.

[71] MONUC, "Facts and Figures"; (2005); at http://www.un.org/Depts/dpko/missions/monuc/facts.html (These facts and figures bespeaks of the notion hat the peacekeepers are from a wide array of nations, of these: Bangladesh, France, India, Morocco, Nepal, Pakistan, and South

Africa, to name a few, while the Special Representative of the Secretary General and Chief of the peacekeeping mission is William Lacy Swing, an American).

[72] Marc Lacey, supra note 10. Where, he explains that peacekeepers have become more aggressive in their efforts.

[73] Ibid.

[74] See: S.C. Res. 1592, ¶ 7; U.N. Doc. S/RES/1592; Mar. 30, 2005; (The document shows the authorizing of the MONUC, to "use all necessary means, within its capabilities and in the areas where its armed units are deployed, to deter any attempt at the use of force to threaten the political process and to ensure the protection of civilians under imminent threat of physical violence, from any armed group, foreign or Congolese, in particular the ex-FAR and the Interhamwe . . . ." ); [415-416].

[75] See: Marc Lacey; supra note 12. & also: Colum Lynch," U.N. Envoy to Resign in Wake of Sex Scandal"; WASH. POST; Mar. 2, 2005; at A14. Also informative is: Emily Wax; "Congo's Desperate 'One-Dollar U.N. Girls"; WASH. POST; Mar. 21, 2005; at A1. Also: Wax, supra note 26.

[76] Emily Wax; Supra note 26.

[77] Ibid.

.

# 4

# Hegemony

## and the

# Profitability

## of

# War

****

*The promotion of 'democracy' abroad has been a feature of US foreign policy since the earlier part of the twentieth century, accompanying its rise as an international actor. It provided the ideological basis for its opposition to rivals in the form of imperialism, fascism and then communism. The end of the Cold War, which signaled the emergence of the US as the sole superpower, accelerated this process. With the ideological fusion of democracy and capitalism credited in large measure for the defeat of communism and the state-planned economy, the promotion of democracy alongside capitalism as the only viable, legitimate mode of governance emerged as an increasingly important component of US foreign policy.* [1]

To me, and to many a scholar and admirer of history, the Roman empire embodies the notion of imperial domination or, at least, some such expanded power wielding, and efficient methods of subjecting the mass peripheral poor classes. Poor, as it regards the average Roman citizen, in general, and the typical Roman citizen residing in Rome in particular. On several occasions and amidst a random group of intellectuals, and more so random historical conversational themes, at Carleton University, where I spent my undergraduate years; these seemingly trivial, yet heated conversations tended to end up in the majority of opinion makers, glorifying the Roman legacy. As a measurement or litmus test for the success or failure of other civilizations, Rome, to a greater extent than the pinnacle of Athenian democracy, I feel; was, for westerners, that standard that was a constant when comparing all other known, past and present civilizations. The aforementioned is true to the extent that, at the same time, "the Rome of Cicero and Virgil stood for high culture, Caesar's assassination was a triumph of republican virtues, Augustus's principate embodied imperial greatness, and the excesses of Caligula and Nero were cautionary tales about corrupting influences of imperial power. As such, Rome is the springboard from which, I believe, it is best to start off from, a backdrop to convey the similarities and differences between contemporary and classical forms of hegemony. As will later be shown in this chapter, empire building has progressed to take on a new form, a more detached version of control or hegemony, through cultural 'infiltration'/occupation or the more antiquated military, socioeconomic and political forms and tactics of occupation, and thus, control of vital national resources.

The British, as with some voices within the US, are quick to leap at the inclusion of Britannia into the Roman Empire, upon which, and after a much later time, the southernmost parts of the isle were significantly Latinized and Christianized. The telling of the history of the Roman Empire, or at least as bespoken of by the consensus, is infused with western bias, or some semblances of 'white pride'. That the aforementioned interpretation is made to fit the status quo ideologies, is a trap made especially easy to fall into, since, most classical Roman historians and geographers spoke robustly of Roman empire building, yet their descriptions of "barbarians", those newly subjects of empire, cannot be taken unassumingly. Ancient historians and geographers, Strabo, Tacitus, Cassius Dio, Suetonius, and Zosimus, to name but a few, offer up vibrant and consistent descriptions of the processes, methods and successes which so led to Rome's enrichment. Such popular histories falter, in part, as a result of the authors' primary need to focus on domestic matters, as such, they used the empire as a backdrop when critiquing, or showing dissent towards Roman politics and the direction taken by their society. However, thanks to archeological, geographical, and historical discoveries of epigraphs, legal texts, bronze copies of discharge diplomas, and even the data collected for several census periods, aid in the accurate contextualization of Roman civilization as it relates to our globalized hegemonic system of capitalism. More than passed on tales, and far reaching assumptions befitting a certain narrative, fields of study as archeology are better relied upon to advance discussions, since an ostensibly better sketched-image can be seen from their uncovering, of how people actually lived, rather than the tales told about them by others. Still, there is much to be considered about the approach most archeologists take in uncovering past legacies, for one thing, "simple farmsteads and ubran dwellings remain largely unexamined," with most of the attention borrowed by grand monuments and estates, and stately villas.[3]

Far from the picture often illustrated by mainstream historians, more so during the early and middle 20th century than in contemporary times, the Romans' policies of assimilation and their tact for diplomacy far surpassed their military conquests. Such grandiose assimilation capabilities were made possible, in part because race, as the construct it has grown to represent, our modern conceptions of this social category was nonexistent; instead, cultural resemblance was the sought after quality. However, it is important to keep in mind that actual cultural assimilation, bringing with it socioeconomic benefits, was something predominantly linked to the local elites and merchants of the conquered land. Much like the neo-liberal and democratic professing ideologies of what makes one American, being Roman, or "Romanness" was not in so terms of race or blood -this is at least one less antagonistic factor, compared to US society- rather, having a distinct and strong sense of their identity; as inherently superior only to those who shared not their culture and morality. Hence, in spite of having borrowed from Greece, and profusely used the term and conception of "barbarian" to refer to most foreigners, the Romans were known to as well freely, and readily borrow from cultures (or discriminated social locations) under their dominion, regardless of the fact that they simultaneously despised said cultures. Note though, contrary to modern day conceptions of Roman assimilation policies, it was not a conveying of blanket equality, and neither did it release the masses from their responsibilities as it regarded serving the empire, via tribute, as well as labor. Brimming with confidence over the mere notion of "Romanness" and the connoted superiority with which it inferred, the empire builders assumed that "tribal" groups became easier to deal with once the embracing of Roman culture was established. Therefore, assimilation was more so coercive and an administrative tool, and so too an affirmation of Roman preeminence, than any granting of equal status, or any such 'genuine' and progressive ideological benevolence.[4] In this regard, Rome is no different from any other imperial civilization's proscribed means of action. Also no different is the influence on the US's morals and perceptions, of themselves and of the external world, by the societies they have seized hegemonic control over.

Cicero would later war, address the prevalence of misrule by the abusive governor in Sicily, that:

*"Within the bounds of Ocean there is no longer any place so distant or so out of the way that the wanton and oppressive deeds of our countrymen have not penetrated there in recent years. Rome can no longer hold out against the whole world- I do not mean against its power and arms in war, but against its groans and tears and lamentations."*[5]

This efficient system that saw money accrued, centralized to the local elite hotspots, before being offered up as tribute to the Governing Roman Authority of the respective jurisdiction. Indeed, at the height of Empire, and during the peace years, the Romans were uniquely adept at creating sustainable systems of bureaucracy, efficiently drawing the process out, exploiting the masses within imperial boundaries. Much as has been discussed of and attributed to US society, from the top down, these aforementioned institutions of bureaucracy seem rational, somewhat benign, yet the abject reality tells a tale of much a morbid and gloomier atmosphere. Intimidation, with tribal locales subjected to prolonged bouts of terror and naked force, inclusive of which ills was the institutionalized slavery that produced almost all the grand monuments, and significantly shaped the cultural triumphs of the ancient monde. Unlike in today's well connected globalized world, Roman Imperial globalization objectives were not hidden, nor was there a bother to sell the populace on the benefits of empire; only elites occupied themselves with the discussing of such matters. Typically, only males from elite families had the right to run for senate. Rather than public uproar and outrage directing the limitations and circumspections to expansionist and belligerent policies, the Roman elites, as it regards managing societal antagonisms, were restricted more so by communication and the limits of travel in the ancient world. Indeed, in the senate, the heated discussions were often sparked by fervently protesting Senators, often questioning whether the representatives of Roman institutions are capable of including the often, trouble-yielding disparate alien populations. Further attesting to the influences of marginalized peoples have over the dominate hegemonic group, is the Roman fear of civil collapse of morals, the degenerative decadence imported by the Greeks, with their high praise of and appreciation for arts and material luxuries.[6] As such, a problem arising from imperial expansion and the exploitation of a people, not only tilts the scales of morality, passively lulling the nonresistant populace, but it furthermore aids in the influx of said foreign culture. This infusion of some parts of cultural material from the subjugated culture into the mainstream of Roman civilization, comes in various forms, such as actual persons, with migration en masse; the proverbial 'chickens coming home to roost'. Antagonisms became quite evident when food shortages became a daily occurrence for citizens, who once and not too long ago, were receiving free grain, and the benefits and higher probability for opportunities, which came with being a resident of Rome.

Indeed, external cultures on the peripheries brought trouble for Rome. For me, Rome, the epitome of empire, best bespeaks of the benefits and pitfalls involved in the benefiting of a few, for the peril of the many. Today, in US culture, for example, and as could be said of any western civilization, the fear of the 'other culture', with 'our culture' linked to Christianity, is a player in the phobia of Islam and a facilitates discursive reactions, seldom leading us into ideological justifications, to explain the validity of our fear of integration, much rather preferring assimilation. A major factor for the incitation of the aforementioned fear, among several geo-political reasons, are the changing tides of technology, and the accretion of wealth, more especially of the financial, speculative variety, within not only national societies, but on a global scale. Alas, though good and profitable for western countries were the inequalities in knowledge/expertise, and skill, and the inequalities in trade conditions, imposed on the poorer nations, now, the fact these poor nations are so far behind in terms of development is impugning on western civilization's way of life. While for Rome, the limits of travel and communication was a great cause for concern, in that institutions abroad were reigned in less than those societies nearest to Rome, the same sense of loss of control, ostensibly is affecting developed nations in general, and in particular the US, with military bases on all inhabited continents. The need to control a world, whereby a priori limits to communication and travel notwithstanding, though not accessible to all in all its modes, is made relatively more possible than in times past; a world that is ever more cognizant of the unequal share of global wealth afforded to them, by the socioeconomic global capitalist order, and its history of subjugation. Alas, the uncertainties, made more unsure by the onwards ascending, and significant share that finance capital takes relative to all other forms of wealth; aid in antagonizing the mass populace, in societies, global, with the poor needing to emigrate, and the wealthier societies grappling with the backlash of exploitation, noticing slightly hidden antagonisms in their society. Ideology has the charmed effect of concealing the suffering within one's own society, when, for the most part, there's an abundant circulation of wealth and opportunities, for a significant part of the population, and the upper middle class and elites notwithstanding, as in the United States in the 1950s. It was a different and 'cold' world then, indeed, a different form of capitalism, and a nascent hegemonic force. As foreign and disparaged and ignored cultures infiltrate through the seams of western civilization, a wave of persons, cultural material, antagonistic ideologies (relative to one's own), and security fears and labor fears ("they get all the cheap jobs, for cheaper!!!") floods into wealthier societies; a socioeconomic osmotic flow if you will. Human collectivity, in pursuit of socioeconomic stability, if not socioeconomic grand amassment, seeks to tilt into equilibrium, the scales of political, juridical, and other forms of supplementary institutional power. As such, the set motion of the global economic order, in favor of wealthier over poorer and ignored countries, may result, if unaddressed, I believe, in implosion, be it moral degeneration as it regards treatment of other humans, or economic turmoil, with more financial collapses happening more often. It may end up being that, as in the words of a lamenting Pliny, in the wake of Roman triumph over Greece, "through conquering we have been conquered".

# Comparing:
## Aspects of US & Western European Policies and Roman Imperialism

It is of some note to appreciate that, in contrast to twentieth century western empires, which played the pretence game, of the just imposition of benevolent governance, over the subjugated poor dark nations; the Romans made no apology as it regards their project Imperium Romanum, by violent conquest not unlike the colonial period. Initially, for the Romans, there was no disagreement between imperial expansion and democratic institutions. In fact, it happens to be the Roman republic that constructed and established the imperium Romanum. Not unlike the US in this regard, the Romans invoked their destiny for universal rule, as in the words of republican statesman Cicero in 56 b.c., who was without restraint in his glorification of how "it has finally come about that the limits of our empire and of the earth are one and the same."[7] The United States, if not militarily, maintains its coercive reach and control around the globe, through ideological, and as such cultural, imposition through eased and creeping infiltration. The US, maintain the semblance of democracy, and democracy promotion, or the promotion of rights for the subjugated and oppressed of the world, through "manufacturing consent", and using their socioeconomic position, and thus legitimacy, to speak on behalf of "good" against "evil", through "American exceptionalism". The Romans, however, were well aware of the need to avoid acquisition of foreign lands and the wealth ensuing from said undertakings, with most territories engulfed through piecemeal and even somewhat surreptitious means. The exception, and not the rule, is Claudius' planned invasion of Britain, predominantly, Rome during the post-Augustus era were preoccupied with stability and maintaining control than with expansion for its own sake.

Contemporarily, in a US in search of socioeconomic consolidation, foreign and conquered elites are used to maintain the coercive hegemonic control. Further elaboration on the aforementioned US foreign policy of democracy promotion, and coercive means of control, will be undertaken later in this chapter, as well as in chapter 5. For now, it is significant to note the similarities inherent in imperial pursuit, and how not one such hegemonic force can be everlasting. The Romans, our backdrop for comparative discussion, were cognizant of the limits of brute force, and thus shared power with cooperative local elites. The small group of conquered locals acted much like an extension of Roman state power, only a locally translated variant, with intimate knowledge of their own customs and dogmas. In the ancient world, such compromises were necessary for the maintaining of revenue flows to the ruling Polis. Communication and the ease of travel are a limiting factor for both the Roman Empire and the US, as global hegemonic influences, only, for altogether different reasons. In the case of Rome, it is needless to say that the limits to communication and travel were a restraint on effective control. It is difficult to know and regulate what the ruling governor of Alexandria endeavors in, and the mobilization of military forces necessitated both resources and time; lots of both, just to name a few eventualities that did not go unheard. As for the US, the ease rather than (dis)ease of travel and communication, in a globalized and relatively technologically advanced mélange of societies, needing to justify any actions of belligerence; it becomes incumbent upon the imperial power to play a highly geo-politicized game, and swift maneuvering in gaining the minds of the global community. Indeed, as was shown in the preceding chapter, that injustices happening in poor nations as the DRC, by both local and external influences are more often than not overlooked, does not negate the often observable 'truism' that power wielding involves the interplay of several influences, and not unilaterally/centrally exhibited and propagated, in spite of its unequal distribution across the board. Thus, communication and travel are variables that play a significant role in determining an imperial force's modi operandi as it regards the mass accretion of resources, and therefore, socioeconomic, and military capabilities. In the case of Rome, it was more partial to exerting influence semi-autonomous client kings, the so-called "friends of the Roman people" by the Roman Senate. To that extent, the Romans were in the habit of supplying these a priori mentioned client monarchs with direct coin payments, and seldom material goods, helping them to remain in power. In this regard, the Romanum imperium should be lauded for its lack of duplicity relating to their ambition of control and dominance, through an administrative grid, imposing their rule over a multitudinous populace, diversely structured local settlements and cultures.

In one regard, and as it relates to the mainstream media institutions in a highly communicative world, much like imperial Rome, the US in a need to justify its foreign policy, in our contemporary era of human rights advocacy and an affinity towards activism, find themselves calling upon higher virtues, as well as national values not harmful to their main allies, in a concerted attempt at winning support. That democracy, and the "exceptionalism" of a predestinated freedom loving nation, as the best chanced for maintaining peace, freedom and order in the world, is something long evidenced in US foreign policy since the beginning of the twentieth century. Perhaps the most effective tool is the relevance of a certain presidential policy, linked to a war or meddled action, as necessary for the security of the nation, of which is embodied in the Patriot Act in the wake of the September 11 attacks in 2001.[8] Hence to win the hearts and minds of the people, more importantly at home, and to a lesser extent abroad, there exists a need to use vague and ideological language, with the thematic uttering related to "American exceptionalism", and democracy, and freedom, and even constructions of "good vs. evil" rhetoric. As shows recent history, for forty years a dichotomy of starkly black/white was the cliché of the détente between the United States and the Soviet Union.[9] Although the nature of mainstream media institutions will be the focal point in furthering our discussion, of class or socioeconomic antagonisms, for the moment, I wish to simply make note of an example that bespeaks of a method, among many, of power struggles, fought on ideological grounds. In retrospect, the revelations that spawned from the Chilcot Inquiry in London of 2010, pertaining to the investigation of the Blair government, and its responsibilities towards the contributing of fabricated evidence of Saddam Hussein's possession of weapons of mass destruction. Indeed, to remain within the legal bounds mandated upon the US by its Senate, granting the US military permission to wage war against the perpetrators of the 9-11 attack, and their affiliates; the investigation in London subverted the a priori justification and fraudulent evidence of Saddam colluding with bin Laden. My point being that, in retrospect, one is forced to question the integrity of American and Western investigative journalism, and the extent to which they've failed to mitigate and rebalance the scale of inequality. The Chilcot Inquiry's revelations, among many other, yet less known publications, attest to the ostensibly seen, spoken and heard of conclusions, by an increasingly weary and aware global public, in pointing the finger at closely linked ties between the interests of the press in the West, and that of politicians, than the tether biding the citizens said media institutions are duty bound to inform. That the armed intervention in Iraq was illegal as it regards to principles of international law, is scarcely made mention of in the influential arenas of public discussion. Evidently, international legal bodies under the purview of the wealthier nations of the world, have, as they're purpose, not the genuine reprimanding of all rule breakers, but, collectively, these institutions act as a global apparatus for maintaining the socioeconomic status quo. The aforementioned illegality is severe in and of its own, regardless of the scant professionalism of western media organizations, and the plethora of lies they propagated in supplement to the manipulation of information. It is often readily forgotten that Saddam Hussein, at one point, was not only considered an ally by the West, but was mounted onto the pinnacle of Iraqi elite society, by influences closely tied to the interests of US and other Western Capitalist elites, and their respective state apparatuses which sustain their entrenched socioeconomic positions. So far, despite the cruelty with which Saddam Hussein ruled, and the carnage he brewed, his death came about under unjust circumstances. Iraq, once a promising milieu, counted among the ranks of the more modernized Muslim countries in the 1970s, and boasting a literacy rate of 74 percent, is now a desolate country, a society left in shambles, and a hotbed for unruliness and radical living. Of course, societal collapse was well underway by the time that the concerned western countries invaded Iraq, in violation of both human rights for the average Iraqi and international law, in relation to subverting a country's sovereignty.[10]

The US, as a republic, although having various and other reasons for pursuing its foreign policy, in a manner further discussed, in both later segments of the present chapter as well as the subsequent chapter; behaves much as Rome during its period as a de facto empire. The period that marked Rome's greatest imperial expansion took place during its days a republic. As such, constricting our attention to only the late republic, ignoring middle and early periods, Rome came into possession of Greece, significant portions of Spain, Libya, Gaul, Syria, Numidia, the Balkans, and extensive lands in Asia Minor. "Where the early republican leaders were initially reluctant to make their annexations permanent, after the civil war of 81 b.c., ambitious senators and military men often seized territory to further personal ambitions."[11] Not unlike in today's global society, particularly focusing on elite circles in the US, despite reluctance from the buffering agent of societal antagonisms, or the state apparatus; these true rulers of society, in pursuit of further aggrandizing their personal prestige, lurk behind the veneer of state legitimacy. Much like the duplicity of the West, in that the rhetoric often diverges from the observed actions, reflected upon which, are the perceptions of Roman civilization from the social location of the prevailing 20th century ideologies; portrayed and lauded the egalitarian virtues of the Roman Republic. However, that popular history extensively mentions Roman egalitarianism, relative to the rapacious plunder and fighting bespeaks more about our society than of the Romans. For me, that at least 1.5 million enemies were slain between 509 b.c. and 19 b.c., alludes to the extent to which violence was practice, and instability revealed as a truer fact of life, more than a conceptualization of an almost equal, or democratic society.[12] Our perception and narration of the Roman Republic, focusing most on their 'egalitarian' practices, is a reflection of the workings of the collective sub-conscious of our western societies. Our rhetoric and discursive arenas are replete with the mention of themes, along the lines of promoting democracy, and freedom and peace, yet our belligerent actions countervail such aspirations, and are furthermore alluded to much less.

"*Historians of empire often equated this Romanization with the twentieth-century concepts of modernization and westernization on the assumption that it entailed the progression from barbarism to civilization.*"[13] However, of note is that at the elite level, subjected and conquered peoples learned Latin, adopted the mannerisms of their Roman patrons, going so far as imitating Greco-Roman architecture and perceptions of beauty, as well as substantially partaking in the purchase of Roman products. What is however missed, whether purposely or as a consequence of constricted viewing due to locked-in paradigms, is the acknowledgement that Romanization did not entail the dominion of one culture over the other, due to "exceptionalism" or inherent superiority, more than it was an acceptance of Roman authority. Imperial Roman society never was uniform at the grassroots level, and exploitation of the masses by their respective local elites turned the wheels of empire.[14] Hence, much like the justifications brought to the van by historical apologists of western imperialism, in general, and US hegemonic expansion in particular, Roman imperial apologists likewise overlook the exploitation, a taking advantage of not unlike the US' and that of other nations' track record; in favor of lauding the 'civilizing', and material benefits 'gifted' to the relative few over the majority. Thus, the supposed and proposed reasons for intervening abroad have changed since imperial Rome, yet the paradigms that encouraged inequality in favor of accelerated wealth gain, are still evident, and in fact inherent in global Capitalism, as it manifests itself today. These aforementioned imperial apologists make it a point to assert the seldom occurrence in the historical account, of educated slaves, and also how freedmen had taken possession of significant positions of authority in the Imperial home. Manumitted slaves, according to apologists, were more than worth mention, they exemplified the high probability for upward mobility, at all levels of the socioeconomic stratum, thus attesting to the success of Romanization (in reference to its inclusiveness) and its affinity for democracy.

"*...enslavement did not mean permanent stigmatization in the modern sense, and Pertinax, who became emperor in the late second century a.d., was the son of a freedman. Yet these were exceptional cases, for the vast majority of Roman slaves were the meanest type of manual laborers.*"[15]

The Britons, under the yoke of Roman imperial dominion, were settlers of a land, which collectively, amounted to the least contributing region/province in the Western Roman Empire, as is evidenced by the relatively meager returns reaped. Yet still more, alluding to the need for some form of legitimacy in the eyes of the British people and the world alike, for its imperial global expansion; the British state apparatus allowed for the institutionalize figuring of Roman Britain, often in a prominent manner, among Anglophones' historical recounting. The aforementioned circulation of such a notion, places significance on the contribution of an inherited Roman legacy; of Romanized Britain as an enlightening happenstance in the nation's history, the predestined beginnings of much a larger destiny. For some, the linkage of select parts of their history to further certain "truths," permits for the pretence of Great Britain as direct heirs of the glorious Roman Empire. Contrary to widely held notions, the Roman period as a feature of British history was not as enlightening, nor as uplifting, or as influential as modern imperial loyalists conceptualize. Greco-Roman classical sources when referring to the inhabitants of Britannia did so disparagingly, depicting Britons as well suited models for imperial subjugation. For the Romans, these peoples on the outskirts of empire were giant forest dwellers, barbarians who, according to Strabo, had "no experience in gardening or other agricultural pursuits." The patronizing perceptions of the early British settlements by the Romans lingered, in spite of Caesar's visit and recognition that the southern "tribes" were more cultured or civilized, as a result of their contacts with the more developed continental Gaul. Conversely, Caesar also defined the Northerners of Britannia as brutal and savage-like tribesmen, living exclusively on the meat of reared animals and their milk, tribesmen who, bafflingly, shared their wives and dyed themselves blue in preparation of war.[16]

*"For Roman authors and readers, Britain was an alien, exotic land that was literally beyond the known world. The English Channel was no mere maritime body. It was "Ocean," a watery boundary that marked the limits of civilization... In Roman eyes they were a different order of humanity that deserved conquest."*[17]

# Democracy Promotion
## (Fueling the Global Socioeconomic Inequality)

Across the board, the observable trend has been the more recent of the strategies of democracy promotion in the Middle East, with the US, in a gradual fashion opting instead to replace a priori supported authoritarian governments, with elite-centered democracies. From a neo-Gramscian perspective (to be later discussed), the shift in US foreign policy can be interpreted as movement from more coercive to more consensual implementations of social control. The idea is that, in a globalized and highly connected world-community, the a priori mentioned form of control ensures for a more lasting version of stability for the respective, concerned states in the region. Of course, though the consensual form of hegemonic rule is not a precedent in US foreign policy, evidenced in earlier times in Latin America, the manner of its implementation on a large scale is novel, as it regards to US-Middle-Eastern sociopolitical and socioeconomic relations. Although Gramscian ideologies will be later touched upon, momentarily, it calls out to me to, in passing, point out and state that; the desired aims of US foreign policy strategy is the attainment of a Gramscian-styled hegemony. The predominant Gramscian or cultural hegemony imposed on most Middle-Eastern societies, by the US, largely entails the internalization of the US' ever varying variant of 'democracy', as the natural order. To ensure stability and protect US interests, the western hegemonic power has, throughout the twentieth century, long relied on authoritarian regimes and governments to maintain control. In the early 1980s, however, a reassessment by the United States of the habituated posture abroad, marked the shift away from support for dictatorial societal rule, in favor of an ostensibly more democratic order.[18] The general preferred direction of the global society, judging from the actions the state apparatus has both, consensually and coercively ceded, could in my view, be conceived as working towards a twofold purpose. The first purpose or desired effect of elite-imposed US foreign policy is to preserve stability in the Middle-Eastern countries of concern, thus, to assert control, at both the state (governmental) level, and for the wider society. The United States of America has sought to maintain several interests, among which range from economic, political, and military concerns, peculiar to each country subject to US intervention or influence. A good example of the importance placed on stability can be viewed through the lens, and rhetoric projected by 'free market' economic ideologies, a significant concern for the global capitalists; that is, the preservation of the status quo system of wealth creation, for them, the few, at great expense to the 'others', the many. In the 1980s, in support of what was to be later partially accredited to the demise of the Soviet Union's communistic hold, on large swaths of the world, consensual and 'democratic' forms of control of distant lands was the opted strategy for the US, champions of the USSR killing liberal free-market economics. Democracy, as was strategically claimed by US and western European Capitalist elites, was the inherent societal structure, which permitted for conditions conducive to free-market economics, as such, allowed for freedom, prosperity and happiness to reign. The elite-based democracy that predominantly replaced the previously backed proxy-authoritarian modi operandi, the former rule entailing "a system in which a small group actually rules and mass participation in decision-making is confined to leadership choice in elections carefully managed by competing elites".[19] Therefore, the elite-based democratic form of rule incorporates consensual means of governance, and more than the authoritative rule, is likely to engender popular support, both for the populaces of the US and the conquered, a nuanced form of US interest pursuit abroad, one which ensures enduring stability. As it regards US policy in the Middle-East, having the first purpose of US/Western-elitist hegemonic consolidation as stability; politically, economically, militarily or otherwise, the second aim of US foreign policy, as seen contemporarily, is the achievement of hegemony in a Gramscian manner. The aforementioned hegemonic manifestation, can be said to have worked successfully only once promoted ideologies are internalized, and largely welcomed as 'natural' by society, the very society upon whose consent a Gramscian/cultural hegemony is dependent.

As far back as the Wilson administration in the earlier part of the last century, even as recent as the Ronald Reagan era, the ideological push towards 'democracy' rose into prominence, as a guiding principle of US international policy; invoking vague contextualization of our sense for "freedom" and the need to vanquish the "evil empire", the USSR.[20] An institutional branch of the Federal Government, the National Endowment for Democracy (NED) first appeared on the scene during the Reagan administration. The NED, an institutionalized body, pursuant to the interests of US elite-backed global Capitalism, implemented reforms in conjunction with the "infrastructure of democracy" that it set out to erect. Not long after the introduction of the NED into the public discursive sphere, were reform initiatives implemented in several countries, among which were the Philippines, Poland and Chile. The National Endowment for Democracy, as an elite apparatus, comes instated at a time when it is realized by the ruling circles that the preservation of the status quo, necessitated the disregard and disuse of coercive and authoritarian governments, a form of past rule that was in the long run unsustainable, or sooner prone to destabilizing revolutionary movements. Carl Gershman, president of the NED, I believe, made the case clear in 1986 when stating that:

"*In a world of advanced communication and exploding knowledge, it is no longer possible to rely solely on force to promote stability and defend the national security. Persuasion is increasingly important, and the United States must enhance its capacity to persuade by developing techniques for reaching people at many different levels.*"[21]

According to Gershman's argument, it was through the promotion of US-variant democracy abroad that the US, and indeed one may just as well make complicit its allies in Western European; would "enhance its capacity to persuade". No different from his predecessors was George H. W. Bush, who as a result of soviet collapse, needed to take a more pragmatic position than Reagan's ideologically charged administration. However, the global elites, mostly 'based' in the US, had already decreed the adoption of a certain order or template to be followed, thus Bush, though more pragmatic than Reagan, was circumscribed to a prescribed sociopolitical and socioeconomic framework, leaving little room for variations in new policies in relation to those of the past decade. William Robinson goes on to notice, and point out that US state mounted programs for the promotion of democracy, as evidenced between 1984 and 1992, entailed the erection by the NED of said programs in 109 countries around the world. Of the aforementioned 109 countries having succumbed to US democracy promotion initiatives, 30 of these are in Africa, 24 in Asia, 21 countries in Central and Eastern Europe (former USSR states included), as well as 8 and 26 countries from the Middle-East and Latin America & the Caribbean respectively.[22]

The representative democracy practiced by the United States, once a major sociopolitical factor in checking and balancing power distributions within the nation, now, and going back to at least the last century; it has seen its clout gradually diminish. As such, the rhetoric of democracy promotion by the US about itself is coherent and complimentary to the discursive of democracy they promote abroad. As mentioned several times prior, the evidenced policies practiced by the US, at home and abroad, differ sometimes markedly from the pragmatic rhetoric which appears in the intellectual discursive, let alone the idealistic aspirations of what democracy ought to be. To the extent that the talk of democracy, in the intellectual discursive, in the US parallels rhetoric on foreign policy democracy promotion, the same comparative attributions could be concluded of US divergent and hypocritical practices of democracy at home as abroad. Since the 1980s, the predominant economic version practiced globally has attested towards the loss of state power to the global capitalist elites, as could be evidenced throughout the workings of America, as in the significance of presidential campaign financing. Therefore, consistent with the foreign policy of 'democracy promotion' of his predecessors, even in his turn, President Bill Clinton upon assuming office, made known 'his' vision for the post-Cold War; a uni-polar international system, with mention of the need for "democratic enlargement".[23] In fact, it was the Clinton administration that coined the term "market democracy", and thus begun the emphasis by institutionalized state and private entities on the intrinsic relationship linking free markets and democracy/democratic governments. The collapse of the Soviet Union was a milestone for the newly forming neo-liberal economics championed by the West, it thus became a truism that democracy and the development of democratic governments, was contingent on the free markets. The effect of coupling free market economics with democracy, now amidst the absence of any contention from any other ideology considered as valid, has been establish broad parameters for the post-1991 ideological contextualization of the world. To the extent that the aforementioned contextualization is malleable and porous, the 9/11 attacks under G.W. Bush became the underlying reason for democracy promotion programs around the world, in general, and the Middle East in particular. The amount of funds provided for these a prior mentioned democracy promotion programs bespeaks of the extent to which global stability, of civil society and the government, is taken seriously by the political elites and their economic elitist counterparts. Under the Bush administration, after the tragic 9/11 attacks, funding for democracy promotion programs increased from $500 million annually in 2000, to approximately $1 billion in 2004. The amount of funds flooding US-state backed programs for democracy promotion was almost $2 billion in 2005, indeed, including spending in Afghanistan and Iraq.[24]

*"The G.W. Bush administration took the advocacy of political reform to unprecedented heights, situating it in the only region so far immune to previous 'waves' of democracy, the Middle East...The US came to regard the Middle East as a vital sphere of interest at the end of the Second World War, motivated initially by the presence of oil, and later by a key ally in Israel. It consolidated its position as the predominant external power in the aftermath of the Suez Canal Crisis of 1956."*[25]

Since then, I believe, the US has come to relate to and regard the Middle East, in almost as comparable a fashion to the degree of penetration by the US into Latin American society, America's backyard, and former testing grounds for democracy promotion initiatives and experimentations on societal revolutions and reforms.

Latin America provides a favorable context for one or two measure of comparisons, of US practices of foreign policy elsewhere in the world, and hints at the underlying motives of socioeconomic elites, both locally and as it regards the pursuit of global clout-bearing interests. The aforementioned comparisons, it should be noted, should be undertaken within a broader context, especially as the strategy unfolding in the Middle-East is still in its stages of infancy. For a significantly longer time than the current period of global 'democratization', the US favored authoritarian regimes both during the initial stages of penetration into Latin American society, as was evidenced of their actions in the Middle East in times past. Indeed, authoritarian regimes were favored as the effective guarantors of stability in Latin America, South East Asia, the Middle East, and the world around. As was argued by National Intelligence Council chairman, Graham Fuller; "democratization is not on the American agenda in the Middle East...Washington finds it more efficient to support a range of dictators across the Arab world as long as they conform to US foreign policy needs."[26]

*"...it is a common fallacy that holds that the US has had little to no interest in promoting democracy in the contemporary Middle East. Time and again, particularly in the face of popular opposition and the prospect of instability, the US has abandoned authoritarian allies in favor of transitions to elite-based democracy- the Philippines, Chile and Panama are all cases in point."*[27]

The backing or encouragement, by the US, of transitions towards elite-based democratic forms of control, largely owes itself to the viability/probability of such a strategy as a success, as it relates to the domestic political atmosphere in the foreign society of interest. As such, the chances of such elite-based democracies succeeding, is centrally dependent upon potential political and influential actors (religious or otherwise), conducive to the US' power consolidation through the ballot box. The Clinton administration was, for me, the point that marked the moment from whence the US increasingly begun placing emphasis on democracy being contingent upon liberal free market reforms and practices. It was believed that following the aforementioned prerequisite Western economic edicts would translate to a new era, ushering in a time and realm where political, economic, and as such, social stability reigned supreme. When Clinton was at the helm of US political machinery, the doctrine followed involved the accentuated promotion of economic initiatives in the region, in support of the much favored "increase in growth rate" and similar proxies for economic evaluation; done so, in the belief that alongside the externally motivate cultivation of civil society, political reform would readily, though eventually be implemented. One may readily conclude that free-market based democracy, exported by the US, changed in foreign policy, especially as it relates to the Middle East under the G.W. Bush administration. Yet, the same implemented policies from the Reagan administration all through to the Obama administration; are evidenced, and aforementioned in this section, accompanied by rhetoric imbued with systematic advocacy for democracy abroad. Despite the ostensible deviation from the initiatives that champion democracy abroad, due to the belligerent military stance, taken by the Bush administration in the wake of the September 11 attacks; the penetration into Iraq and Afghanistan drew significantly on the traditional premises of economic and political reforms, as effective methods, and key contributors to US national security.

For most advocates of the application of liberal economic principles in conjunction with 'democracy', the West is often reinterpreted as a culture having undertaken linear progression, leading these societies into achieved desired purpose; the liberal democratic model. To the extent that the liberal democratic model is championed by the wealthy western nations, it accounts for the exclusion of democracy from undergoing critical interrogation, or constant re-evaluation as to the credibility of its evidenced benefits, compared to the downturns inflicted by the devices of said policy on the societies of concern. After all, who in their right mind would be against democracy? As such, the question that arises in the discursive realm on democracy is one of "how" best to champion and export it, rather than inquisitions on "why" or "whether", such policies, with respect to each society, are amenable to the majority of the people.[28] In most observable cases, the intelligentsia, or scholars of the world have digressed from investigative templates, ones which would allow for the two a priori mentioned "why" or "whether" structured questioning. Of course, not all scholarly accounts are restricted to the mono-template of "how". Robert Dahl voiced his perceived distinctions, "between democracy as an ideal system and the institutional arrangements that have come to be regarded as a kind of imperfect approximation of an ideal."[29] One such other eccentric, yet well respected thinker is William Robinson, who endeavors to analyze US foreign policy, or democracy promotion as it regards Philippines, Haiti, Nicaragua and Chile, under the strobe light of Gramscian theory (consensual cultural hegemony). Unlike most scholars of his time, Robinson went so far as to expose what he saw as global transnational elites, pursuant to interests of little benefit to the national society. However, on a vast scale, the scholarly literature shaping society's direction, fails to situate democracy cloaked in liberalism, as a universal ideology. Liberal democracy, as contemporarily championed, is, after all, a western construction, despite its abstraction and subsequent universal characterization. Best exploring the above stated notion is Fukuyama, in his reference to "the universalization of Western liberal democracy as the final form of human government."[30] In contention to seeing democracy as an essence only suited to a particular framework, Larbi Sadiki argues for an "Arab" variant of democracy, one not necessarily congruent with Western dogmas, norms and values, especially as it regards the use of capitalism as a founding or prerequisite precept.[31]

"*[I intend] not to say the literature has been uncritical of US [-Middle-Eastern]…policy, far from it, but rather that as elsewhere, it has failed to critically interrogate the strategy of democracy promotion…Adopting an institutional definition of democracy, the academy has for the most part sought to facilitate its diffusion in the region.*"[32]

# Cultural Hegemony

Extensively demonstrated and relatively profusely discussed in Marxist theory, as well as the subsequent analysis by Antonio Gramsci, is the concept of the rule of one culture over another. Since then, several other notable scholars have approached and furthered the notions of consensual control or rule. However, as for Gramsci, he provided a generalized and encompassing definition of what he perceives hegemony to be. Gramsci describes hegemony as "the 'spontaneous' consent given by the great masses of the population to the general direction imposed on social life by the dominant fundamental group."[33] For Gramsci this deliberate giving away of power to the elites was a form of perk, he attached this to the world of production, whereby a wealthy minority gained confidence and sociopolitical prestige within the society. The idea that cultivates and supports Gramsci's rendition of hegemony, and that of other cultural contemporary publications; is predicated on social contracts that run deeper than the state's social cohesive capabilities. As such, enmeshed in the strategy of control is a subconscious social agreement, of significant enough clout to counteract the varied divisiveness and antagonisms, this maintenance of the status quo happens on an ideological platform. One should be cognizant of the ideological struggle to win over the hearts and minds of the global population. Therefore, it is in the normalizing of elitist propagated and often antiquated norms, beliefs, perceptions, and values that support and continue to shape the structures of central authority, and thus, to add constant fuel to the engine of socioeconomic inequality.[34]

Contemporarily, Dionysis Markakis has made an extensive rendition of Gramscian theoretical framework, as a precedent, adapting or superimposing the ideational framework onto US democracy promotional tactics in the Middle East.[35] Markakis' approach proposes venturing beyond the notion of security, however valid the fear, as well as the materialistic analyses (the hunt for resources), and in spite of such analyses extensively featuring in the literature. Instead, the different prism of view, and as according to Gramscian theory, should be situated in civil society. That is to say, as it regards the US' promotion of democracy in the Middle-East; by enveloping the promotion of democracy in several other prerequisite qualifications and policies- of an economic, a political and cultural persuasion- control of civil society can be attained. Therefore, US foreign policy seeks to strategically "penetrate not just the state, but civil society...and from therein exercise control."[36] In this regard, it becomes easily observable once aware of civil penetrations, that civil society, or its consent, is the central desired output of US democracy promotional programs globally. A shift in US foreign policy strategy is hence perceivable, with the move away from support for authoritarian regimes abroad, the shift to elite-based democratic rule thus ushered in instituted reforms, from not only above the societal cage, but likewise from within civil society, moving away from the prior practice of solely top-down forms of asserting control. The reason of my and other contemporary scholars' interest in the Middle-East as it regards American foreign policy is, in small part, owed to the region's relative imperviousness to the process of democratization, which has so characterized the rest of the world in the modern period. That the Middle East remains to this day a vital locus of the US' and the West's geo-strategic aspirations, is abundant throughout academia, and the local 9 pm news alike, however, the reasons that necessitate US and Western intervention in the region is, in my view, insufficiently explored, and within a limiting pre-established framework if extensively covered. From all appearances, the Middle East is currently undergoing, and has for the last three decades undergone a transitory metamorphosis, in view of the US and Western global elites. It is in our contemporary times that we find the existence of two worlds concomitantly, with one side of the dichotomous view of the Middle East by the US coming in the form of their support for authoritarian regimes. The second manner, in which the Middle East is perceived by the US and its Western allies, is as a fertile terrain for the instituting of a more secure form of control, that is, through infiltration and penetration into the civil societies of the region. Successful consensual forms of control from the imperializing force can be evidenced once the ideologies, norms and values of that hegemonic force are perceived as: intrinsic to, and congruent with the expectations, values norms and dogmas of the local people. Thus, the masses of persons within the foreign lands must truly believe that the implementation of democratic governments, the principles of liberalism and liberal economics are precepts of their choosing.

*"The Middle East illustrates the fundamental tension posed between America's ongoing relationships with authoritarian governments in the region, in the hope of maintaining the status quo and in particular stability over the short-term, and its desire to encourage political reform and spread of its ideology, so as to ensure a more sound, enduring form of stability over the long-term."*[37]

As in the United States, so abroad; the erecting of institutions and 'non-governmental' organizations at the grass roots level, with actors eager to enmesh their message together with that of big moneyed foreign influences, grasping for the opportunities offered them for amassing wealth or power, or both. NGOs are only a small aspect of asserting consensual control from afar, regardless, these organizations are given leeway due to the good that they do. I mean, why would the devil come off as scary during your initial encounter, he of course, "wears Prada". Predominantly, the erection and reforms of legal institutions and policies, as well as institutionalized political maneuvering (funding one or two or all opposition party campaigns); allows for this hiding in plain sight, and aids in the launching of minority groups' agendas into the fore of societal importance. More on the media's role to aid in this public relational stunt, particular to each audience (region), local, European, African, or American, will be elaborate on in the proceeding chapter. For now, what's of note is the conceptual realization, of the intricate many number of ways that one culture's modes of thinking, their values, norms and dogmas, or rather said, the importance that that ruling society places on economic and political forms of rule, finds itself within and among the subjugated, received and even later championed by these masses.

Throughout the Middle East the trend has been to largely resist the liberal democratic political initiatives, programs and reforms that were consistent with an unbalanced free market economy, which saw to the favorable placement of US and European nations and their elite ruling circles. These US and European elite-backed institutions and corporations were well entrenched and assured in their global socioeconomic position, in matters of trade and capital accretion, resource, speculative or otherwise. Middle Eastern societies, for the most part, as other developing nations in Latin America, Africa, Asia and Eurasia, have made concerted efforts at veering clear of the social and cultural values to which American ideology is beholden. In spite of these aforementioned vilification of American social and cultural values in the religious domain, as the political; elements of what is considered popular culture by Americans, and significant portions of the world, as attributable to the notion of cultural trafficking, have received widespread appeal among populations in urban settlements.[38] American values, are social constructs of theories of morality, of which collectivization of values as 'American', is in fact a product of a dominant group within the society, one which identifies itself as a member within the makeup of communities in society. The dominant group is afforded the prestige, through its established institutions, and a variegation of gradually reformed policies that parallel the interests of the most powerful among them; as such, this group largely dictates the framework for acceptability on all matters moral, political, socioeconomic, religious or otherwise. In possession of the resources and facilities, with which to carry out their strategic acts of power consolidation, the socioeconomically top tiered within US and European societies, both locally and globally, hinder accessibility to the centralized levers of control, denying subjugate groups or individuals the chance to be heard or effectual on a stage where it matters.

*"For the past hundred years, and more especially since 1918, the English-speaking peoples have formed the dominant group in the world; and current theories of international morality and the view that they are consummate international hypocrites may be reduced to the plain fact that the current cannons of international virtue have, by a natural and inevitable process, been mainly created by them."*[39]

Gramscian theories of hegemony, alternately perceive hegemony, less so in rigid terms of one state's dominion over the other, rather offering a more intricate and nuanced interpretation.[40] Gramsci explored further, or more significantly than most of his contemporaries, the distinctions attributable to coercive, as consensual mechanisms of social control. It is worth noting that the use of the more currently favored consensual variant of rule, does aggregate to the exclusive use of such passive, and ideologically centered social controls on the populace. Instead, coercive or violent retaliation is deployed, as a subsidiary measure, when the success of hegemonic practices fails. Once failure arises within a consensually ruled society, that is when the means for mitigating conflicts, within the institutionalized system, that is, within the framework of forums, practices and procedures (e.g. through periodic elections). In Gramsci's words, the strategy in concern could be seen as "hegemony protected by the armor of coercion."[41] How internalization of the dominant global ruling groups ideology is effectuated, through spin and the allure of benevolence, said elite groups "articulate a social vision," one that purports to be subservient to "the interests of all".[42] As such, incentives as socioeconomic opportunity for the people, support for human rights, contingent upon liberal democratic and free market principles, mobilize support from subjugate groups and individuals, precluding any opposition, for lack of an alternative ideology, within the predetermined framework, to sublet the status quo state of affairs. For Gramsci, hegemony is evidenced in a range of forms, that is, from strong to weak forms of hegemonic rule or control. The former incorporates an elevated level of social integration, evidenced by a strong consensual bond between elites and the masses, the US and the United Kingdom being two such examples of strong hegemonic state influences. While, as in the case of Pakistan or Greece, there seems to be little evidenced incorporation of the masses, with the elites instead highly socially integrated.

Some oriental societies attest to the widely held misconception about US and European forms of control, much like the literate person who environed by infestations of advertisements, "pays no attention to ads."; the mere incorporation of western industrial technology, contingent upon its political consequences, hints at the proverbial chips having already fallen. The spiritual, moral and cultural reservations had by those in the orient, towards technology, is non-existent in the realm, or on the level of opinions or concepts, instead, the incorporation of external technology only under certain socioeconomic and sociopolitical restraints, works towards altering patterns of perception, gradually, and thus effortlessly shifting our ratios of sense; our paradigms.[43]

> **"**In all societies…two classes of people appear- a class that rules and a class that is ruled…The first class, always the less numerous, performs all political functions, monopolizes power and enjoys the advantages that power brings, whereas the second, the more numerous class, is directed and controlled by the first, in a manner that is more or less legal, now more or less arbitrary and violent.**"** - Gaetano Mosca

## Societal Sell-Out and the Legal System
## (Triumph of the Contract)

The emphasis and weight placed on the legitimacy, and sometimes infallibility of the legal contract, backed and mediated by the grounded belief in the impartiality of the legal system, has been a gradual reform dating back centuries. As with democracy promotion discussed in the prior section, it is in the interests of the global socioeconomic elites to standardize or align institutions, and civil systems. The systematic standardization of economic, and political, and even cultural institutions and assimilated norms and values, a movement all global societies are ostensibly heading towards. Of course, as was discussed, as it regards cultural exchange, the subjugated societies have a reciprocal influence on the domineering influence. Therefore, even though a standardized and fully integrated global economic order dances to the tune the elites play for their own pleasures, to some extent, a negotiation of the terms and conditions takes place between local elites, and the intruding larger force wishing to impose its institutional modus operandi, inclusive of which is the coercing of the marginalized to commit, as signatories, to the rule of international bodies, as the ICC. Or be ensnared by economic debt and the lingering presence of imposed austerity by grand monetary institutions, which set the trends and propose the course that nations should take; by definition, they define the geo-political atmosphere. Still more, the influence of one society, or one group of elites over another society, or its elites, is not effectuated in a single direction. The reciprocal influence or the interplay of power struggles on display is one where, the dominant force has to concede some ground to the local elites and/or the fervent incessant demands for change from the larger population. This allows for a more smooth sailing state of affairs, in short; stability. An example of one form of concession having arisen between banking elites in the West, and those of the Middle-East is the use of Islamic banking system. Granted, this form of banking is unique and common to Islamic majority countries, as a form of slight defiance to the occidental culture, several authors have attested to the little difference in divergence between the several practices of Islamic banking, and the diverse yet, as with the former, narrowly circumscribed framework evident in occidental societies. The relatively narrow constraints placed upon what is deemed as acceptable practice and policy, aids towards standardization and continual calibration of a socioeconomic order. With the advent of international legal bodies, most notably the International Criminal Court, there has been an emphasis placed on the law, particularly with regard to its inherent properties as credible, impartial, and infallible. The judicial and legal systems, both locally and on an international order, have in fact grown into their role of institutions for elitist power projection and protection, more especially in the last century.

Morton J. Horwitz, a prominent American legal historiographer, and Law professor at the Harvard Law School, endeavored, in a manner almost unprecedented, with shrewdly lent focus, on the deconstruction and examination of nineteenth-century American legal ideology. However piece meal Horwitz's developments and perspective were, in a deconstructionist sense, in "The Transformation of American Law", his efforts bespoke a different tale. Horwitz's examinations and research, in his concluding chapter "The Rise of Legal Formalism", led the astute thinker to observe that, "the special power of the legal profession in American society has always been grounded in some theory of distinctively objective and autonomous nature of the law." Furthermore, he pointed out, and I believe rightly, that for him factions of the antebellum legal theory, boldly advanced a 'formula' or equation of law and science, while in actuality systematizing and classifying, in a manner that prevents coherence of content (hiding inconsistencies) and method. In effect, a chasm separates the society into factions that speak different languages from one another, with institutional checks and balances within this framework contributing to a pile up of processes, the evidenced time it takes to institute reforms not complimentary to elite interests. The intended purpose, Horwitz believes is to separate "politics from law, subjectivity from objectivity, and laymen's reasoning from professional reasoning".[44]

*"This combination of pretense and genuine concern to root the law in "science" produced some extraordinary results which expose the reigning ideological biases and raise complex questions about the influence of the law on economic theory."*[45]

Indeed, Horwitz points out how G.C, Verplanck, among other prominent scholars and influential, institutional legal trend setters, be given the stage highest stage to do so, propagated theories counter to traditional modes and doctrinal conceptions of the law. A priori, the legal traditional doctrines were predicated on an objective theory of valuing commodities, and allowed for contracts to be justly substantiated. However, the preeminence of a focus on economic science, and as such, a subjective approach of valuing, contingent upon individual and distinct desires as the deciding principle to evaluation; a more substantive approach is followed as it regards the judicial substantiation of contracts. As such, as with the three brunches of the government, although not having had started with partiality towards the elite, a gramscian approach of consensual control was utilized by the latter to gradually gain ground over the latter. Among several factors, as the influencing of political actors, and successful lobbying tactics, for example, the adaptation and enforcement by socioeconomic global elites in the US, of a subjective manner of adjudicating value within the judicial system, brings in line, the law with the interest these elites.[46] Eugene D. Genovese, in his review of Horwitz's "The Transformation of American Law, 1780-1860", attributes the aligning of elite "commercial interests" with the legal community's view, bespoken of by Horwitz, as:

"...[meaning] *much more than that the law simply was swinging into line with the emerging economic rationale of the world market. The victory of economic subjectivism at law enormously strengthened its supporters within the economics profession itself. The ideological struggle within the legal profession may well have had as great an impact upon economic thought appealing to the newly prevailing subjectivism of legal doctrine...*"[47]

Therefore, the adoption of occidental industrial technologies, by oriental cultures in the twentieth century, was also a move towards systematic approaches, or a methodological yet standardized mode of thought and ingenuity, allowing for readier assimilation of Western values, as the gradual reliance on contracts and the 'scientific' nature of the law.

The father of the Austrian republic, promoted these emergent ideologies, maintaining the faith in the scientific nature of the law, and legal procedures, asserting that "there is no equality outside society in a fictitious pre-social state. Equality", he maintains, "is a creation of law and society". For proponents of subjective evaluation of judiciary and legal systems, in particular as it regards the contract, there was a push for an ideology that could work towards undergirding the notions of liberal freedom. The form of liberties pushed for was of the individual, however, maintaining that freedom can only be achieved through law, predicated, of course, on the assumption that the law is infallible, or at least close to, needing only minor reforms here and there. With the freedom of individuals, much as the efforts to uphold rights for all humans, this freedom becomes less meaningful the lower the global-socioeconomic scale one ventures. Therefore, the question to be posed becomes not so much one of development than, as pointed out by Horwitz, the kind of development.

> "...*since even workers and farmers...accepted a developmental perspective while having as yet no model of their own, they fell under the hegemony of a legal system committed to the enhancement of commercial interests.*"[48]

As such the ownership of private property, and individual wealth, along with the emphasis on the contract was not only followed through, but with dashing enthusiasm. The focus now should be lent towards deciphering the extent to which the varying socioeconomic interest groups, in a move for power consolidation, launched a consistent and protracted assault on traditional relational concepts between freedom, individual property rights, and social security.

Horwitz maintains that as far back as the seventeenth century, the legal undertakings emergent were underpinned by a reformulation of notions, concepts, in effect doctrines of common law. In his view, the socioeconomically influential within US society were gradually spared the heart-wrenches of subservience to the legal system, with commercial profits deemed beneficial, and in fact as the sole essence for all upper-middle and elite classes (among whose ranks some legal and judicial professionals were a part). For Horwitz, in reference to these "commercial interests", the reforms implemented upon doctrines of common law, would amount to the creation of "...immunities from legal liability and thereby...provide substantial subsidies for those who undertook schemes of economic development".[49] Most importantly, at least for me, Horwitz makes mention of the capitalist ideology that reshaped the paradigms of social construction, what he terms as the "triumph of contract". No longer was inheritance group related, by this I mean; the notions of "inherent justice" or "intrinsic value" were subverted by a "will theory of contract". It is the aggregation of the most nuanced concepts of societal perceptions and values, as well as the scale of importance placed on other socially constructed, and as such, fictitious paradigms which amount to the subversion of a priori norms. As of the first half of the nineteenth century, and in the words of Horwitz, "all economic relationships" were redefined "in terms of contract". He opined that the first half of the nineteenth century was the turning point, when "all economic relationships" were reformed and restated "in terms of contract", the very contract which, for him, bespoke of a "market conception of legal relations...[whereby] all pre-existing legal duties were inevitably subordinated to the contract relation."

## WALLS

The shift towards ridding society of the former civil relations, of a more trusting substance, in favor of interpersonal commercial and private relations (e.g. marital contracts) mediated fully, and solely, by the law. In effect, judges and the judiciary order elevated the social construction or "paradigm of contract to its supreme place in nineteenth century legal thought."[50] The establishment of a system of law that was predicated on the capitalist economic order, during the heyday of the slave societies in the New World, was one that followed a subjective approach. Thus, the reliance on contracts, and with economic incentives for a few infecting the legal system; these modes of civil relations through legal mediation were soon wrought with contradictory ideologies. On one side of the coin, the featured prominence of contracts in the legal system, although lacking in substantive action, speaks of and alludes to notions of freedom and equality. On the other face of the aforementioned proverbial coin, "there is the perplexity of property in persons, of commerce in human beings, and of human chattel equated with inanimate things."[51] Hence, one would not be misguided, I believe, in questioning the very precepts that undergird our subjective ratings of value within the legal framework. No longer objectively weighing matters and concepts, it is easy for such 'standardized'/calibrated or in-sync institutions of law (or even as regards the politics of the land) to succumb to the interests of the socioeconomic elites.

# The
# Military-Industrial
## Complex

*Every gun that is made, every warship launched, every rocket fired signifies, in the final sense, a theft from those who hunger and are not fed, those who are cold and are not clothed. This world in arms is not spending money alone. It is spending the sweat of its laborers, the genius of its scientists, the hopes of its children.* - Dwight D. Eisenhower, April 1953

The notion that an influential circle of a few, within a local society, say the US for example, dictate the military direction taken by a nation, either through policies of detente or belligerent confrontation (boots on the ground), or otherwise, is of no novelty. To better accentuate the rough sketch that this book is intended to portray, a brief discussion must be undertaken, on militarism, power elites, and the institutionalized economic elements fueling technological innovation and progress. Indeed, the world of generals and incessant trivial wars is one of several platforms upon which the vying for power takes place, between elite circles or individuals. Apart from a few needles in haystacks in a barn, dominating the literature on the military industrial complex (MIC) is the support for situating, on the widely accepted timeline of the modern human story, the dating of the origins of the MIC as no earlier than WWII. Particularly, it is widely purported by analysts and other pundits, although wrongly, as I will show, that the Cold War period under the political leadership of the Eisenhower administration was the flare in the sky, which signaled the initial point at which the conception of the MIC on the timeline of the human story was realized. Indeed, the order of the day for contemporary scholars, as it regards their portrayal of the MIC, has been the pursuit of a framework laid down by C. Wright Mills. Mills formulated and spoke of a model whereby elites, whom he referred to as "power elites", influential persons, forming informal groups and ties, and having their interests aligned with high levels of defense or military spending. Almost every attempt at analyzing and defining the MIC in the scholarly literature can be deconstructed into bespeaking of two paradigms. Namely, the first of these paradigms can be labeled as the functional form, on which rests scholars' depictions and analyses of the MIC, while the second, we may tag as the structural form/paradigm that animates discussions. According to the structural standpoint that scholars assume, as it regards the incentives or drivers that sustain, promote and initiate the interplay of several institutions linked to the military, some of which are industrial; the debate still rages on as to whether the culpable segment of the MIC is the military, or business (commercial interested), or political elites. Hence, within this functional paradigm of the origins of the MIC, and its driving force/reason d'être, almost every scholar agrees with the notion of influential persons/elites, although not in full control, as manipulators of the public's perceptions, for purposes of instituting a war-like and on-edge atmosphere. Patriotism, issues pertaining to the nation's security and the need for readiness, faced with an external foe, as communism or the USSR, or simply terrorism (i.e. warring against a fear tactic); these are public perception changers that have been relatively effective in the past. Conversely, the second of the aforementioned paradigms that predominates the literature on the MIC, and what we termed as the structural form, or standpoint from which to view civil society; is a view centered on bureaucratic principles, as complimentary to the elite interest groups. Yet in rapport with the main postulates of this brief discursive undertaking, and in step with Thorstein Veblen's broad definition of what he deemed as an institution; the structural as the functional forms of perceiving the MIC can be seen as composite pieces of a bigger institutional puzzle. In spite of the antagonisms within both the bureaucratic framework and the elite circles of the socioeconomically opulent, the military cadre, and the political personalities; the systemization of life for the disenfranchised, as seen from a quotidian level, is the embodiment of institutional. I predicate the insignificance that I attach to antagonisms within elite circles of the political, commercial, military or other such domains, on the notion that social constructs, which institutions are, grow into animals in their own rights. Complimenting the aforementioned post-modern school of thought is the notion of reciprocal influence between the dominant and subject groups or individuals, previously discussed in the first half of this chapter. Thorstein Veblen sees an institution as behavior or a mental construct that finds itself well entrenched within a culture.[52]

The military industrial complex, thus, can be portrayed and even defined as an amalgamation of institutions, as with any other in society, and much like orchestras, beholden to instructions imposed by maestros, whereby:
*"Military procurement in peacetime is largely through private contractors. This [military-industrial]institution spawns, and in turn is*

*sustained by a transactional nexus of groups that benefit from the flow of defense funds generated by the state; the most obvious groups being military officers and procurement officials, congressmen as authorizers of funds, and private firms as recipients of contracts and other benefits."*[53]

However, we would be amiss in our discussions if lacking in the mention of power, it's definitions across different scholastic schools of thought, the most promising of these theories, and how they relate to our current discourse, on the extent to which inequality persists in aspects of everyday life.

# Notions of Power

At the root of almost every outspoken theory on power is an inquisition, of whether or not contemporary/post-modern societies have estranged themselves, as evidenced in discourses and actions, from their primitive inclinations towards war, as a means of survival, protection or as relates to the engulfment of additional territory. Notions of power, and the societal implications of said influence/force, are age-old topics that need constant attention. Throughout the ages, in literary conversation with the likes of Aristotle, Thucydides, and even Marcus Aurelius, one finds evidences of attempts at defining power, and the subsequent implementations of power theories onto the civil order. Concepts as the nation-state and globalization, as are perceived today, are sorely lacking in such antiquated discussions on power relations, yet, does that translate to the obsoleteness of these theories, and their descriptions of the fundamental ways in which groups/settlements interact, in our post-modern, developed societies? Before expounding further on the constructivist school of thought that is closest to this book's hypotheses on inequality, as regards national and international relations of power, I deem it best to begin with a brief, yet broad description of the concept of power, as well as a brief undertaking on prevailing notions and theories of power in scholastic fields of international relations. Before any further discussions are to be undertaken on the military-industrial complex, and how this profitable industry serves as one of the many tools in the elites-toolbox; a brief exposition of the realist and liberalist views on power will be explored. This will then allow for a short description of the school of thought of interest to us, the constructivist view on power and power relations in the international arena.

## The General Approaches to Descriptive Theories of Power

Inherent, or taken for granted, is the overarching notion of power, despite the numerous ways in which it has been defined. The earlier scholars have defined and described power in ways of force and militarism, neglecting the principle of soft-power forms of concession that the thinkers closer to our age have championed. Commonly, power has been imbued with characteristics that bespeak authority, control, or the dominion of one's will over the other(s). In the case of Aristotle, as Machiavelli, these aforementioned characteristics inherent in power needed no further elaboration as to their meaning, it simply was a given. Indeed, conversely, Machiavelli implored the use of terms as "authority", "strength" and "potency", however, he too sought not the trouble of defining further what, to him, may have seemed obvious, terms that speak for themselves, they just are what they are. Max Weber, in his own right saw power as "the probability that one actor within a social relationship will be in a position to carry out his own will despite resistance…"[54]. In the late 1950s and early 60s, C. Wright Mills, aforementioned, was a great believer in what he coined as "power elites" who dictate the directions taken by civil societies on a global order. Mills thus believed in the (omni)potent prowess of military power and violence, relegating to the margins any other forms of power, as diplomatic power for example, which accounts for inter-nation stability and security. Indeed, "[a]ll politics is a struggle for power", yet to presume that "the ultimate kind of power is violence"[55] is customary of a past world replete with 'us' versus 'them' dichotomies, of an absolutist regard. It is I believe, unfortunately for Mills, not that easy. Predominantly, indeed, although not always, the a priori mentioned theorists, and the masses of scholars they have inspired, focus on power within the narrow constraints of strictly defined communities or states, with allusions to interactions between states less prevalent. Moving away from the rigid extrapolations of power as principally cloaked in the garb of violence, with self-serving affinities, thinkers of the likes of Talcott Parsons and Hannah Arendt, in the 1980s, entertained more consensual forms of power, although not to the extent afore-spoken of in earlier segments of this chapter. Parsons attributes the source of power as coming from the political elite class. Parsons, for the most part, ignores military and commercial interests; still, he perceives power as "a circulating medium, analogous to money, within what is called the political system"[56] than he sees it as resultant from actions or inactions from said political elites. Of course, that some aspects about all the above mentioned thinkers are counter to both the premised paradigms of this book, as well as the constructivist views on power relations (to soon be discussed), is no reason enough to toss the proverbial baby out with the bathwater. Hannah Arendt was indeed onto something in her description of power as "correspond[ing] to the human ability not just to act but to act in concert." Arendt remarked that:

> *"Power is never the property of an individual; it belongs to a group and remains in existence only so long as the group keeps together."*[57]

A common theme that finds itself weaved into the ideational fabric of several prominent theories on power relations, as regards both elementary communities and nation-states, is the notion of the outcome of a situation having been already decided by the manipulator or temporary holder of some power. Such notions feature extensively in the literature of concern, with subtle variations between authors, contingent upon the respective authors' world view of international relations. Alas, common are the assertions that view power "…as the ability of an actor to get others to do something they otherwise would not do…"[58] (Keohane and Nye (2001)); a notion wrought with patches and holes. Can power be said to have been asserted when an agent/actor is willing, and in fact about to perform a certain act, an act that happens to coincide with the very act dictated to him/her by the power wielder? The view of consensual forms of control spoken of in this chapter, indicate the viability of the above question, that is, yes power in the above and simplistic scenario was asserted, while, conversely, the notion propagated by Keohane and Nye, and others, precludes us from perceiving power in action through consensual means. Another theory in accord with the precepts espoused by the hypotheses of this book, and by no means the only theory of this kind, is that of Robert Cox, whose definitions of power point to its relations to production (of capital, value etc). Cox describes all social phenomena as being primarily and secondarily a result of power's control over means of production, which, in turn, engenders more power, and thus; he relegates all other observable phenomena, as manifestations of this power-production relationship.[59] Although the above mentioned theories on power can be said to have several merits to them, the prejudices of the various writers cannot so easily be dismissed, as is evidenced in their writings, thus must their social location must always be considered. While Arendt, Keohane and Nye imbue their writings with liberalist mannerisms, Cox on the other hand, shows Marxist leanings.

> *"It is necessary to recognize that there are different kinds of power, and different ways in which it can be used. Additionally, power is not always a oneway process; its use will always have consequences*

> *or side effects upon the user. If an idea of consensus power is adhered to, logically it is not possible for an actor to use power without this power also affecting the user. Thus, the way in which power is defined in international relations also depends on the view taken of what kinds of power exist, and how states or international actors interact using those kinds of power."*[60]

The general theories that are given clout by the prevailing institutional norms and dictates, often of a conservative nature, respectively, and for the most part; reflect a narrow framework, demarcating the somewhat linear coordinates from which future works are to be based. To iterate what has often been paved allusion to in every chapter thus far; the production of wealth leads to the garnering of power, as is evidenced in the onward rising costs of running an election campaign in the US. Furthermore, institutions; legal, political or otherwise, formerly established out of goodwill and earnest need for libertarian promotion, have succumbed to influences from within and without their midst, forces under the control of socioeconomic, political, power elites, among others, or in short; the powerful ruling global elite class. The reasons for briefly mentioning the different theories of power relations, in part, is to account for the different ideological inclinations that the varying elite factions, around the world adhere to, which in turn is translated in the perceived actions and positions taken in power struggles with other powerful influences.

## The Realism and Neo-Realism Approaches to Descriptions of Power Relations

Undergirding the notions of traditional realism is the conception of the world, as a dog-eat-dog one, with a lingering anarchic atmosphere the only way of perceiving international relations. According to this mode of view, the evidences and inequalities that persist globally are chalked up to the relations between states/nations, as the basic units of measuring variable agents. The above perceptions of the world true vary in degree, and as is contingent upon the individual biases of the respective authors. However, this notion or paradigm used to account for both the past and contemporary state of affairs in the world, is best illustrated in the words of John Mearsheimer, who sees "international relations [as] not a constant state of war [than]…a state of relentless security competition, with the possibility of war always in the background."[61] Thus, realists, of whom it can be generally said, although not exclusively, view military force or power as the true source of power, and thus the principle contributor to the systematic imposition of inequality the world round. All other forms of power evidenced within the collective societal order were, in the 1980s and some of the 1990s, secondarily entertained, relegated to the margins of the scholastic discursive realm, and rather seen as begotten from militaristic ventures and hubris. Furthermore, realist and neorealist views, predominantly, have extensively put forward assertions that the international system can only be kept in equilibrium through means of power balancing between states.[62] Thus, there was a factional need to maintain a bipolar or dichotomous worldview, between routine servitude and freedom, between democracy and despotism, or better said, between the US, and its allies, and the USSR, and its allies. As such, the neorealist approach to descriptions of global power relations, although slightly ameliorated from the realist angle to account for the events that lead to Soviet collapse, leave little room for notions of soft-power exertions between and among states.

*"[T]he idea that only coercive forms of power are of any use within the international system has become ingrained in the minds of Western politicians, diplomats and many academics over centuries...the concept of power itself has come to be seen as realist, without due consideration of other ways of viewing it."*[63]

Many historians share the realist view that lays claim to states as the principal manipulators of power, particularly military power, in a world attuned to chaos. However, as of late, the realist view of the world has been losing credence, although still popular among certain influential interest groups. This decline in legitimacy in the mainstream discursive platform can be owed, in part, to the ascendency of groups like Al Qaeda, and other organizational networks that promote and inflict terror. A more nuanced view, of world affairs as regards factional power struggles, now extensively features in the intellectual and scholastic, and even political airwaves. Still more, realist currently have amended their views on power and relations between individuals and groups, still steadfast about their assignment of blame to the state/nation; neorealist schools of thought have given terrorist groups and other non-state, or sub-state actors the light of day. Still more, however, neorealist views postulate that, these terrorist or rogue groups are in essence sponsored by different states.[64] That the state is seen as the source of power, rather than a legitimizing tool for rule by an elite circle, is the chasm that divides the overtone hypotheses espoused by this book. Indeed, it is not farfetched to link terrorist groups with certain states, wishing to covertly put in action their conception of the world, however, I postulate that, as the state an institution, made up of many others, for implementing of the will of the 'masters', so too can such groups of terror find their origins as having stemmed from a minority circle of interested power, political, and commercial elites.

> " …one could go and pick out at random any foreign policy pursued by the United States from the beginning to 1919 and one would hardly find a policy…which could not be made intelligible by reference to the national interest defined in terms of power- political, military and economic… " [65] -

Hans Morgenthau (1952)

In spite of the "pessimistic" attributions to Morgenthau's descriptions of sources of power, and his perceptions of international anarchy, hailed from a conservative and somewhat socioeconomically well-off, social location; his incorporation of a more multilayered and interwoven power structure within his realist descriptions, is, for me, worth mention. Still more, the concepts championed by proponents of realist ideology do us no good when analyzing power relational structures as is evidenced among and between European Union member states. Neorealist theories, as others, do not measure up to credible standards of analysis, an approach that would allow for a descriptive deconstruction of power plays endeavored, in the absence of any such notions of militarism among EU member states. That Germany and France, once sworn enemies who plunged one another into ceaseless bouts of wars for hundreds of years, as the sole means of settling disagreements, should today be thought of as almost kindred, indeed only almost, and with the probability of war breaking so miniscule that it is of little significance. Therefore, the failure to superimpose realist notions onto the contemporary global order, gives credence to their growing irrelevance, as regards descriptions and prescriptions on matters of international relations between states, non-state, and sub-state entities.

*"That the rise and decline in the pervasiveness of realist perceptions of power seems to have reflected the current world-view of US administrations additionally points to questions about its universal applicability, and US bias."*[66]

## The Liberalism and Neo-liberalism Approaches to Descriptions of Power Relations

Soviet Union collapse brought in the demise of mainstream ideologies in the West, which in part sparked and fueled Cold War-era international relations. There was a vacuum created as a result of the discrediting of the realists' approach, due to the inept manner with which realist theories generally prescribed and described the mannerisms of power on a global scale. Rushing to fill this vacuum was a much sidelined social identity, inspired by liberalist scholars and thinkers. The collective of theories and concepts of which we will assign to the category of liberalism, can be viewed as a mélange of trickled down ideas from philosophers of the likes of Jeremy Bentham, Immanuel Kant and John Locke, expressed in the seventeenth and subsequent century. However, I say liberalism is a product of a mixture of trickled down bits of ideologies, in that, it was developed from the "idealists", as Woodrow Wilson, which, in turn, is a derivative of the aforementioned seventeenth and eighteenth century thinkers. Woodrow Wilson, a proponent of the so-called "idealists", during humanities period of soul searching, in the wake of WWI; sought to direct the international system, through the several institutions that prop it up, so as to live up to a Utopian like transcendent global society of an ideal. Indeed, the cold war era marked a brief period when "American exceptionalism", as espoused by Woodrow Wilson, was sidelined, with the realist paradigm championing democracy and American exceptionalism, except, done within the context of national security. During the Cold War, the idealist view of power was deemed more acceptable for maximizing profits, by powerful influences in concert, at a time when America knew more wealth than ever in its past. Still more, Soviet demise was the boost that liberalism needed to assert itself within the mainstream and acceptable discursive realm, which was to influence states' policies. Liberalism would eventually lead to the subtly varied derivative, namely, neoliberalism.[67] Or otherwise said, it was of interests for elites on both sides of the world, the US and the Soviet, to call it quits on their strategy for maximization of profits through war, or rather through preying on the fears of war of the general populace. A new era, one of liberal democracy, and a rule predicated on consensual forms of rule had dawned. Although, this adherence to consensual forms of rule, and soft power relations between actors does not preclude the prospect of violence to curb varying resistant, and hard to deal with factions, in nations of the Global South.

> *"A central theme of liberalism is that individuals are free to make their own choices. Therefore, people's and states' actions are not necessarily dictated by an anarchical system, but they can co-operate by looking after each other's interests in order to bring about security for all."*[68]


Evidently, liberalist and neo-liberalist show an affinity for advocacy for and focus on individual actors, than nations states, in their analysis, as the origins of power in a globalized and highly communicative world. More than military prowess and dominance or fortitude, the focus of such schools of thought, which influence perceptions towards policies for international relations, has been on economic and institutional power, as well as consensual forms of power that subsequently account for cooperation between actors.[69] Such notions of power by liberalist, and neo-liberalist thinkers in particular, are in stark contrast to the more reactionary and anarchic views embodied in realist ideologies. Indeed, some liberalist thinkers credit the state's reduced role in contemporary matters of international relations, to the level of a multi-national corporation, due to its burden of constantly needing to affirm its legitimacy. By this, I mean that, the state/government finds itself entangled in several deep commitments to and social contracts with its citizens, the base that upholds the legitimacy of this elite-infiltrated institution. These commitments from the state come in the way of security guarantees of 'borders', social security/welfare guarantees of varying degrees, and debt payments/relief, among other required civil functions, upon which governmental rule in developed nations, particularly in the West, are contingent. Keeping this in mind, in spite of the vast resources available to developed states, that they are entangled in such long-term commitments, makes for a reduced amount of resources available, to mobilize for use in the international order, replete with vying entities of juggernaut proportions. Thus a state, judging from the resources at its disposal, can be thought of as reduced to the influence of a multinational corporation. Each state, of course, distinct in its treatment of citizens within its bounds; allocates its resources to the principles and sectors that it deems most profitable, that is, in spheres of socioeconomic wealth and power and security; done by joining global legal or monetary institutions (IMF, WB, ICC, etc), for example, or through militarily and economically aligning their interests with other nations (compromise for the ultimate good). However prescriptively accurate liberalist and neo-liberalist notions on power are, in regard to international relations, they tend to only be feasible in relations between, among and within developed nations. Neo-liberalists, predominantly, marginalizes and fails to account for the evidenced relations between, among and within developing nations, and their relationship with developed and industrialized states. Developed states fit the liberalist framework owing to their freedoms of trade and movement vis-à-vis one another. The emphasis, therefore, on the effect of a scholar's or speaker's social location/identity on theories, and the like notions, respective to their times, must ceaseless be reiterated, for better contextualizing of the discussions thus far covered.

*"Consensus power is based upon the free choice of individuals to co-operate with one another. It need not be incompatible with the idea of competition, and is a necessary component of liberalist thinking. All power*

*derives from the consensus of a group; even in a totalitarian state, the power wielding dictator can only control that power with the co-operation of his administration and military...*"[70]

A proverbial baby not to be thrown out with the bath water, among many others, is the notion of the accumulation of wealth by individual and their subsequent use of economic power to direct the global order, indeed, done in likeness to state actions. A corollary of this is when, for instance, an individual acquires shares in a company, this acquisition of shares, often, directly translates to a certain influence that said individual holds over the management strategies, and the direction that that company is to take. According to Utpal Vyas, in "Soft Power in Japan-China relations", the influence of an individual in a company, as aforementioned, is relatively insignificant, on its own, to countervailing or curtailing other global influences/antagonisms. Indeed, in line with the notions of cooperation for garnering influence, Vyas explains how the exercising of this sought of 'buy-in' power into a company, by several individuals, in concert, can amount to not just influence, but decisive control of that company. Much in the same way, this kind of economic power can influence the global system, with international corporations merging and 'buying-in' into other companies, asserting control over institutions in the long-run, which, in turn, perturbs the spheres of interests espoused by a state, and thus, can affect international relations. However, one must be wearing with theories that lay blame to the economic and institutional forms of power, as the nexus of all global societal inequalities, as do liberalists and neo-liberalists. That liberalist thinkers hold dear such precepts of international relations is, partly, as result of the undergirded conceptions of political power, as being in the possession of individual actors, as other sub-state actors alike. The autonomy and relative freedom given these nongovernmental, transnational, and international and supranational organizations (EU, NAFTA, IMF, Apple etc), can be thus seen as a source of power, contingent upon their inter-relations and transactions. Vyas describes the liberalist views on sources of power, held by large non-state, as state actors as defined by interplay of interdependence in an increasingly connected and inter-connected world. Let us ignore the irony that this era also marks a period of huge disconnect between the opulent minority and the destitute global majority, as well as the ostensible disconnect from the real and an opting for, rather readily, an emersion in virtual spheres and realities. For Vyas, the transactions between the concerned actors "include flows of money, people, information and other goods and services…with [t]he value of these transactions [having] grown to a point where actors and states are mutually dependent". Thus the state of affairs arising from such interdependence is an institutionalized social construct that is imbued with power, by the consortium of individual influential members. That some actors may be less dependent upon a transaction than others is also a source of leverage/power.

> " ...elements of consensual power can be seen in that true economic competition can only occur in a system with certain ground rules, i.e. international laws or practices. " – Utpal Vyas (2011)

## Constructivism

### (A Viable Approach to Contemporary Descriptions of Power Relations)

The approach so far taken in this book, setting nothing in stone, and as such, acknowledging the facts that, my and other scholars' lack of knowledge of our lack of knowledge is of significant weight, as regards the biases we take to create or justify a pattern out of the unknown and unknowable. For this reason, and in admittance among several other reasons, could this collective of our discussions be said to fall under the categorization of constructivist school of thought. Although, I will be the first to unrepentantly fess up to there being a few eccentric deviations from the constructivist norm. Regardless, it is from these theoretical coordinates that we find ourselves discussing the evidences, and notions of inequality through different prisms, propagating a long line of works on inequality, each unique in their own right, adding to the discursive dialogue/debate. The collective yet different concepts, termed "constructivism", is an approach taken, more and more, to analyze the 'geographically' interconnected and highly inter-communicative world of international relations today. This approach combines several elements of the human sciences, particularly esoteric ideas from philosophy, psychology, and indeed, sociology; this newly favored eccentric method of analysis, and critique, are intended to decode the varying social identities/locations and interests, which define international relations, or, at least, it's for which descriptive and prescriptive aims they strive.[71] In line with the notions afore discussed about the importance of ideology, that is, norms and values (mental/social-constructs), in the distilling of control through Gramscian means of hegemony, vyas asserts that:

"...*the international system, as with the domestic systems, is defined by the ideas and ways of thinking of the actors involved in them. Hence, if key actors within a system strongly believe it is anarchic, then it will be...*"[72]
Indeed, as persons are the pieces that make up the collective puzzle that is the nation, the raging fears of a society, spreading like wildfire, in the hands of a powerful group of individuals; could be used to maintain and propagate pessimistic perceptions. It could readily happen, of course, that the interests of adherents, of said fear and fear-mongering precepts and rhetoric; are translated into policy, with a pessimistic approach readily opted for, defining the diplomatically taken stances, as regards international relations. However, one problem, I believe, with most constructivist schools of thoughts, and their adherents, is their continual placement of accentuations on the state's role, as the most influential/fundamental actors in our contemporary global village (e.g. Wendt 1999). Once more, this view, for me, is limited, in that the possibility of the state as a legitimizing tool for the ruling class, now more than before, also, it maligns the growing influence of terrorist groups and corporate mercenaries (soldiers for hire), and thus mislead us, as to the pragmatic severity with which to handle such factions, vying for power.

> " ...states and other actors build up ideas about each other in order to predict others' behaviour and tailor ways in which they should use power appropriately...when the constructivist approach is utilised...[it embraces]...the complexities of the global system, rather than the reductionist tendencies of the previous theories... "[73]

That war is an economic industry in its own right is of no novel notion. However, I wish to extend the conversation in light of some of the precepts espoused throughout this collection of works, of consensual or psychologically manipulative forms of control. It is necessary to revert to aspects of the military-industrial complex, as the product of inter-relations between several institutions, in varying civilizations, whereby, the most influential actors in global-society have the right of setting the global trends of belligerence, and with the evaluation of acceptability given only to other, relatively influential powers. Therefore, this segment of the chapter will focus more on the evidences of fear, used as a tool in putting forward policies, or changing the perceptions of the collective within a nation, which in turn legitimizes belligerent or quasi-belligerent or Cold-War-like actions from a hawkish state. Hence, through the use of fear by the ruling classes, as a tactic deployed on the unsuspecting masses, can war be seen as necessitating a strong ideological base, to redefine the story a nation tells itself about itself, that is, its culture and history.

## Distracted by Our Own Panics

Leading up to the collapse of the Soviet regime, extensive were discussions that entailed the US' use of fear on its own people, and how this tactic was subsequently distilled into the world, a world forced to choose between two ideologically contrasted lightening-rods of power. Prevalent explanations of the gluttonous and dangerous state of affairs of the arms race, varyingly and to some extent, drew their percepts from notions of fear, particularly, fear of the ever present and ever lingering Soviet threat.[74] Sheldon Ungar, in his analysis of the military-industrial complex, maps out the fluctuations of inflictions of fear on the populace, which bespeaks, even more than he does, of the consistencies or parallels of fluctuations of levels of societal fear with fluctuations in the arms race. He thus brought to the fore and developed an analysis of institutional legislature and the ensuing practices, as seen through the lens of what he termed "moral fear". It is on a few of the findings offered up by Ungar (1990), relating to concepts of geopolitical and economic manipulation by some circles of the ruling class, (commercial, political, or otherwise) that I will develop further how inequality, as a driver, factors in, even on such a globally influential level. He postulated, and, for me, to a significant extent demonstrated credibility to his argument that, "…the generalized and relatively constant fear of the Soviet threat was punctuated by moral panics unleashed by the spectacular and startling Soviet challenges to American nuclear hegemony."[75] That the discursive realm, or the rhetoric spewed in the political arena in the US and the USSR was filled with antagonisms for the 'other', indeed, at fluctuating periods, between 1948 to 1964; accounts for, in huge part, the public consensus that stoked the "Great Fear"[76], in effect, there was a more favorable view on massive nuclear expansionist programs I n the US. As such, the prolonged anticipation of war and the perpetration of war itself, within the collective of societies, as such a shaping mechanism for values and norms of said societies; meant for a lucrative commercial sector. Sheldon Ungar demonstrated an increase in US military arsenal "came in three large waves". For him, the Soviet atomic bomb, the Sputnik/Cuban missile crisis, the window of vulnerability, were directly resultant from the fears induced by the Truman, the Eisenhower/McNamara, and the Reagan administrations, respectively, which allowed the state to increase the US' arsenal, with each subsequent "wave" endeavoring in unprecedented arsenal build ups.[77] Shying away from too many absolutist commitments in his hypotheses, Ungar noted the initial insufficient atmosphere or cloud of panic in US society, when only perceptions of quasi-belligerent Soviet advances, and no other significant tactics, were distilled into the discursive realms of 'merit' or clout. Indeed, the narratives that allow a society to form and transform their social location/identity or reality, were, during those initial stages of antagonistic rhetoric propagation, still at the rudimentary stages of panic creation, or rather said; the ideologies hadn't yet simmered. Therefore "…it was incumbent on elite groups to impart direction on" these newly brewed fears. The military-industrial complex, as such:

"…dramatized the fear…by creating an affinity between nuclear supremacy and both national security and the sanctity of the American way of life."[78]

Several authors and scholars, since its coming into preeminence, have offered up similar yet distinct theories and notions of the role in which fear, or "moral panics" is often seen to be directly used for its symbolic nature, that is: the ontology of antagonisms of different parties in conflict, with the dogmas, mores and values of a 'superior' civilization imposed on the ostensibly inferior. Thus, with the perceived threat of mutilation to their way of life, civilizations have been seen to react with intense anger, sometimes to the point of irrationality. Such reactions persist, despite the mass populace's knowledge of only part and parcel of the political, geo-political (power) and commercial interests involved. These interests initiated, and in fact endlessly accompanied the religious/cultural/ideological contrasts in the political and scholastic sphere of rhetoric, and prevalent perceptions, of the 'other'. To clarify, the interested elite factions who endeavor in such fear-mongering tactics, in an attempt to secure further power, which, in turn, leads to the production of more wealth; have no hold or control (monopoly) over these evidenced socially engineered fears. On the international level, Ungar perceives the ruling classes as having greater control over the direction in which events precipitate, upon the repeated and efficient distillation of fear, more than the little control they posses over the timing, that is; between the time of perceived introduction of moral panic and the time in which tensions finally spew over.

*"The inability to directly redress threats that often implicate sacred national symbols can unleash ritual responses, domestic moral crusades that have little bearing on the threat, but dramatize insecurity and prime the populace for titanic struggles."*[79]

The angst and moral panic stirred up by the ruling class, through institutional means, especially as seen in both US and Soviet societies, and their respective 'staunch' allies, during the Cold-War era, was, in and of itself, an effective form of control, of the consensual variety. Exaggerated fears of the other's nuclear capabilities, and thus of the high potentiality, for the other to set global trends in norms and values, or rather, has made for the hand-in-glove tactic that the ruling class of concern now partly endorses, as a substitute for antiquated social contracts, with the throne and altar.[80] The Soviet launch of the H-bomb, was the wakeup call, an "awesome mystery", that amplified the latent fears Americans had of communistic ideology, in the wake of the "Red Scare" of 1919. In this regard, the inducement of moral panic within a society, in and of itself is incapable of, or insufficient for mobilizing public opinion. And thus, were it not for already present and deep-seated fears and antagonistic sentiments of the 'other'. From 1947 onwards, the fear of the bomb instilled a lingering state of fear, and sometimes intellectual paralysis around the world, and in the US in particular. The atomic age, or Anthropocene period, could thus be easily conceptualized as an age when the image of vaporized cities will be a fact, and not a nightmarish imagining. Conversely, our growing realization of the advantages and advances brought about by tact diplomatic relations between state, sub-state, non-state entities, as a global collective, provides for a more optimistic view of the future of international relations.

**"**…primitive fear, the fear of the unknown, the fear of forces man can neither channel nor comprehend. This fear is not new; in its classical form it is the fear of irrational death. But overnight it has become intensified, magnified. It has burst out of the sub conscious, into the conscious, filling the mind with primordial apprehensions. **"** [81]

# Notes

[1] Robinson, W.; "Promoting Polyarchy: Globalization, US Intervention and Hegemony"; Cambridge University Press; 1996; p. 15.

[2] Timothy H. Parsons; "The Rule of Empire and why they always fall"; Oxford University Press.; New York; 2010. Parsons was citing: Catharine Edwards; "Introduction: Shadows and Fragments," in "Roman Presences: Receptions of Rome in European Culture, 1789–1945"; ed. Catharine Edwards; Cambridge; Cambridge University Press; 1999; pp. 3, 9.

[3] Timothy H. Parsons; "The Rule of Empire and why they always fall"; Oxford University Press.; New York; 2010.

[4] Benjamin Isaac; "The Invention of Racism in Classical Antiquity"; Princeton: Princeton University Press; 2004; pp. 190–92, 503. Also see: P. S. Wells; "The Barbarians Speak: How Conquered Peoples Shaped Roman Europe, in Roman Imperialism"; pp. 244–46.

[5] Naphtali Lewis and Meyer Reinhold, eds., "Roman Civilization"; Source Book I: "The Republic"; New York: Columbia University Press; 1966.

[6] Timothy H. Parsons; "The Rule of Empire and why they always fall"; Oxford University Press.; New York; 2010, pp. 26.

[7] Citations from Susan Mattern; "Rome and the Enemy: Imperial Strategy in the Principate"; in Roman Imperialism: Readings and Sources; ed. Craige Champion; Oxford: Blackwell; 2004; pp. 202–3.

[8] Melvyn P. Leffler endeavors best in portraying the relationship between core values and national security, see: Melvyn P. Leffler; "National Security," in Michael J. Hogan and Thomas G. Paterson, eds., "Explaining the History of American Foreign Relations"; 2nd ed.; New York: Cambridge University Press; 2004; pp. 123–36.

[9] John et al.; "Going Public, Crisis after Crisis: The Bush Administration and the Press from September 11 to Saddam." *Rhetoric & Public Affairs*, vol. 10 no. 2, 2007, pp. 195-220. *Project MUSE*, doi:10.1353/rap.2007.0039

[10] Loretta Napoleoni; "Maonomics: Why Chinese Communists Make Better Capitalists Than We Do"; Seven Stories Press; New York; 2011; pp. 497-499.

[11] Timothy H. Parsons; "The Rule of Empire and why they always fall"; Oxford University Press.; New York; 2010, pp. 28.

[12] David Mattingly, "An Imperial Possession: Britain in the Roman Empire, 54 B.C.–A.D. 409"; London: Allen Lane; 2006; pp. 6.

[13] Timothy H. Parsons; "The Rule of Empire and why they always fall"; Oxford University Press.; New York; 2010, pp. 37.

[14] Ibid.

[15] Ibid. pp. 39.

[16] Strabo; "The Geography of Strabo", book 4: "Gaul"; trans. Horace Leonard Jones (Cambridge, MA: Harvard University Press, 1988); pp. 255–57. & also: Julius Caesar, "The Conquest of Gaul"; trans. S. A. Handford (Baltimore, MD: Penguin, 1951); pp. 135–36. & also: Tacitus, "On Britain and Germany"; trans. H. Mattingly (Baltimore: Penguin, 1964); pp. 61–62.

[17] Timothy H. Parsons; "The Rule of Empire and why they always fall"; Oxford University Press.; New York; 2010.

[18] Robinson, W.; "Promoting Polyarchy: Globalization, US Intervention and Hegemony"; Cambridge University Press; 1996; pp. 15.

[19] Robinson, W., "Globalization, the World System, and "Democracy Promotion" in U.S. Foreign Policy"; Theory and Society, Vol. 25, No. 5; October; 1996; pp. 623–4.

[20] Reagan, R.; "Address to Members of the British Parliament"; 8/6/1982, at: www.reagan.utexas.edu/archives/speeches/1982/60882a.htm; accessed 15/8/2012.

[21] Gershman, C.; "Fostering Democracy Abroad: The Role of the National Endowment for Democracy"; American Political Science Foundation Convention; 29/8/1986.

[22] William Robinson; "Promoting Polyarchy: Globalization, US Intervention, and Hegemony"; (Cambridge Studies in International Relations); Cambridge University Press; 1996; pp. 332.

[23] Brinkley, D.; "Democratic Enlargement: The Clinton Doctrine"; Foreign Policy, No. 106, (Spring) 1997.

[24] Melia, T.; "The Democracy Bureaucracy: The Infrastructure of American Democracy Promotion"; Princeton Project on National Security; (September) 2005; pp. 13-14.

[25] Dionysis Markakis; "US Democracy Promotion in the Middle East: The Pursuit of Hegemony"; (Routledge Studies in US Foreign Policy); Routledge Press; 2015.

[26] Fuller, G.; "Muslims Abhor the Double Standard"; Los Angeles Times; 5/10/2001, at http://articles.latimes.com/2001/oct/05/local/me-53771; accessed 16/7/2012.

[27] Dionysis Markakis; "US Democracy Promotion in the Middle East: The Pursuit of Hegemony"; (Routledge Studies in US Foreign Policy); Routledge Press; 2015.

[28] Christopher Hobson delivers a valuable deconstruction of the history of democracy. See: Hobson, C.; "Beyond the End of History: The Need for a "Radical Historicisation" of Democracy in IR"; Millenium Journal of International Studies; Vol. 37; 2009. Also; Milja Kurki speaks of the contested nature of democracy and the potential effects of its promotion; See: Kurki, M.; "Democracy and Conceptual Contestability: Reconsidering Conceptions of Democracy in Democracy Promotion"; International Studies Review Vol. 12, No. 3; (September) 2010. Also: Kurki, M.; "Democratic Features: Revisioning Democracy Promotion"; Routledge; 2013.

[29] Dahl, R.; "Polyarchy: Participation and Opposition"; Yale University Press; 1971; p. 9.

[30] Fukuyama, F.; "The End of History"; National Interest; No. 16; (Summer) 1989.

[31] Sadiki, L.; "The Search for Arab Democracy: Discourses and Counter-Discourses"; Hurst; 2004.

[32] Dionysis Markakis; "US Democracy Promotion in the Middle East: The Pursuit of Hegemony"; (Routledge Studies in US Foreign Policy); Routledge Press; 2015.

[33] Gramsci, A.; "Selections from the Prison Notebooks of Antonio Gramsci"; edited and translated by Hoare, Q.; Nowell Smith, G; Lawrence and Wishart; 1971; p. 12.

[34] Femia, J.; "Gramsci's Political Though: Hegemony, Consciousness and the Revolutionary Process"; Clarendon Press; 1981; p. 39.

[35] Dionysis Markakis; "US Democracy Promotion in the Middle East: The Pursuit of Hegemony"; (Routledge Studies in US Foreign Policy); Routledge Press; 2015; pp. 20.

[36] Robinson, W.; "Globalization, the World System, and "Democracy Promotion" in U.S. Foreign Policy"; Theory and Society, Vol. 25, No. 5; (October) 1996; p. 643.

[37] Dionysis Markakis; "US Democracy Promotion in the Middle East: The Pursuit of Hegemony"; (Routledge Studies in US Foreign Policy); Routledge Press; 2015.

[38] Ibid. pp. 17-18.

[39] Carr, E. H.; "The Twenty Years' Crisis, 1919-1939"; Palgrave Macmillan; 2001; pp. 74-5.

[40] Although Prys et al. consider hegemony as a different from traditional forms of imperial domination, I believe it to still be the same mode of rule, using updated tactics. For more on cultural hegemony and rule by consent, see: Prys, M.; Robel, S.; "Hegemony, Not Empire"; Journal of International Relations and Development, Vol. 14, No. 2; (April) 2011.

[41] Antonio Gramsci; "selections from the prison notebooks of Antonio Gramsci"; ed & trans. Quintin Hoare and Geoffrey Nowell Smith; pp. 263.

[42] Rupert, M.; "Marxism and Critical Theory"; in Dunne, T.; Kurki, M.; Smith, S. (eds.); International Relations Theories: Discipline and Diversity; Oxford University Press; 2007; p. 157.

[43] Marshall McLuhan; "Understanding Media: the extensions of man"; critical edition; Gingko Press; 1994; p. 31.

[44] Morton J. Horwitz; "The Transformation of American Law, 1780-1860"; Harvard University Press; 1977; pp. 257.

[45] Eugene D. Genovese; Harvard Law Review; Vol. 91, No. 3; (Jan., 1978); pp. 726-736.

[46] Morton J. Horwitz; "The Transformation of American Law, 1780-1860"; Harvard University Press; 1977; pp. 183.

[47] Eugene D. Genovese; Harvard Law Review; Vol. 91, No. 3; (Jan., 1978); pp.731.

[48] Ibid.

[49] Morton J. Horwitz; "The Transformation of American Law, 1780-1860"; Harvard University Press; 1977; pp. 100.

[50] Ibid.

[51] "Dominion and Dependence in the Law of Freedom and Slavery"; Amy Dru Stanley; Law & Social Inquiry; Vol. 28, No. 4; (Autumn, 2003); pp. 1127-1134; Wiley on behalf of the American Bar Foundation.

[52] Cited in: "Institutional Origins of the Military-Industrial Complex"; Bruce G. Brunton; Journal of Economic Issues, Vol. 22, No. 2; Jun., 1988; pp. 599-606; Taylor & Francis, Ltd.

[53] Ibid.

[54] Max Weber; Economy and Society; 1968 [1925]; pp. 53; New York: Bedminster Press.

[55] C. Wright Mills; "The Power Elite"; 1959; pp. 171; New York: Oxford University Press.

[56] Talcott Parsons; "Power and the social system"; Lukes, S. (ed.) Power; 1986; pp. 101; Oxford: Blackwell.

[57] Hannah Arendt; "Communicative power"; Lukes, S. (ed.) Power; 1986; pp. 44; Oxford: Blackwell.

[58] Robert O. Keohane; Joseph S. Nye; "Power and Interdependence"; 2001; pp.10; New York: Longman.

[59] Robert Cox; "Production, Power and World Order – Social Forces in the Making of History"; 1987; New York: Columbia University Press.

[60] Utpal Vyas; "Soft Power in Japan–China Relations: State, sub-state and non-state relations"; 2011; pp. 15; New York: Routledge Press.

[61] John Mearsheimer; "The false promise of international institutions: International Security"; 1994; 19, 3: pp. 9.

[62] Tim Dunne, and Brian Schmidt; "Realism"; in Baylis, J. and Smith, S. (eds); "The Globalization of World Politics"; 2001; Oxford: Oxford University Press, pp. 141–161.

[63] Utpal Vyas; "Soft Power in Japan–China Relations: State, sub-state and non-state relations"; 2011; pp. 15; New York: Routledge Press.

[64] Joseph E. Thompson; "Virtual regime: a new actor in the geopolitical arena"; Political Science and Politics; 2002; 35, 3: pp. 507–508.

[65] Hans Morgenthau; "Another "great debate": the national interest of the United States"; The American Political Science Review; 1952; 46, 4: 961–988.

[66] Utpal Vyas; "Soft Power in Japan–China Relations: State, sub-state and non-state relations"; 2011; pp. 19; New York: Routledge Press.

[67] Charles W. Kegley; "Controversies in International Relations Theory: Realism and the Neoliberal Challenge"; 1995; New York: St Martin's Press. Or see also: Michael Doyle; "Liberalism and world politics revisited"; in C.W. Kegley (ed.); "Controversies in International Relations Theory: Realism and the Neoliberal Challenge"; New York: St Martin's Press, pp. 83–105. Also: Mark W. Zacher; and Richard A. Matthew; "Liberal international theory: common threads, divergent strands"; in C.W. Kegley (ed.); "Controversies in International Relations Theory: Realism and the Neoliberal Challenge"; New York: St Martin's Press; pp. 107–150.

[68] Utpal Vyas; "Soft Power in Japan–China Relations: State, sub-state and non-state relations"; 2011; pp. 20; New York: Routledge Press.

[69] See: Charles W. Kegley; "Controversies in International Relations Theory: Realism and the Neoliberal Challenge"; 1995; New York: St Martin's Press. Also: Cynthia Weber; "International Relations Theory: A Critical Introduction"; 2001; London: Routledge.

[70] Utpal Vyas; "Soft Power in Japan–China Relations: State, sub-state and non-state relations"; 2011; pp. 20; New York: Routledge Press.

[71] See: Alexander Wendt; "Social Theory of International Politics"; 1999; Cambridge: Cambridge University Press. & Also: Ted Hopf; "The promise of constructivism in international relations theory"; in International Security; 1998; 23, 1: pp. 171–200. Also: Steven Lukes; "Power and the battle for hearts and minds"; in Millennium: Journal of International Studies; 2005; 33, 1: pp. 477–493.

[72] Utpal Vyas; "Soft Power in Japan–China Relations: State, sub-state and non-state relations"; 2011; New York: Routledge Press.

[73] Utpal Vyas; "Soft Power in Japan–China Relations: State, sub-state and non-state relations"; 2011; pp. 35; New York: Routledge Press.

[74] Lester Kurtz; "The Nuclear Cage: A Sociology of the Arms Race"; 1988; Englewood Cliffs, NJ: Prentice Hall.

[75] Sheldon Ungar; "Moral Panics, the Military-Industrial Complex, and the Arms Race"; The Sociological Quarterly; Vol. 31, No. 2 (Summer, 1990); pp. 165-185; Wiley on behalf of the Midwest Sociological Society.

[76] See: Paul Boyer; "By the Bomb's Early Light"; 1985; New York: Pantheon.

[77] Sheldon Ungar; "Moral Panics, the Military-Industrial Complex, and the Arms Race"; The Sociological Quarterly; Vol. 31, No. 2 (Summer, 1990); pp. 165; Wiley on behalf of the Midwest Sociological Society.

[78] Ibid.

[79] Sheldon Ungar; "Moral Panics, the Military-Industrial Complex, and the Arms Race"; The Sociological Quarterly; Vol. 31, No. 2 (Summer, 1990); Wiley on behalf of the Midwest Sociological Society.

[80] William McNeill; "The Pursuit of Power: Technology, Armed Forces and Society Since AD 1000"; 1982; Chicago: University of Chicago Press.

[81] Paul Boyer; "By the Bomb's Early Light"; 1985; pp. 8; New York: Pantheon.

# 5
# Media
## and the
# Selling
## of
# Audiences

*****

*"Three hostile newspapers are more to be feared than a thousand bayonets."* -Napoleon Bonaparte

Often referred to as the fourth-estate, an institution engendered to mitigate excessive power use, where and when the constitutional system of the three branches of government falter, the media has long had a distinguished responsibility, as the people's eyes and ears; the bearer of both good and bad news. Indeed, it was the much beloved member of the house that served as both another level of communal association within the family, as it did alerting the household to nefarious activities unfolding, which may have been of concern to them. That the media has the freedom of speech when issuing to the public their investigative reports, was an ideal placed on the pedestal and included into the constitution by the founders of the USA. It is also a concept that bespeaks the ideals of a contemporary world, having survived two World Wars and countless atrocities of genocidal proportions. However, presently, and for some time, as prominent media organizations further embroil themselves in the web of commercialism, they now mean to ensure institutional consensual control, measured through lack of resistance to elite policies. We take for granted the journalists and scholars who strive to leave up to the lofty ideals of a libertarian society, they are much to be touted, and to which ideology our global collective, zealously and genuinely should aspire. What then happens, when our rhetoric contrasts, at times severely, our ostensible actions and policies, both at home and abroad? Indeed, hypocrisy in an international relations arena that relies on soft power forms of approaches, by the dominant actors vis-à-vis their 'inferiors', may result in entanglements that typically make for pyrrhic victories, as such, worth re-telling. Carrying on with the precepts redundantly invoked by this book, I wish to undertake a loose discussion on the infiltration of exterior elite interests, particularly commercial, which have gradually seized hold of society's afore-reliant watchdog, reliant, that is, relative to contemporary times. At the time of writing of this book, common within the discursive airwaves, the world round, is talk of "fake news" and false reporting, or the untrustworthiness of the mainstream media. Therefore, this concluding chapter aims to offer, even in the least bit, some insights or approaches to perceiving the interactions between the ruling classes, and the highly lucrative media corporations that aid in their sustained rule. Media, indeed, is a power, in and of itself, and thus the underestimation of the ability for symbols and images to mold people's beliefs, more and more, no longer finds itself viewed by cynical observers.

Works of De Tocqueville, in his analyses of the French Revolution, rightly described some of the effects of media on a group of societies, explaining, in some ways unprecedented, the significance of the printed word in bringing about some cultural homogeneity to the French people. The uniformity of social constructs, or of the French's social location/identity vis-à-vis themselves and the outside world, was a top-down occurrence, whereby, the elite/noble classes were the segments of society that were in-sync with each other, imposing similar forms of rule to their respective surfs, merchants and smiths. The ease with which printed forms of media were distributed and assimilated within literate European societies, after the era of reformation, allowed for notions of relative similarity among peoples of a nation, with the French in the north able to relate more to those in the south. Alas, the prevalence of principles of uniformity, linearity and the ability to more accurately continue the rhetoric that so defines a society's norms and values, meant that prior intricacies, associated with the antiquated feudal and oral society, were supplanted by the written word. Such a period is concurrent with the rise of the legal contract into preeminent reliance, in European and New World societies. Indeed, it was the new literati and lawyers who saw to it that the French Revolution was the sparked phenomenon that it was.[1] Marshall McLuhan in "Understanding Media: the extensions of man", discerns that some of the inscribed perceptions of De Tocqueville about media in its printed form, bespeak not of only his astuteness, but exemplifies the differences between the nations of France and England. For McLuhan, England was sequestered and undergirded by ancient traditions of common law, with its reliance on oral approaches for cultural material/information transfer. Indeed, the credibility of forms of rule and modes of questioning, founded upon oral paradigms, was the basis upon which the English parliament, as an institution stemming back to the medieval period, was centered around. It is partly because of this oral-centrist approach of socially constructing the values and norms that account for a society's culture that English, more than French society, did not succumb to the paradigms supported by notions of uniformity or continuity, which accompanied the new visual print technology taking Europe by storm. McLuhan, for this reason, claims that the "result was that the most important even in English history has never taken place; namely, the English Revolution on the lines of the French Revolution".[2] Local British rulers or aristocrats based not their power base on literate culture, as a means of distinguishing themselves from the masses that they ruled, and this, for several scholars in more uniform European societies, alluded to their barbarism. McLuhan's analyses of some of the popular cultural material artifacts, within British traditions, offer meaningful discursive spaces from which to begin one's deconstructions, analyses on what the culture that educates us actually says about us, and not what it itself purports us to be. According to him, E.M. Foster's "A Passage to India" offers a great example of a dramatic rendition of the clash of civilizations, more precisely; between the oral and intuitive oriental culture and the European visual paradigms or approaches to perceiving human relations. That the legal contract has gained prominence in our Western societies, is, in part, owed to the fact that 'uniformity' and 'continuity' in one's rhetoric or ideology, as well as the perception of 'sequential' progression is seen as 'rational'. McLuhan portrays the contrasts in oriental and western societies, as expressed by E.M. Foster, as between sound (oral) and visual (print). To this effect, when in Foster's novel, Adela Quested was out of the Marabar Caves, whose affinity for resonance over apparition was the epitome of what Indian society or human relations were like. After leaving the caves, "[l]ife went on as usual, but had no consequences, that is to say, sounds did not echo nor thought develop. Everything seemed cut off at its root and therefore infected with illusion."

"The ultimate conflict between sight and sound, between written and oral kinds of perception and organization of existence is upon us. Since understanding stops action, as Nietzsche observed, we can moderate the fierceness of this conflict by understanding the media that extend us [or that are an extension of our human collective] and raise [and support] these wars within and without us."[3]

# A Match Made in Washington (DC):
# Media and the Presidency

We have come to expect and, for some, come to eagerly look forward to the annual State of the Union address by the president of the American republic. And although a few scholars have come to contest the notion that US presidents in the nineteenth century were in several regards similar to modern presidents, when dealing with public opinion and the subsequent rhetoric that emanates from the White House. "The Rhetorical Presidency" by Jeffrey Tulis makes for a good example of works that argue that twentieth century American political life lacked the mechanisms, or the institutional know-how, to mobilize public opinion effectively. However, Richard J. Ellis and Alexis Walker, among others, have argued against Tulis in this regard. Instead, Ellis and Walker lay forward meaningful arguments to the contrary, by asserting that presidents, during the mid-nineteenth century encountered antagonisms, as came up with solutions to mitigate the civil pressures flung at them, and their administrations. Some of these antagonisms, in the way of conflicting ideologies, is resultant from the idealist aspirations of the founders of the nation, and societies (re)telling of said glorious myth, their (hi)story. On one hand, the founder fathers envisioned, we hope, the presidency as a responsibility, an office that was impartial, above the fray of party politics, while conversely, the heavy head that wears the crown is wrought with conflictions due to the role that the president plays, as de facto party leader.[4] Faced with these conflicting ideologies, among many others, the presidency has long had a tradition of balancing its interests with the power structures that aid in its conceptualization, actualization and maintenance. Of course, there are just as many, if not more dissimilarities, than there are parallels between nineteenth-century and modern presidencies. Indeed, in the 19th century presidents seldom came out and spoke on their own behalf, paradoxically, done as a means of maintaining a certain image of the president by the public, molding perceptions to line up with the ideology of what the US of A was. Presidents at that time, wished the presidency to not be muddied by waters that portrayed them in the light of the "unseemly", in their ambitions, and as practitioners of "demagoguery"; thus, the notions of democracy that undergird and legitimize their rule needed such 'safeguards'. In spite of George Washington's consideration of oratory prowess and skills of persuasion, as would maybe make Plato proud, as vital to the practices of democracy in a democratic republic; he, as his immediate successors, thought of such conduct as direct interchange with citizens as beneath the auspices of the presidency.

> "*Indeed, the founders designed the presidency to be insulated from public opinion, fearing that popular passions could become a crucible for tyranny.*"[5]

Although the approach taken by presidents in times past has varied according to the ruling ideology of the day, and the extent to which the society is reactionary, among several factors; the similar need to know and curb public sentiments and reactions differs little from today. Mel Laracey makes a poignant remark in comparing the presidency's use of news papers in the twentieth centuries, as the equivalence of our "going public" today, on the several media forms and platforms available to us. He makes the distinction that although radio and magazines, as other embodiments of media were common and of mainstream use in US society, dealing with a newspaper or three was the much preferred means of conveying information by the office of the presidency. These newspapers, indeed, served as a means for reproaching closer to the common people, one of the few partisan tools available to early American politics. Although, more and more, the age of the television taking centre stage in American life, the radio would soon be relied upon for presidential addresses. An example of late eighteenth and nineteenth century uses of newspapers was Alexander Hamilton's erection of The Federalist Gazette of the United States, in 1789, as a platform for molding public opinions, on local tax or employment issues, as with international relations and the need to have public support for a war or two. Thus the Federalist Gazette by several prominent federalists, Alexander Hamilton among the ranks, made for a "reliable political organ" for President George Washington's administration. With time, news papers as the Federalist Gazette took on prominent roles within the discursive space, for presidential administrations, as a means of reaching "the public with information on national affairs and administration policy" as well as to "present the administration's position" on their stance towards certain policies.[6]

The need by political actors to invoke past injustices and other emotionally charged memories, from within a nation's collective, partly owes itself to the useful strategy often evidenced of the ruling US political elites, in conjunction with others, to shape contemporary understandings and assimilation of the gravity of matters being faced. Shock is used to catch the populace unawares, as mentioned in the concluded phase of the last chapter, this shock and awe doctrine mobilizes reactions from the masses, at times, little in the way of reason. For this reason, often than not, presidents "simplify and reduce stories to conventional symbols for easy assimilation by audiences," with the imploration of historical allegories and analogies, as well as metaphors, to offer the most emotionally powerful and readily identifiable justification (logic) for a certain policy or act. Paralleling Saddam Hussein to Adolph Hitler, needless to say, evokes dreary sentiments and antagonistic perceptions of both him, and to a lesser extent of the society he hails from, by the segment of the US public alienated from investigative proofs and articulations to the contrary.[7] Thus, by paving allusion to the notion that nuclear weapons supremacy by the US, couple with technological ascendancy could render obsolete nuclear weapons from the 'other', thus Reagan found successful the toying with fears of the American public, curbing and manipulating public opinion in favor of his administration's proposed policies.[8] Hence, rather than the framing of the discussion in terms of US oil excavation missions in the Middle East, costing human lives on both sides of the equation, needless to say, policies are best left advocated for by precepts of "liberty", "democracy promotion" and "human rights", never straying far from past Euro-centric-like justifications of "civilizing missions" and the spread of Christianity to Africans.

**"**I simply made up my mind what they [the American people] ought

to think, and then did my best to get them to think it.**"** - Theodore Roosevelt

Prior to President William McKinley, as alluded to by Stuckey, presidents were expected to rise above the socioeconomic and political fray, and so, if a presidential predecessor of McKinley, by and large, were to speak on issues that had no direct bearing "to his administrative function", meant for the president "to speak inappropriately and risk his legitimacy."[9] The prevalent theme painted and the stance taken by the founders of the United States, as regards to popular leaders were nothing short of contempt and disapproval, with such writings by Alexander Hamilton appearing in the Federalist no. 1, warning against "those men who have overturned the liberties of republics", and how most of these tyrants came to be so "by paying an obsequious court to the people; commencing [as] demagogues…".[10] However, to play the part of the uncompromising representative in political relations, as regards political dealings with commercial interests, as is the case for other interests, is, in and of itself, a strategic form of communicating with the public. Furthermore, the limiting of presidential addresses to entail nothing but matters central to administrative progress or failure, and with opinions by the presidents, and his advisors, funneled through to a single form of media, print via newspapers, also meant the elimination of political noise, and an efficacy in passing along a much needed message, for the shoring up of US public support. Hence, regardless of the period of focus in our studying of the US' history of presidents and their varying means and methods for swaying public opinion; one commonality, between predecessors and successors of McKinley, remains the ability to maneuver seamlessly through the ideological maze of the day. James K. Polk embodies the nineteenth-century president, willing to implore all means and tools available, so as to line up the collective perception that people had of themselves, and of others, with the policies promoted by the 'reigning' political administration. Since, as Jeffrey Tulis points out, for Polk to deliver speeches during the Mexican-American war would have gone against the predominant ideologies du jour, and rather than garner support, would amount to gross indignation from the constituency, at large. Indeed, Polk "judiciously avoided popular appeals because they contradicted the 'custom' of the period". According to the prevailing paradigms of his day, for the president to attempt to influence public perceptions and opinions, through direct discourse, would have been seen as a "sacrifice [of] his dignity", whereby, it was mostly perceived, it necessitated that he "beg in person for support".[11] Although Polk was confined by the norms and values of his time, that did not preclude him from performing the duties expected of the presidency, by the aristocrat/elite classes who, through the American version of representative democracy, as well as lobbying (done more discretely then), significantly factored in ascent to the highest office. Presidents that led the country during such times as Polk were not excluded from the expectations of curbing public opinions and sentiments, at least of some factions in society, which varyingly and for diverse reasons, more than seldom saw their interests as counter to the differing elite interests. Rather than speak directly to the people, to justify the need to go to war against Mexico, Polk instead mediated the matter with a letter to Congress, requesting an immediate declaration of war, due to the Mexican attack on US forces. One can thus draw a parallel from the stratagems used by the George Bush administration and that of Polk. Much as the Chilcot report detailed the fraudulent ways in which war, and the invasion of a sovereign Iraq was undertaken, so too, in hindsight, was it revealed of Polk's letter to congress, asking that they trust the president in the absence of proof that was still at the printer's. Polk's request to the representatives of the general US public was enthusiastically answered, with his order voted in, with 40 to 2 in the senate and 174 to 14 in the House, in favor of war. Another example of Polk's political prowess was the use of his own news paper, the Washington Union, bought for $50 000, "in U.S. Treasury funds… [through] a bank in a small town in Pennsylvania"[12]; when promoting for the annexation of Texas.[13]

> "*Polk used the [Washington] Union to frame and spin the progress of the Mexican war…he was so closely engaged with the daily operations of the Union, not only exercising direct editorial control over its content but…[wrote] anonymous article that appeared in the paper trumpeting his policies…*"[14]

Not until the McKinley administration, and its approach for garnering support for the Spanish-American War, would the office of the presidency have as a significant prerequisite the ability to sell war, and, indeed, foreign policy. One, I opine, should ask where influence ends and manipulation begins, since the line separating the two is so fine as to conceal the seams. For this reason, any effort to influence public opinion by its government could be said to have the society already docked on an inclined slop, leading to, as in the words of Bertrand Russell in 1950, "…no nonsense so arrant that it cannot be made the creed of the vast majority by adequate governmental action". As the American public nominally gained in affluence, in the period immediately subsequent to the Gilded Age, so too did the literacy rate increase, and even for the skilled yet illiterate, more than ever, there was the economic possibility of taking an apprentice or two into the fold, who would read to them the news reports of the day, from regional, national and international newspapers. It was after this period, eminently prior to the Spanish-American War, up till today, that Presidents, beginning more noticeably with McKinley, felt the need for oratory transmission of their message for the gathering of public support for their administration's elitist mandated policies on matters international. McKinley marked the moment when presidents, under the guise of liberating the unfortunate citizens of the world, the American nation, having, for itself, fought for its independence from King George of Britain; propagated myths about democracy promotion and "American exceptionalism". Thus the norms and values of a society were transformed with a transformation of the role the presidency occupied, a people previously thinking it dishonorable for a president to directly address the crowd on matters non-administrative. McKinley's approach to international relations was also a turning point from American isolationism from the rest of the world, to be subsequently embroiled in European-elite matters in both World Wars. What was the style of rhetoric supporting American elite interests to branch out, and spread their wings to other lands? Touring the country, closing the gap between the people and their leader, McKinley, now in Savannah, touted the nation's exceptional ideals, proceeding to ask, "…who will shrink from that responsibility, grave though it may be?" The providential responsibility he spoke of, was to guide the foreign peoples out of the darkness that was their ignorance, lack of means for self-defense, and their barbarity, and so, for him, if "following the clear precepts of duty, territory falls to us, and the welfare of an alien people requires our guidance and protection, who will shrink from that responsibility…".[15] The trip down south was, for William McKinley and his administration, an overwhelming success, with his address to the Georgian legislature in Atlanta incurring a thunderous roar of applause, one inscribed in the book of legends, with images of a trembling dome of the state capitol building invoked by the mere mention of his speech. However, that such a trip was made by the president, stopping several times in settlements of the south, alludes to growing importance attached to the mobilization of public support, in favor of interests that entailed venturing beyond the republic's borders, both ideologically as geographically. Thus, with the McKinley administration began the journey towards following through with the nation's latent imperial ambitions. In spite of the depiction of McKinley as a spineless puppet, readily swayed by public opinion, more especially by historians of the period immediately subsequent to his custodianship as president, latter intellectuals and historians, however, have come to overturn the notions of him as spineless. An appreciation of McKinley's uses of populism, to direct public perceptions towards a needed stance, has contemporarily been the theme of many a scholastic journal. Indeed, McKinley's ability to make it seem as though his actions were driven by an aroused public was of itself a mark of success in public relations, and today, is viewed as "one of the nation's more effective chief executives."[16] Having honed his skills in politicking, as both congressman and governor of Ohio, McKinley, it can be seen more clearly in hindsight, was the most suitable candidate for most of the influential elite factions, for the presidency. In so far as William McKinley was a great leader, he exemplified what Greenstein labeled the "hidden-hand", a phenomenological style of leadership that allowed for strong exertions on the public's collective mind, without the appearance of doing such.[17]

> *"[McKinley] moved quietly and unobtrusively toward his goals. His studied ambiguity concealed his intentions. He skillfully neutralized opposition and closely directed the political battle while seeming to remain above it."*[18]

In October of 1898, a dozen days into that month, a touring President McKinley drove home the point for the need to go to war with Spain in Omaha, and to a nation still adjusting to the changing stance towards modernization that the country was taking. The nation, at this point, was still recovering from the bloody dispute, which saw the kinfolk from the North mercilessly end the lives of their kin in the South, and vice-versa, this war would, in some respects, reunify the nation, rallying behind a common goal. Indeed, freeing Cuba from clasps of Spanish tyranny was an ideal that painted an intensely prettier portrait of what it meant to be America, and lined up with the ideals associated with the myth of the founding fathers. It was in Omaha that one finds the use of the words "manifest destiny" featuring in his speech, to a people already willing to go to war, for incentives ranging in shape, from idealistic to economic forms. Much as with the Romans and the British, the use of the term "destiny" within the political discursive realm offered an opening, within the collective-social construction, for the justifications that would allow both North and South to belong to the "good", and permit the tainting of the Spanish, as the antagonists in this eternal confrontation. McKinley played it cool, and fed off the already primed US public's insecurities in once falling short of the lofty ideals they purport for themselves, asking; "[s]hall we deny to ourselves what the rest of the world so fully and justly accords us?"[19]

> *"Territory sometimes comes to us when we go to war in a holy cause, and whenever it does the banner of liberty will float over it and bring, I trust, blessings and benefits to all the people."*[20]

War is as beneficial as it is detrimental for a society, indeed, war is morally wrong, according to the predominant compass for morality somewhat globally in use today; however, one can attach unification of antagonistic factions in US society, several times in its history, to the rallying behind a war, of one sort or the other. Thus the office of the presidency has come to perfect strategies for selling war, through trial and error, for over a century, and has come away with the realization that war, induced by fear, is as potent an ideological tool for manipulation as any gun. It is through the different media platforms available to commercial interests as political ones alike, that efforts are focused at guiding the rhetoric of civil society, in effect, to control the development of the mores and dogmas to be labeled as "acceptable". William James, the philosopher goes as far as to opine that the political arena is greatly challenged during peacetime, needing to reduce pressure from a multitude of antagonistic forces, and to keep the nation collected; there's an ostensible readiness towards war, as LBJ's "war on poverty", or Reagan's "war on drugs".[21]

66
Public sentiment is everything. With public sentiment nothing can fail, without it nothing can succeed. He who molds public sentiment goes deeper than he who executes statutes or pronounces decisions. He makes

99
statutes or decisions possible or impossible to execute.      **-Abraham Lincoln**

# Media:
## Institutions
## of
## (Mis)Information

The early twenty-first century, at the time of writing of this book, is undergoing an information revolution, as the agenda setting societies experience a relatively rapid shift in societal norms and values; the old media institutions that had unanimous market share find themselves in competition with online independent journalists, broadcasters, satirists and sundry. One notices a certain amount of distrust emanating from the so called millennial-segment of the US population, of the "official stories", realizing the extent to which commercial interests, particularly in the form of advertisements, are embroiled in the Media, agenda-setting institutions. It has, indeed, not eluded many, that the agenda-setting Media, such as the New York Times, CBS, and Fox News, are first and foremost profit seeking organizations, as is any corporation of their caliber. These media corporations that have long run the show, it should be remembered, are owned by larger corporations, forming a mere branch of the likes of General Electric, or Westinghouse. One cannot ignore the hierarchic structures inherent in corporations, with an almost dictatorial atmosphere, wrapped by a façade that bespeaks notions as "job satisfaction", "we are a family", et cetera; a structure that entails dictatorial demands conceptualized at the top of the river, to be passed down stream for only implementation. It would of course be inaccurate to claim that everybody in these elite/agenda-setting media institutions is in on the game, that's just nutty. Noam Chomsky, for me, during a talk at Z media Institute, in June of 1997, best draws the sketch of how the mechanisms that account for the system's modus operandi, in a large media corporation. I would, thus, be amiss not to quote him extensively:

" Those of you who have been through college know that the educational system is highly geared to rewarding conformity and obedience; if you don't do that, you are a troublemaker. So it is kind of a filtering device which ends up with people who really, honestly (they aren't lying) internalize the framework of belief and attitudes of the surrounding power system in the society. The elite institutions like, say, Harvard and Princeton and the small upscale colleges, for example, are very much geared to socialization. If you go through a place like Harvard, a good deal of what goes on is a kind of socialization: teaching how to behave like a member of the upper classes, how to think the right thoughts, and so on. .. When you critique the media and you say, look, here is what Anthony Lewis or somebody else is writing, and you show that it happens to be distorted in a way that is highly supportive of power systems, they get very angry. They say, quite correctly, "Nobody ever tells me what to write. I write anything I like. All this business about pressures and constraints is nonsense because I'm never under any pressure." Which is completely true, but the point is that they wouldn't be there unless they had already demonstrated that nobody has to tell them what to write because they are going to keep to the rules. If they had started off at the Metro desk and had pursued the wrong kind of stories, they never would have made it to the positions where they can now say anything they like... The same is largely true of university faculty in the more ideological disciplines. They have been through the socialization system...

Take the New York Times. It's a corporation and sells a product. The product is audiences. They don't make money when you buy the newspaper. They are happy to put it on the World Wide Web for free. They actually lose money when you buy the newspaper. The audience is the product. For the elite media, the product is privileged people, just like the people who are writing the newspaper, high-level decision-making people in society. Like other businesses, they sell their product to a market, and the market is, of course, advertisers (that is, other businesses)...

Whether it is television or newspapers, or whatever else, they are selling audiences. Corporations sell audiences to other corporations. In the case of the elite media, it's big businesses...the obvious assumption is that the product of the media, what appears, what doesn't appear, the way it is slanted, will reflect the interest of the buyers and sellers, the institutions, and the power systems that are around them. If that wouldn't happen, it would be kind of a miracle....

What about their institutional setting? Well, that's more or less the same. What they interact with and relate to is other major power centers: the government, other corporations, the universities. Because the media function in significant ways as a doctrinal system, they interact closely with the universities. Say you are a reporter writing a story on Southeast Asia or Africa, or something like that. You're supposed to go over the university next door and find an expert who will tell you what to write or else go to one of the foundations, like Brookings Institute or American Enterprise Institute. They will give you the preferred version of what is happening. These outside institutions are similar to the media. The universities, for example, are not independent institutions. There are independent people scattered around in them (and the sciences in particular couldn't have survived otherwise), but that is true of the media as well. And it's generally true of corporations. It's even true of fascist states, for that matter, to a certain extent. But the institution itself is parasitic. It's dependent on outside sources of support, and those sources of support, such as private wealth, big corporations with grants, and the government (which is closely interlinked with corporate power that you can barely distinguish

them)- they are essentially the system that the universities are in the middle of. **"** [22]

 

     Thus, when one internalizes values and norms, the very ones that maintain certain socioeconomic and political centralized powers within society, it cannot always be said that you're imposing a form of censorship. As Chomsky illustrates, there just some thoughts that don't come readily to you once you're at a certain level within the corporation, sufficiently embroiled in the dog-eat-dog world, chasing the next sound bite. Why fault someone's ambition to claw to the top, when the system said person is found in, often than not, has little to no rewards for persons that deviate too far from the script? It needs that we focus our efforts, I believe, towards amending the antiquated education system for one that is suitably more dynamic to keep up to the demands of the information and high-tech revolution; such notions begin by teaching our teachers to teach society mental tools for escaping the human collective, self-inflicted reigning prison-paradigm. Of course, as with the presidency, or any other high-level office in any US institution, as the world around, there are exceptions, whereby, someone steps up in an attempt to change the system from within the system. This notion of change from within has been discussed in sections prior, to the extent that, influential factions within society are just as incumbent upon pressures from factions they marginalize, so that; the conceding of some Jim Crow measures could happen, sooner than it would've happened. Indeed, that racial integration happened throughout the US, allowing for a period of adjustment, was for some scholars and pundits an inevitable eventuality, and the injection that the crony capitalism we practice needed; more people with the capacity to buy more products and services. Still, to relegate the power of mass movements too far behind economic incentives for change, as with the emancipation of slaves and the abolition of Jim Crow laws; is also to give too little credit to forms of soft-power manipulation and propagation.

# Media's Role

# in

# Garnering Support for War

### The Establishment-Media's Invasion of Iraq

Scholar, American Attorney and former child actor, Jeff Cohen was embedded in fervent discussions on the Middle-East in general, and Al Qaeda in particular, with his adamant opposition to the eminent invasion of Iraq made clear, it wasn't long before his stretched nineteen weeks of airtime on MSNBC came to a close. The television show that took the nation's attention replaced the balance only made possible by differing expert opinions, embodied by Cohen; "Countdown: Iraq," was a daily show that ostensibly sprinkled glitter on the potential of war, rather than scrutinize or systematically subject such notions to questioning. There indeed was a direction away from accommodating voices, as Cohen, who warned that such action would serve to "undermine our coalition with Muslims and Arab countries that we need to fight Al-Qaeda". Instead, the ruling classes were in favor of inviting military analysts close to the pentagon, into their media instituted studios, which amounted to significant contribution to US public sentiments, towards Saddam Hussein, and even towards the Iraqis they wished to liberate, through "Operation Iraqi Freedom". "Countdown: Iraq", this daily show was successful, in that it achieved what it was partly erected for, the validation of a certain framework, from which discussions of this nature are to be posited; the sorts of questioning that will pass as permissible/acceptable. Cohen later remarks, in commenting about the MSNBC television show, with retired generals using "props, maps, and glitzy graphics to spin invasion scenarios"; that for him "it was excruciating to be silenced while myth and misinformation went unchallenged."[23] Paving the way for suitable grounds, on which to till, and subsequently sow the seeds, and reap the fruits of the ideological tree; are established institutions' shaping of the rhetorical frame. That war had to happen, however, was a given, from which then sprung the discussions dominating the airwaves, mostly in influential media institutions in the West, but this could be extended globally, with exception to some countries (in the Middle-East, even in Europe and beyond).

Hans Blix, was the diplomat elected to lead the weapons inspectors under the directive of the UN, that November in 2002, with his name trending many a news channel of all forms of media; a military analyst on "Countdown: Iraq" was asked, "what's the buzz from the Pentagon about Hans Blix?". The analysts' response was, to some extent, candidly revealing, in saying that Blix amounted to "something like the Inspector Clouseau of the weapons of mass destruction inspection program…who will only remember the last thing he was told- and that he's very malleable".[24] As such, in a world where "fake news" is prevalent, in the wake of the invasion of a sovereign Iraq, however despicable their leader was, undertaken fraudulent circumstance, is a world that is increasingly suffering the birth-pangs of big data and an intercommunicative and globalized village. Not knowing what to believe from all media platforms some of the time, and with the knowledge of the increased ease, for poor people from the Global South, to reach Europe or the US, lingering firmly in the back of the collective mind; a fearful tension builds, partly due to the uncertainty of information given to us, and gradually, we lose focus of intelligibility of discourses and pay attention to our primitive responses of fear that our territory will soon be over-ran. Yet the continuation of all such antagonisms, the lot of which was covered throughout this book, still hint at the-like ideological stances as beneficial for the few more than the many, within the global society.

*"The problem for US media was that there was wide disagreement among WMD experts, with many skeptical about an Iraqi threat. The problem only worsened when UN inspectors returned and could not confirm any of the US claims."*[25]

Among several outlets, CNN hosted David Albright, the former UN inspector, who was vociferous in accusing Iraq of harboring chemical and biological weapons, on several an occasion, never lacking in the mention of such notions, prior to the invasion of Iraq. Later, when his claims were found wanting, and when asked about his confident assertions to the contrary, Albright pointed at the White House, saying, "I certainly accepted the administration's claims on chemical and biological weapons. I figured they were telling the truth." At another time, former CIA analyst, and then CNN expert, Ken Pollack, came on the air, in a bid to calm the global shock, emanating from some, and the cynical jeers from others, upon he himself having once made mention of Saddam's "building [of] new capabilities as fast as he" could". Pollack was not hesitant in pointing the blame elsewhere from him, blaming his remarks on a "consensus" that within the world of intelligence, now asserting in atonement that, it "was not [him] making that claim; that was [him] parroting the claims of so-called experts."[26]

Nowadays, more than in times prior, the most significant stories of the ill-use of power by our political representatives, by and large, go unmentioned, and not out of a journalistic need to conceal the stories. Rather, serious rumors are seldom investigated by journalists, due to the growing expectation, within the public/acceptable/mainstream discursive space, of substantial evidence of a courtroom standard, a story that convinces the public, as in the words of Ted Turner, "beyond a reasonable doubt". Thus the justifications for holding the press to such high standards of evidence, as shown by Gary Webb, in "The New Rules for the Millennium", paradoxically leads to a lessening of journalist standards in spite of the mainstream consensus that unsubstantiated stories a left out, thus resulting in higher standards across the board. The press was never meant to be beholden to such standards for substantiating their stories, indeed, too little research done, with the main reliance on rumors, for the telling of the story is a hallmark of tabloid-like media. Thus, it isn't hard to imagine a world where 'unsubstantiated stories are kept out of circulation, as, US society embodies the muffling phenomenon on several stories, in spite of the possibility that most are undergirded by truths.

*"Such a standard would have kept Watergate out of the papers. Lover Canal, the CIA's mining of Nicaragua's harbors, the El Mozote massacre in El Salvador- all would have been suppressed."*[27]

Author and journalist Gary Webb points out, quite rightly, how things have been turned topsy-turvy, with the mainstream dismissing the notion that journalists and reporters, unlike the police and legal prosecutors, are incapable of conducting 24-hour long surveillances, and bound by a code not to pay off informants for information. It is through reference to the public record that most of the information is gathered by journalists, as such, much can be said of a civilization upon analyzing the extents of the transparency of the state-apparatus. Thus, if influential people, our representatives, cannot be held to account for their public and on-the-record statements, saying different things of the same thing, at various times (inconsistent), then we continue to make difficult the ability for integral (often independent) journalists to perform their duty.

# Propaganda and Perception

Until the rise and spread of Nazism, championed by the German Third Reich under Hitler, the word propaganda had connotations significantly contrasted to our perception of what the word entails today. One could think of the term "Public Relations", a friendlier face to the state operations that amount to digging out the desired reactions from the public, supplanting the term "propaganda". The institutions which have come to set the trend, and direct social mores and doctrines, were long put in place, as early as the 1916. Although, the McKinley administration was well adept at using the state apparatus, in a manner well adept at invoking the necessary public reactions; not until the Wilson administration was a legal infrastructure coupled with the political maneuverings. The irony of course not eluding many a history scholar was that Wilson was elected on an anti-war platform, to conclude his string of presidential campaign rallies the country round, that year, 1916. His slogan, classic, "Peace without victory", was not sufficient a thing to preclude the US from participating in the much dreaded war, by the US public, taking place in Europe.

> "...how do you get a pacifist population to become raving anti-German lunatics so they want to kill all the Germans? That requires propaganda."[28]

Nazi-Germany's use of propaganda to gain mass appeal among an economically disenfranchised German public, after the loss of the First World War, was a response by the then German state apparatus, under the leadership of Hitler, which showed the extent to which the US and British use of propaganda in the first world war was appreciated. Indeed, The US pubic, still wishing to maintain their isolationism in the Western hemisphere, were vehemently opposed to any notions of US involvement in the First World War, unfolding at a gory pace in Europe. Public relations, as the lucrative and seriously taken industry we know it to be, although evidenced in sporadic moments throughout history, say when a person was hired to make more appealing Rockefeller's image, the industry we know emerged in the US, during the First World War. The man to head this propaganda initiative, to convince the American people of their want to go to war, was none other than Edward Bernays. Bernays is known for excellence in what he does, which is to sell you something, anything. As a man, and outside of work, one could say he was a man of the people, a liberal at heart even. Today Bernays is best remembered for the role he played in successfully selling to women the idea that it was hip and cool to smoke cigarettes, appealing to a great many modernists and encouraging the long desired, indeed, the long needed feeling of independence and rebellion. Though Bernays was but one man, his endeavor at convincing the US public to join the war was successful, only in so far as the committee on Public Information (aka the Creel Committee), this agency of state propaganda, backed him. The Creel Committee, an unprecedented state propaganda agency in the history of the United States, was the first of several agencies for monitoring and influencing public opinion. Thus, as has been premised throughout this book, the erection of an institution, as the Creel Committee, was a necessary instrument by the ruling class, aimed at maintaining, or at least, beginning to toy with the idea of rule via consent. Edward Bernays' book, released in print in the late 1920s, became the preeminent manual on matters of public relations, in which he points out that, by applying precepts used in the First World War, it was possible to "regiment the public mind every bit as much as an army regiments their bodies." Such tactics of regimentation, of course, and as according to him, were to be wielded by the "intelligent minorities", in order to ensure that the masses follow the intended path, pursuant with interests beneficial to the many, only within elite circles.

*"...there is a new art in democracy called "manufacturing of consent"...By manufacturing consent, you can overcome the fact that formally a lot of people have the right to vote."*[29]

## The Treatment of a Peaceful King

The role of the establishment, big corporation media companies, is to write the script, or frame, to be parroted by other media platforms, each respective to the interests of the owner(s). The frame has long been set, the frenzied casting of nets and hooks in hopes of a sound bite, or ten, culminating in the journalist's recompense, advancing his or her career, is a framework that undergirds the reward systems in almost all institutions; media, research and education, the law and countless other props/institutions of power. As such, if the New York Times or the Rolling Stone appear to be partial to a musical artist, showering nothing but praise for the artists' work, then, often than not, the flood gates open, in terms of opportunities for these musicians. Every other think-piece and critique from other media corporations, if not counter to the 'boss" interests, thus, lend themselves to lauded acclamations, in agreement with the trend-setting media's perceptions of talent or excellence. The same, of course, is true when an artist is disparaged or rejected by these establishment media corporations, in that other corporations follow suit in their marginalization of the musician(s). This is not to say that, writers, musicians and artists who are initially rejected by the cultural-trend-setting corporations never make it any further down the pipeline of their career. Rather, I wish to allude to the assortment of obstacles that may arise for a great artist, due to the complacency of establishment cultural institutions, who enforce a system where only a handful of opinions and critiques matter out of a possible pool of dozens (if not more), of these cultural institutions. Howard Bloom, author, and once publicist of musical icons of the likes of Billy Joel and Prince, gives voice to the significance with which public relations influenced the manner in which stories were covered.

> *"Public relations taught me a good deal more about why facts were not, after all, what a good reporter wanted. He wanted a story that would either titillate his audience, fit his own clique's political prejudices, or replicate a piece of reportage he'd read somewhere else."*[30]

Thus with the chase after that sound bite that's always around the corner, you know the one, the type of story to either make you or break you as a journalist, depending on how you reel in the bait; violence, and the ability to chock audiences is a premium for many a television network. Edward R. Murrow, the reporter who covered everything Soviet and CIA related, as well as the Watergate scandal, recognized his increase likelihood of featuring on the CBS Evening News, were he covering a "black militant talking the language of 'Burn, baby burn!' than with moderates appealing for a Marshal Plan for the ghetto.[31]

Every year, like clockwork, we ritualize the passage of film footages onto our screens, of Martin Luther King Jr., on the anniversary of his assassination. The clips shown on the network television, are the ones we've tirelessly seen over and over, namely; of a King, struggling for racial desegregation in a polarized Birmingham (1963), or still in the same year in Washington as he recited his much quoted "I have a dream" speech. Notably, the other two footages of King were, his march for voting rights in Alabama, Selma in 1965, and lastly, the motion picture of a still-lying, dead on a motel balcony, Martin Luther King Jr., in Memphis of 1968. Besides these clips of the reverend, no other clips of him speaking in 1966 and 1967 have ever made the annual highlight-reel in remembrance of him. All the speeches King made during those years were filmed, some attesting to his ever diligent organizational capabilities, yet today they are not shown on television. Once King and other civil rights advocates, of many walks of life and 'races', had accomplished the first step towards the dismantling of the Jim Crow way of life in the US, the change was initially imperceptible on a day-to-day, for some, and drastic for others, the essential was that a legal acts were erected. King did not cross both hands in satisfaction, having guaranteed his name in the history books, as a thing of legend; instead, King understood the nature of the reigning form of capitalism, which dictated everyday lives. The reverend "began challenging the nation's fundamental priorities. He maintained that civil rights laws were empty without "human rights"- including economic rights" for the segments within society who find themselves unable to finance their stay at a restaurant, or unable to afford decent accommodation. King acknowledged that a majority of Americans who found themselves below the poverty line, were, in fact, white, although this is in absolute numbers, and not in per capita terms. Thus, the rhetoric to follow suit from this realization was one that was framed in class-conscious terms/perspectives. Calling for "radical changes in the structure of society", so as to share or redistribute wealth and power, he, like many today, pointed the finger at the huge income gaps between the varying factions in US and global civil society.[32]

> "True compassion is more than flinging a coin to a beggar; it comes to see that an edifice which produces beggars needs restructuring." – Dr. Martin Luther King Jr.

Yet before this version of Dr. King flung himself at the public, as he did so well, and so often, he was made to go through hoops and hurdles, particularly by the media, and its structure of reportage. He fought for what he initially thought would be the true emancipation of black people; a trial by fire, which would allow him to better understand matters of inequality, as arising from the ill-distribution of wealth and power. Indeed, the much outspoken revolutionary of peace, the reverend Dr. King was, in 1967, one of the country's prominent anti-Vietnam war activists, a staunch critic of belligerent and hypocritical US foreign policy stances. At Riverside Church in New York that April 4th, 1967, with only a year to live, he exclaimed in denouncement of US actions, in his "Beyond Vietnam" speech. King questioned the US' "alliance with the landed gentry of Latin America," while proclaiming his view of the United States of America, as being "on the wrong side of a world revolution", as also regards its position in Vietnam and South Africa. For King, and I believe rightly so, the US was going counter to the professing of its big-brother/sister forms of support for the downtrodden and captive, since, the state apparatus actively worked towards suppressing the revolutions "of the shirtless and barefoot people" of the Global South. Although this speech of King's is not well known and does not, in view of the corporate media institutions, merit a featured during the annual commemoratory film clips of his life, several media groups of his day made sure to discredit and delegitimize his presence. Life (magazine), in reaction to the reverend Dr. King's speech, denounced it as "demagogic slander that sounded like a script for Radio Hanoi." Concurrently, The Washington Post remarked on the speech in claiming that "King has diminished his usefulness to his cause, his country, his people".[33] As my brother James remarked, "Are not his country-folk his people?" Indeed, King was American, and a patriot, only in so far as he stuck to the script. Thus when the media back –lash to his speech was launched at him, it had to be insisted upon, particularly for those non-blacks who saw King as a true patriot, that "his people" were not the American people, and his energies would only best be appreciated when lent to matters of racial discrimination, with no mention of wealth and power disparities. Hence, today, King is remembered for his fight for the rights of black people, and not for his protestations of socioeconomic inequality by elite circles.

Howard Bloom, while at CBS in early February 1968 was out and about, as all other journalists during those incendiary, counter-culture years of the 1960s, in a bid to feature on the evening news, let alone extract the sound bite of the year, attended a news conference in Washington. At the end of the press conference, however, Bloom approached what seemed to be a fatigued and withered Dr. King, seated in an almost empty room, and proceeded to inquire on his seemingly battered spirit. King answered him saying, "because of you and because of your colleagues in television." King candidly followed through with saying that the media, "try to provoke [him] to threaten violence" and if he were not to comply with such expectations, then, the trend often entailed placing on television, "those who do". Rightly so, the reverend pointed out that "[b]y putting them on television, you elect them our leaders. And, if there is violence," he asked, "will you think of your part in bringing it about?"[34]

> "Karl Marx held that history is shaped by control of the means of production. In our times history is shaped by control of the means of communication." – Arthur Schlesinger Jr.

# Notes

[1] Marshall McLuhan; "Understanding Media: the extensions of man"; 2003 eds.; Gingko Press: Berkeley; pp. 27.

[2] Ibid.

[3] Ibid. pp. 28.

[4] Ellis and Walker; "Policy Speech in the Nineteenth-Century Rhetorical Presidency: The Case of Zachary Taylor's 1849 Tour"; Presidential Studies Quarterly 37, no. 2; (June 2007); pp. 248–69.

[5] The Alan B. Larkin Series on the American Presidency; "Selling War in a Media Age"; 2010; Andrew K. Frank and Kenneth Osgood Eds.; University Press of Florida.

[6] Mel Laracey; "The Presidential Newspaper: The Forgotten Way of Going Public"; in Ellis, ed.; Speaking to the People; pp. 67, 69.
Thomas Jefferson, James Madison, and Henry Lee in turn founded the National Gazette in October 1791, in opposition to Federalist propaganda, also to mobilize Republicans across the country. Laracey offers an example of Jefferson's use of the National Intelligencer to shore up support for the administration's embargo against Britain.

[7] Bruce Miroff; "The Presidency and the Public: Leadership as Spectacle"; in Michael Nelson, ed.; "The Presidency and the Political System"; 4th ed.; Washington, D.C.: Congressional Quarterly Press; 1995; pp. 276. On the utility, accuracy, and effectiveness of historical analogies for policymakers, see: Richard E. Neustadt and Ernest R. May; "Thinking in Time: The Uses of History for Decision Makers"; New York: Free Press; 1986. See also Frank Costigliola; "Reading for Meaning: Theory, Language, and Metaphor"; and Robert D. Schulzinger; "Memory and Understanding U.S. Foreign Relations"; in Hogan and Paterson, eds.; "Explaining the History of American Foreign Relations"; pp. 279– 303 and 336–52.

[8] The Alan B. Larkin Series on the American Presidency; "Selling War in a Media Age"; 2010; pp. 4; Andrew K. Frank and Kenneth Osgood Eds.; University Press of Florida.

[9] Mary E. Stuckey; "The President as Interpreter-in-Chief"; Chatham, N.J.: Chatham House; 1991, pp. 15. Also for more on the conceptions of the day in civil society, in a nascent republic, see: Jack N. Rakove; "Original Meanings: Politics and Ideas in the Making of the Constitution"; New York: Knopf; 1996; pp. 268.

[10] Alexander Hamilton, John Jay, and James Madison; "The Federalist: A Collection of Essays, Written in Favor of the Constitution of the United States, as Agreed Upon by the Federal Convention, September 17, 1787"; ed.; by Michael Loyd Chadwick; Springfield, Va.: Global Affairs; 1987; p. 3.

[11] Jeffrey K. Tulis; "The Rhetorical Presidency"; Princeton: Princeton University Press; 1987; pp. 63, 76.

[12] The Alan B. Larkin Series on the American Presidency; "Selling War in a Media Age"; 2010; pp. 9; Andrew K. Frank and Kenneth Osgood Eds.; University Press of Florida.

[13] Mel Laracey; "The Presidential Newspaper: The Forgotten Way of Going Public"; in Ellis, ed.; "Speaking to the People"; pp. 77-78.
Polk put forward instructions to his secretary of war, to write an article "vindicating the government", to be published in the Union. This was, in part, in response to General Zachary Taylor (the commander of US forces in Mexico), who criticized the president's plans for wagging war with Mexico. Quite regularly, a recalcitrant Congress was also in the line of fire, from the Washington Union's editor, under instructions from Polk.

[14] The Alan B. Larkin Series on the American Presidency; "Selling War in a Media Age"; 2010; pp. 9; Andrew K. Frank and Kenneth Osgood Eds.; University Press of Florida.

[15] December 17, 1898, Speeches and Addresses of William McKinley from March 1, 1897 to May 30, 1900; (New York: Doubleday & McClure, 1900); 174.

[16] The Alan B. Larkin Series on the American Presidency; "Selling War in a Media Age"; 2010; pp. 22; Andrew K. Frank and Kenneth Osgood Eds.; University Press of Florida.

[17] For more on the "hidden-hand", see: Fred I. Greenstein; "The Hidden-Hand Presidency: Eisenhower as Leader"; New York: Basic Books; 1982.

[18] The Alan B. Larkin Series on the American Presidency; "Selling War in a Media Age"; 2010; pp. 22; Andrew K. Frank and Kenneth Osgood Eds.; University Press of Florida.

[19] October 12, 1898; "Speeches and Addresses", 105; Hilderbrand, "Power and the People"; 39.

[20] October 13, 1898; "Speeches and Addresses", 114; Hilderbrand, "Power and the People"; 39.

[21] For more about the infiltration of war and militarization into American culture in the twentieth century, see: Michael Sherry; "In the Shadow of War: The United States since the 1930s"; New Haven: Yale University Press; 1995.

[22] A talk by Noam Chomski; "What Makes Mainstream Media Mainstream"; talk at Z media Institute; June 1997.

[23] Jeff Cohen; "We Were Silenced by the Drums of War"; in "You are still being lied to"; 2009; New York; The Disinformation Company; p. 25.

[24] Ibid.

[25] Ibid.

[26] Jeff Cohen; "We Were Silenced by the Drums of War"; in "You are still being lied to"; 2009; New York; The Disinformation Company; p. 26.

[27] Gary Webb; "The New Rules for the New Millennium"; in "You are still being lied to"; 2009; New York; The Disinformation Company; p. 40.

[28] A talk by Noam Chomski; "What Makes Mainstream Media Mainstream"; in "You are still being lied to"; 2009; New York; The Disinformation Company; pp. 23.

[29] Ibid.

[30] Howard Bloom; "The Puppets of Pandemonium: Sleaze and Sloth in the Media Elite"; in "You are still being lied to"; 2009; New York; The Disinformation Company; pp. 29.

[31] Ibid.

[32] Jeff Cohen and Norman Solomon; "The Martin Luther King You Don't See on TV"; in "You are still being lied to"; 2009; New York; The Disinformation Company; pp. 51.

[33] Cited in: "The Martin Luther King You Don't See on TV"; Jeff Cohen and Norman Solomon; in "You are still being lied to"; 2009; New York; The Disinformation Company; pp. 51.

[34] Howard Bloom; "The Puppets of Pandemonium: Sleaze and Sloth in the Media Elite"; in "You are still being lied to"; 2009; New York; The Disinformation Company; pp. 33.

www.ingramcontent.com/pod-product-compliance
Lightning Source LLC
Chambersburg PA
CBHW050442290526
45786CB00006B/2124